Korea and East Asia

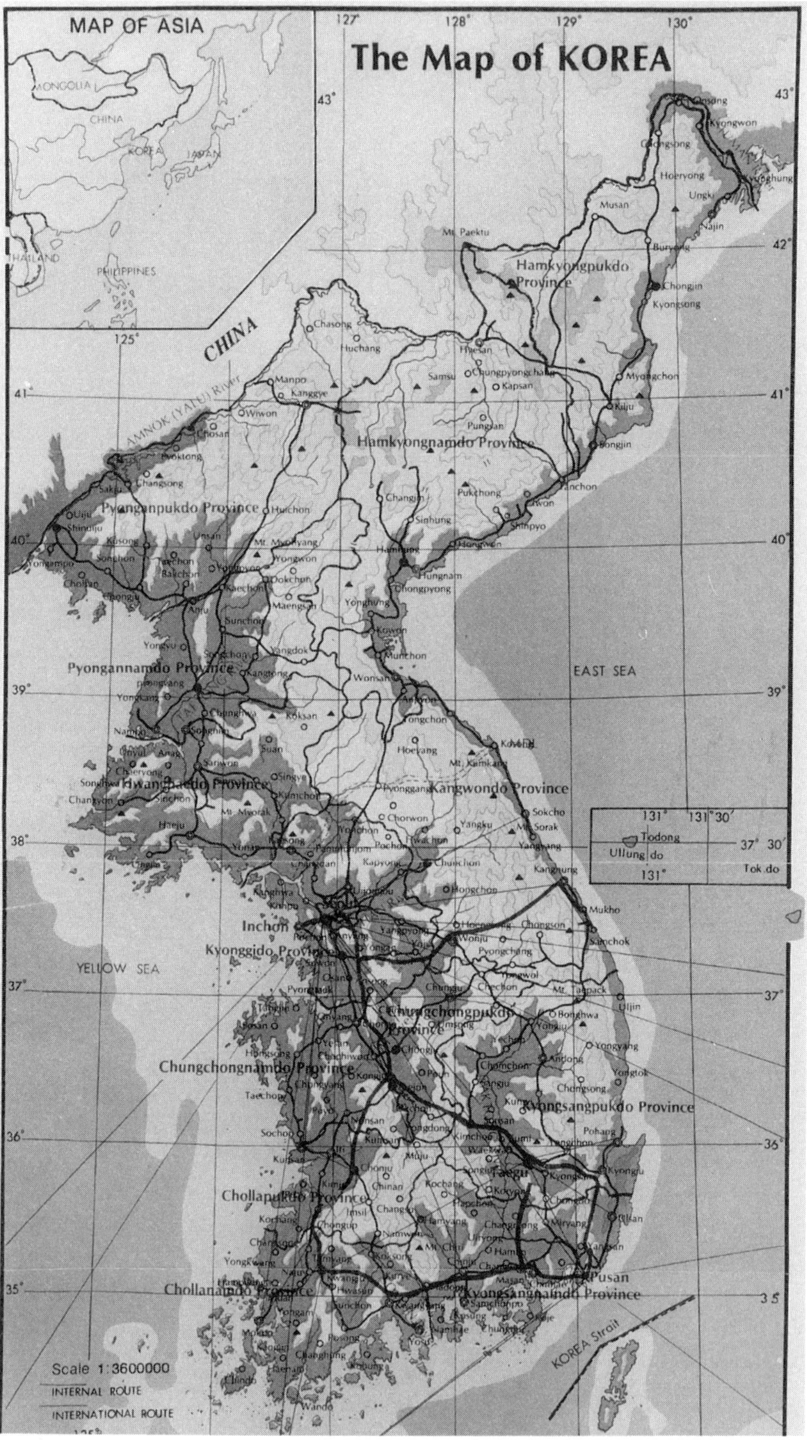
The Map of KOREA
MAP OF ASIA
MONGOLIA
CHINA
KOREA
JAPAN
THAILAND
PHILIPPINES
CHINA
127°
128°
129°
130°
125°
43°
42°
41°
40°
39°
38°
37°
36°
35°
Mt. Paektu
Hamkyongpukdo Province
Hamkyongnamdo Province
Pyonganpukdo Province
Pyongannamdo Province
Hwanghaedo Province
Kangwondo Province
Kyonggido Province
Chungchongpukdo Province
Chungchongnamdo Province
Kyongsangpukdo Province
Chollapukdo Province
Chollanamdo Province
Kyongsangnamdo Province
AMNOK (YALU) River
EAST SEA
YELLOW SEA
KOREA Strait
Inchon
Taegu
Pusan
Ullung do
Tok do
Scale 1:3600000
INTERNAL ROUTE
INTERNATIONAL ROUTE

Korea and East Asia

The Story of a Phoenix

Kenneth B. Lee

Forewords by Edward Olsen
and Kyung-Cho Chung

PRAEGER

Westport, Connecticut
London

Library of Congress Cataloging-in-Publication Data

Lee, Kenneth B.
Korea and East Asia : the story of a Phoenix / Kenneth B. Lee ; foreword by Edward Olsen; foreword by Kyung-Cho Chung.
p. cm.
Includes bibliographical references and index.
ISBN 0–275–95823–X (alk. paper)
1. Korea—History. 2. Korea (South)—History. I. Title.
DS907.18.L44 1997
951.9—DC20 96–44693

British Library Cataloguing in Publication Data is available.

Library of Congress Catalog Card Number: 96–44693
ISBN: 0–275–95823–X

First published in 1997

Praeger Publishers, 88 Post Road West, Westport, CT 06881
An imprint of Greenwood Publishing Group, Inc.

Printed in the United States of America

The paper used in this book complies with the Permanent Paper Standard issued by the National Information Standards Organization (Z39.48–1984).

10 9 8 7 6 5 4 3 2

To my parents

Dr. and Mrs. Lee, Hoon Koo

Contents

Foreword

Korea, its peoples and their history, is of growing importance in world and Asian regional affairs. Too often in the modern era Korea has been overshadowed in the consciousness of Westerners by its larger and more powerful neighbors, China and Japan. Also, negative perceptions of Korea have dominated the news media. These include the dire consequences of the Korean War, political repression in both halves of the divided Korean nation, and bad publicity emanating from societal unrest in Korea. Cumulatively they have tarnished Korea's image. Nonetheless, as the larger world saw during the 1988 Olympics in Seoul, there is much that is positive about Korea's accomplishments, its history, its culture, its contributions to science and technology, and its economic and geopolitical contributions to regional prosperity and stability. Its cumulative positive impact has been very significant. Therefore, it is appropriate that Korea should be the focus of greater international attention.

This clearly is the desire of Dr. Kenneth Lee in this volume. It is a labor of love which reflects his more than three decades as an educator in Korean language and culture at the US Defense Language Institute. He writes as a Korean patriot in the best sense of that phrase, expounding on Korea's seminal contributions to the growth of East Asian civilization. He describes a Korea which has played a key role as a link between China and Japan, but also has carved out a distinct identity in Asia and the international community. The core contention of Dr. Lee's volume is the need to regard Korea as on a par with its two more influential neighbors, to elevate the public's and scholar's appreciation for Korea's many achievements. His treatment of Korea's status may tweak the sensibility of Sinophiles and Japanophiles, and in that sense is somewhat controversial, but it also is a useful antidote to excessive Sinocentrism and Japanocentrism.

Korea and East Asia: The Story of a Phoenix will prove to be a useful addition to the literature on Korean history, Korean national development, and Korea's role in the modern world.

Edward Olsen, Ph.D.
Professor, East Asian Studies
National Security Affairs
US Naval Postgraduate School
Monterey, California

Foreword

In his new book, *Korea and East Asia: The Story of a Phoenix*, Dr. Kenneth B. Lee has painted a timely, many-faceted picture of the real Korea and its heroic people.

This indispensable volume is founded on Dr. Lee's intimate knowledge of his native country and his profound scholarship. The book's style is easily readable, presenting a wealth of material on the long Korean history in relation to Korea's neighbors, as well as the present-day situations of South and North Korea, in the context of broad political, economic, military, social, and cultural aspects. The book describes these subjects most accurately, thoroughly, and objectively.

Indeed, the author has made a great contribution to academia with many new historical theories regarding the development of the Korean and other East Asian civilizations. He has long been a believer in Korea's importance as a strategic factor in East Asian war and peace, and in the peace of the world. I strongly recommend this timely book.

Kyung-Cho Chung, LL.D., Lit. D.
Author of *Korea Tomorrow*; *New Korea*;
Korea: The 3rd Republic;
The Korean Guidebook

Preface

The English historian Arnold Joseph Toynbee, probably the most prominent historian of the world in the twentieth century, classified the Korean civilization as one of the most advanced of all time. Toynbee wrote this in his master-work, six-volume *A Study of History*, while analyzing twenty-four of the world's civilizations. It was an understatement, because Korea has not had one, but four, brilliant golden ages. Each of these has far surpassed the achievements of her neighbors, China and Japan, in arts, technology, and science, especially during the last millennium. In many fields at given ages, Korea was ahead of even Europe by several centuries. This book describes these four golden ages in detail.

The Korean government of the Li dynasty became feeble and corrupt in its last fifty years, from around 1855 to 1905. The government was in no condition to handle the turbulent onslaught of the imperial powers of China, Russia, and Japan. Inexperienced Korean government officials made many mistakes. In the end, Japan, which won the war against China and Russia, proclaimed that Korea was Japan's protectorate in 1905. Japan annexed Korea in 1910. In the long five-thousand-year history of Korea, this was the first time Korea lost its independence entirely.

Korea has consistently been ahead of Japan by at least several centuries, except during the last 150 years of a long history. In the 1850s, Japan made contact with the West, about thirty years earlier than Korea.

When Japan occupied Korea against the will of the Korean people, the Japanese government imposed a total black out of all Korean publications. Any information about Korea, including the historical facts, could come only through the Japanese sources. Japan ignored the fact that its civilization descended from Korea, that the early civilization was transmitted to Japan from Korea. In order to justify Japanese colonization of Korea, Japan set out to depict Koreans as backward people, who could not rule themselves and needed direct Japanese rule. The Western public and historians were fed Japanese propaganda regarding Korea that was either covered up, distorted, or entirely fabricated. This situation prevailed for over one-half century, until 1945. The ill effects continue into the 1990s, as these early Japanese publications have been quoted many times over. This is one of the major reasons why Korean civilization has been grossly underrated and misunderstood by many Western scholars. Some of the major Korean historical accomplishments and contributions were often mistakenly attributed to either China or Japan. Many history books of East Asia, written by Westerners, often omit the Korean civilization entirely. This major part of East Asian history, that of Korea, has frequently been ignored.

In the last two decades or so, Korean scholars and some Western scholars, and even the younger generation of Japanese historians, have begun to publish correct accounts of Korean history. The younger Japanese scholars are more contemptuous of Japan's past wrongdoings than anybody else. However, the dispersion of such new knowledge has been rather slow.

After 1945, Korea became a divided nation, divided by the two great powers, the United States and the Soviet Union. This eventually caused a devastating civil war, involving many world powers. The Korean War cost more than three million human lives. At the turn of the twenty-first century, Korea is not yet free of the tragedies which engulfed the Korean Peninsula for a full hundred years.

Korea has had a long, great civilization, with recurring golden ages. Destruction caused by foreign powers has failed to extinguish the Korean spirit for surviving and for building another golden age. Now, Korea, at least its southern part, is at the threshold of another golden age, despite the handicap of being a divided nation. South Korea has moved well past the stage of newly industrialized country (NIC) and into the exclusive realm of the advanced industrial powers of the world. South Korea is the first nation which has achieved this highest level of socioeconomic development since World War II, only after the Japanese model. Politically, both South and North Korea have had the misfortune of having power-hungry dictators, who seized power by forcible means. However, at least half the nation, South Korea, was on its way to becoming a true democratic country. The corrupt ex-military dictators, who abused power, were sent to jail in 1995. However, as of this writing, people in North Korea were still completely enslaved by the dictators. They were literally starving to death in 1995. Unification seemed to be the only means left for salvation. At the turn of the twenty-first century, there is a ray of hope for betterment for most of the Korean people.

To understand the present situation, one must look back into many thousands of years of Korean history. Contemporary Koreans are the product of a millennium of history. The purpose of this study is to look squarely at historical facts, without distortions. Atrocities committed by the Japanese in Korea in 1592–1598, and again in 1895–1945, have to be mentioned truthfully. By the same token, many mistakes made by Koreans themselves, and the neighboring powers of East Asia, that is, China, Russia, and the United States, are mentioned frankly, without relying on diplomatic wording. Many beneficial legacies left by American civilians and the government in Korea are discussed without exaggeration.

How did Koreans rebuild their country time after time, after destruction by foreign invaders, creating recurring golden ages? How could Koreans (South) in recent years rebuild their economy in such a short period, unprecedented anywhere else in the world? What motivates them? Why is North Korea so different from South Korea? What is the potential of Korea in the twenty-first century? Why are the peace and security of the Korean Peninsula so vital to the peace of East Asia and the world? Why do Koreans have such difficulty unifying their country? Why is unification of Korea so essential for Korea and the world? These and many other questions are posed and discussed frankly in this book.

Acknowledgments

As this book requires original texts of East Asian languages (Korean, Chinese, Japanese) as well as English, the author has needed the help of libraries holding extensive research materials in these languages. The author is grateful to the East Asian Library of the Hoover Institution, Stanford University, and the Defense Language Institute Library for loaning valuable materials without hesitation.

The author would like to pay special respect and gratitude to Dr. Claude Buss, Professor Emeritus, Stanford University, East Asian Studies, who has been his lifelong mentor. Dr. Buss has provided valuable advice and encouragement from the initial stages of this book. His advice is to tell the historical truth regardless of the surrounding circumstances; that advice has given the author courage to write truthfully regarding the facts. Dr. Buss has also reviewed the manuscript and provided invaluable advice.

Appreciation is given to Dr. Edward Olsen, Professor at the U.S. Naval Postgraduate School, National Security Affairs, East Asian Program, who reviewed the manuscript of this book and gave the author valuable advice. Many thanks are given to Andrew Haslett and Erica Olsen, who edited the manuscript and gave excellent advice.

And last, but not least, affectionate thanks are given the author's wife, Alice K. Lee, who is presently the Chairperson, Korean Department A, U.S. Defense Language Institute, and who assisted with Korean materials and provided outstanding advice.

Introduction

This book has utilized resource materials pertaining to East Asia, written by scholars of four different countries, in original texts of four different languages (English, Korean, Chinese, and Japanese). Therefore, there have been some difficulties in transcribing three different languages (Korean, Chinese, Japanese) into English in one single book. A different transcriptive system for each language was employed.

There are several different methods for transcribing Korean sounds and words into English. The most widely used is the McCune–Reischauer system, which is employed by this book. However, the Korean language has the characteristics of vocalizing *t, p, k, ch* consonants sounds into *d, b, g, j* sounds after vowels and *n, m, ng* sounds. For example, the written word *Ko-ku-ryō* is pronounced *Koguryō.* In some instances, these pronunciations are transcribed as they are pronounced. The transcription becomes even more complicated when dealing with personal names. For example, the person's name Li Sūng-man, based on the McCune–Reischauer system, is spelled *Syngman Rhee*, by the person's own choice. *Pak Chōng-hi* was spelled *Park Chung Hee*, by personal choice. The name *Li* was spelled many ways, such as *Li*, *Lee*, *Rhee*, or *Yi*. In such instances, this book gives both spellings, as in the example, Pak Chōng-hi (Park Chung Hee).

The Korean language has a complex vowel system in comparison to some other languages. This vowel system has phonemes, indicating that the meaning of a word changes when the vowel sound changes. In the Korean language there are Round "o" and Round "u" vowels, as well as Flat "o" and Flat "u" vowels. In this book, the Flat "o" sound is expressed with the "ō" symbol, and the Flat "u" sound is expressed with the "ū" symbol. The Korean Round "o" sound and Round "u" sound are written as the English vowels.

In transcribing Chinese words, this book has mainly employed the Wade system, along with Chinese phonetic alphabets: for example, Nan-ching (Nanjing). The Wade system is similar to the McCune–Reischauer system of transcribing Korean words.

For transcribing Japanese words, the system commonly used by Japanese–English dictionaries has been employed.

In research on historical events, the primary sources are more reliable. The primary sources for East Asia are mainly found in Chinese, Korean, and Japanese texts, in the original languages, except for a period covering the last two hundred years or so, when the Western nations became involved in Asian affairs. The author has used primary texts as often as possible. The secondary sources are less reliable because the personal opinions of the users of the primary source are interjected. When source materials are tainted with political influences, those materials become quite worthless. When two nations were involved in the same historical event, the author has used primary sources of both countries, thus balancing the historical findings.

Part I

The Early Period of Korea

1

The Early Beginnings and Racial Origins of Korea

LAND AND PEOPLE

Land

Today the land of the Korean people is the Korean Peninsula, which thrusts into the Pacific Ocean in a southerly direction from the Amnok (Yalu) and Tuman (Tumen) rivers for about 1,000 kilometers (about 625 miles). To the north, Korea borders China and Russia. To the east, the Korean Peninsula faces the islands of Japan, separated by about 180 kilometers (112 miles) of the water known as the Korean Strait, from the southern tip of the peninsula to northern Kyushu. In between, there are two large Japanese Tsushima islands. The Korean Peninsula lies between the latitudes of 43 degrees north and 33 degrees south. The 38-degrees latitude parallel line, which once divided Korea into South and North about thirty miles north of Seoul, also passes near San Francisco and Washington, D.C. on the North American continent. All of Korea is in a temperate zone, although the northernmost portion of the peninsula is colder, influenced by the Manchurian climate. The southernmost Chejudo Island seldom sees snowfall.

The area of Korea is 221,607 square kilometers (about 85,563 square miles). It is about two-thirds the size of Japan and equal to the main island of England. At present, the Korean Peninsula is divided into two parts by the demilitarized zone (DMZ), near the 38th parallel: The Republic of Korea (South) and the People's Republic of Korea (North). The area of South Korea is 99,237 square kilometers (38,503 square miles) and forms about 45 percent of the peninsula. It is slightly larger than the European countries of Portugal and Hungary. The area of North Korea is 121,880 square kilometers (about 47,060 square miles).

The main mountain range runs from north to south, close to the east coast. Lesser ranges run toward the Yellow Sea. Most of the rivers, including the Amnok (Yalu), Han, Tae-dong, and Kūm, run westward, following these mountain ranges, except the Tuman and Naktong rivers, which run eastward. The Korean Peninsula is a mountainous region, with only 20 percent of the areas having less than a 5-degree angle of slope. There are several mountains in the east coast mountain range that are world famous for their scenic beauty, such as Kūmkangsan in North Korea and Sōlaksan in South Korea. There are hundreds of needle-sharp peaks and waterfalls. Most of the fertile plains are located in the south and southwest; most of the farm products, especially rice, have historically come from the southern part of the peninsula. On the other hand, the northern mountain ranges contain concentrations of mineral deposits rarely seen elsewhere on earth.

North Korea has most of the mineral resources of the peninsula, with more than two hundred minerals of economic value. Coal, iron ore, lead, zinc, tungsten, barite, graphite, magnesite, gold, molybdenum, limestone, mica, and fluorite are significant by world production standards. In addition, there are important deposits of copper, nickel, silver, and aluminum.[1] Iron deposits are estimated to be about two billion tons, and coal deposits about eight billion tons.[2] North Korea is better endowed than South Korea in mineral resources; however, South Korea has overcome this handicap with highly educated human resources. South Korea had become one of the ten largest industrialized nations in the world by 1995, with a gross domestic product (GDP) of U.S. $547 billion (see Chapters 17 and 21). In 1995, South Korea's population was 45,554,000, compared with North Korea's population of 23,487,000.

People of Prehistoric Korea: Galloping Horseriders

During the last decade or so, several archaeological excavations have shed new light on the prehistoric society of Korea. The habitation of early man in Korea started as early as five hundred thousand years ago. At Sōkjang-li, near Kongju, Ch'ungch'ōng Namdo, Lower Paleolithic tools representative of the chopper–scraper culture have been unearthed. At the same site, hand axes and cleavers of later eras were also uncovered. At Sangwon, near P'yōngyang, many fossilized fauna remains from the diet of early humans of the Lower Paleolithic Age have been discovered. From caves at Chōmmal near Chech'ōn and Turubong near Ch'ōngju, pre-Neanderthal and Neanderthal dwellings have been found. At Sōkjang-li, human hairs next to a hearth, together with animal figures of a bear, a dog, and a tortoise, have been unearthed. They have been radiocarbon-dated to twenty thousand years old.[3]

A few Mesolithic sites have also been discovered. In the coastal area of the western Korean Peninsula, some pottery of the Altaic Neolithic period with geometric markings, bearing some indications of cultural ties with the Ural–Altaic regions, has been discovered. This pottery is of a half-egg shape, with an open lip and a round bottom. It was produced with clay baked at low heat in an open kiln.[4]

Numerous sites of the Neolithic period were found in Ch'ongho-li, near P'yōngyang, along the Han River near Seoul, and in the Naktong River estuary, near Pusan. These were early Neolithic sites, dating about seven thousand years ago. People lived by fishing, hunting, and gathering wild fruits. They learned to grind acorns and wild grains on saddle querns. Around six thousand years ago, the Late Neolithic period began. People began to use pottery with wavy parallel lightning designs. Much of this pottery was found in the western and southern coastal and river basins. By this time, people had learned to plant grains using horn or stone hoes to dig: an incipient farming culture. They raised cattle and horses. At the Chit'ap-li site, carbonized millet was found in a pottery shard, indicating that harvested grains were stored in pottery. As early as seven thousand years ago people wove cloth and fish nets with spindles.[5] They built huts in round or rectangular dugouts with one to several hearths. These discoveries indicate that early people on the Korean Peninsula were engaged in farming and livestock raising and wove cloth as early as six thousand to seven thousand years ago. They also formed villages.

Previously, scholars believed that the Bronze Age in Korea began around the fifteenth century B.C., which was about thirty-five hundred years ago. The discovery made near P'yōngyang (North Korea) in 1993 appears to set the date back to at least 5,011 years ago (3018 B.C.). Probably the Korean Bronze Age began even before that date. The gilt bronze crown and bones discovered in a ruler's limestone tomb, believed to be that of Tangun, the founder of the Korean Kingdom, were radiocarbon-dated to circa 3018 B.C.[6] A bronze ritual ornament depicting a man plowing the land, discovered at a dwelling site near Taejōn (South Korea), was radiocarbon-dated to 2760 B.C.[7] This puts the date to more than 4,750 years ago, close to the time of Tangun's crown. These recently discovered Korean artifacts set back the date of the Korean Bronze Age to five thousand or more years ago, indicating that the Bronze Age in Korea was as early as that of China.

The Neolithic and Bronze Age Korean cultures were related to the cultures of the Ural–Altaic regions. This was proved by the discovery of similar pottery and artifacts in the two regions. The relationships of the people in the north-central region of Asia and the Korean Peninsula and Manchuria of today were also closely interwoven through similarity of languages (see the next section). It is also known that the people of Korea were galloping horseriders, who moved swiftly, conquering any who stood in their way. The Altaic people in the northwest of China moved into Manchuria and the Korean Peninsula around seven thousand years ago. They drove the original natives to Sakhalin Island, Kamchatka, and the Arctic, and possibly onto the northern Japanese islands.[8]

Among those people who were driven out of present-day Manchuria and the Korean Peninsula were the Ainus, who settled on Sakhalin and the Japanese islands of Hokkaido and eventually migrated down to southern Honshu. The

Ainus were violent people, who used poison arrows against the enemy in battle and in hunting.[9] They fought against galloping horseriders, Koreans of Altaic Turkish stock. But they were driven from the Asian mainland onto Hokkaido about seven thousand years ago.[10] Later, beginning around the second century B.C., Koreans had to fight Ainus again for nearly ten centuries on the Japanese islands. The Ainus were vanquished again and driven back to Hokkaido (see Chapter 4).

By 5000 to 4000 B.C., the new Korean settlers of the eastern regions of the Asian continent had become well established. They engaged in farming, wore woven clothes, and used bronze tools and weapons. They called themselves Puyō and Chin. These two branches of the Korean nation spoke the same language and shared the same culture and customs. For several thousand years, they jointly created the ancient, united kingdoms of Chosōn. The Chinese called them *Tungu(s)* or *Tungi*.

TRIBAL BEGINNING

The ancestral beginnings of Koreans can be traced back to the north-central regions of the northern Asian continent between the Ural and Altaic Mountain regions. Artifacts and pottery are important elements in the determination of such ties. Physical and facial features and customs are other such elements. Similarity of languages is yet another.

The Korean language is a branch of the Ural–Altaic language group, which includes Korean, Mongolian, Manchurian, Japanese, Turkish, Hungarian, and Finnish. These languages have common features of syntax, morphology, and phonology. Korean and other languages of this group put verbs at the end of the sentence with verb endings. Nouns can be placed anywhere in the sentence without much restriction. These languages do not employ tones, as do Chinese, Vietnamese, and Thai. The verb endings that denote questions and statements are also almost identical. These Ural–Altaic linguistic features are unique and very different from those of Indo-European and Southeast Asian languages.

The north-central and northeastern tribes of Asia who spoke similar languages also had similar racial and cultural beginnings. They lived in arid, harsh land not suited for agriculture. Their main livelihood depended on hunting and raising livestock. In order to control and raise livestock, they had to be excellent horseriders. They had to move periodically, seeking better grasslands, when food for the livestock became exhausted in the area where they had stayed for a period. They had to be mobile; hence, they were nomadic. When their food supply became short, they attacked neighboring tribes. Movement, warfare, and turmoil were constant. This situation made them warlike, and they were excellent fighters, skilled in cavalry warfare. These tribes lived in mobile tents by necessity of constant moving. They could move great distances in large tribal groups. One of these large groups were the Koreans.

These ancient Koreans were called different names by different people. Koreans themselves called their own tribe *Hans, Puyōs, Koguryōs, Koryōs,* and later *Chins* (*Nuchens* or *Jurchens* in Chinese) and *Manchus.* The Chinese called them *Tungus,* a derogatory description of their eastern neighbors, just as they called the Westerners who went to China in the nineteenth century Western barbarians. Whatever they were called, they had the same ancestry and settled in Manchuria and the Korean Peninsula by 5000–4000 B.C. Historically their domain was northwest of China. They then moved to northeast of China, later to Manchuria and the Korean Peninsula, and at the latest period to the Japanese islands. The Chinese feared these warlike, swiftly moving horseriders greatly, as attested by the existence of the twelve-hundred-mile-long castle, the Great Wall of China, which extends from the Manchurian border to Western Mongolia. This Chinese fear was justified, as over several millennia, China lost its nationhood many times over as a result of invasion by these northern nations. No great invasion ever came from the southern border of China; hence China did not build a massive fortress such as the Great Wall in the south. Ancient Chinese history books recorded that a large tribal group had been moving from northwest of the Chinese border to northeast of China and Manchuria over several centuries.[11]

This eastward migration of a loosely organized federation of Korean tribes took many centuries. These easternmost tribes spoke the same language and had the same customs and temperament. They created the great empires of Khitan, Chin, Koguryō, and Ch'ing of Manchus in East Asia. Their monotonal language, which was Altaic, was altogether different from the tonal Chinese language. Their physical features had more Caucasian characteristics than those of other Asian races. Archaeologists have discovered that Korean settlers who moved into the Japanese islands were on average several inches taller, with higher forehead bones, than the indigenous Japanese natives in the period from the second century B.C. to the fourth century A.D. Even as late as the nineteenth century, American missionaries noted that of all Asians, Koreans were closest to Caucasians in their physical features, with lighter skin color, high forehead, oval facial features, and taller stature than other East Asian people on the average. The Korean language is closest to the Turkish language and similar to Hungarian and Finnish. This relationship may give some clue to the puzzle of differences in physical features among Asian people. It is believed that such difference was no accident because Koreans originated from the region where Caucasian and Asian races intersected and became mixed in the northwestern Asian continent near present-day Kazakhstan, west of Mongolia and north of Xinjian, China.

Large-scale immigration of Koreans took place in several waves eastward through southern Mongolia, into Manchuria, and then to the Korean Peninsula in the period of the 5000 to 4000 B.C. until they reached the eastern sea. Even the sea did not stop them: When their civilization advanced and acquired riches to build large enough ships, they started to immigrate into the Japanese islands, conquering and assimilating the indigenous Ainus and Kumasos there from the second century B.C. to the fourth century A.D. Large waves of immigrants continued to move into the Japanese islands from the Korean Peninsula until the eighth century A.D., even after the Yamato state was established in Japan.

The warlike horseriders who moved into Manchuria in several waves created two major nations. One nation that was created in the west and central regions of present-day Manchuria was called *Puyō.* The Puyō people had a high level of civilization and practiced sophisticated agriculture in fertile farmlands. It is believed that the Puyō nation was ruled by a clan named Han (the Korean name *Han* had no relation to the Chinese Han Empire). The horseriders of the Puyō moved southward into the Korean Peninsula and created the Three Han Kingdoms; later their descendants created the four Korean kingdoms of Koguryō, Paekche, Silla, and Kaya in the first century B.C. Thus the tribal migration of the Puyō, which started from the north-central Asian continent, took a route through southern Mongolia to southwestern and central Manchuria, where they created a highly developed civilization in the period of the tenth to the first century B.C. Then the descendants of the Puyō people entered the Korean Peninsula in the northwest and south of that region. The "South Koreans" of the twentieth century are essentially the descendants of the Puyō horseriders. As early as the fifth century B.C., Puyō people were using iron tools. From the Kaya and later Paekche Kingdoms of the Korean Peninsula, several waves of migration took place into the Japanese islands from 200 B.C. to 700 A.D.

At about the same time, another large tribal movement similar to that of the Puyōs took place, entering southeastern Manchuria and the northeastern Korean Peninsula. These people were also horseriders, like the Puyōs, and were warlike. However, because they had settled in mountainous forested areas, they had engaged primarily in hunting and livestock raising and were relatively less culturally developed than the Puyō. Nevertheless, on several occasions, these people who called themselves Chins (Jins), and were called Nuchens (Jurchens) later by the Chinese, rose to create some of the mightiest empires in history, including the Chin and Ch'ing empires, which ruled most of East Asia until 1911. Present-day "North Koreans" descended from a combination of Puyō and Chin peoples.

2

Early Korean Kingdoms

MYTHOLOGICAL TALES

The early Korean kingdoms maintained an official department of history in the government, whose members' duties were to memorize historical records and transmit those records verbally to the next generations. Such methods were better than having no recording department; however, after several generations, any orally transmitted records would naturally become distorted. Koreans used the Chinese writing system as early as 220 B.C., and the earliest recorded writing (in 36 B.C.) dates from Korean contact with the Han Empire of China. A written Buddhist scripture of the Silla dynasty proved that Koreans even invented the world's first wooden block printing system in the seventh century A.D. Old historical records other than Buddhist scriptures and inscribed stone memorials are difficult to find for two reasons: because Korea was frequently invaded by foreign troops who burnt and destroyed government buildings, schools and universities, libraries, and any large buildings that kept historical records, and because the historian Kim Pu-sik, who compiled the history book *Sam-kuk Sa-ki* (History of Three Kingdoms) ordered by King In-jong in 1145 A.D., was also the all-powerful prime minister of that time. To ensure that his book had no competitors, he ordered that all previously written history books be destroyed, declaring that his book was the compilation of all other books. The history book *Ku-sam-kuk Sa-ki* (Older History of the Three Kingdom Period) was written several centuries before Kim's book, but the actual text has not survived. The book *Sam-kuk Yu-sa*, written by the monk Il-yōn in the twelfth century, still exists today.

The first kingdom was named *Chosōn*, which may be translated as the "Land of Morning Calm" in English. According to *Sam-kuk Sa-ki* and *Sam-kuk Yu-sa*, Korea was founded by Tan-gun (Lord of Tan) in the year 2333 B.C. These books noted that Tan-gun (pronounced *Tangun*) was the son of a female bear and a god called Kwōn-ung. According to myth, a tiger and a bear were so eager to become human that they tried to endure one hundred days of seclusion. Only the bear succeeded and turned into a beautiful princess, who eventually married the god Kwōn-ung and produced a son, who founded Korea. It is a mythological tale, but with some historical background. Early Korean or Tungusic tribes were represented by totem symbols of animals, and a princess of the bear tribe married Kwōn-ung, a god, representing a union of two large tribes in Korea. Tangun ruled a kingdom large enough to contain the southern part of Manchuria and the northern part of Korea.

Although Neolithic remains of these early Korean tribes have been found all over Korea, the early kingdom was formed by settlers who moved into the southern part of Manchuria and northern Korea, where climate and soil were more suitable for agriculture than fishing and pastoral pursuits. As noted, Tangun's tomb was discovered in the P'yōngyang area and was carbon-dated at 3018 B.C. Archaeological findings, which are more accurate than mythological tales, indicate that the actual founding of Korea occurred more than five thousand years ago.

The second kingdom of Korea was said to be founded during the Chinese Chu Dynasty of the Warring period, when a noted sage called Chi-tzu became disheartened with the lawless state of China and immigrated to Korea with five thousand followers in 1123 B.C. He founded the kingdom of Kija Chosōn around P'yōngyang in North Korea today. This theory has been disputed by most of Korea's historians. Another Chinese tale says that the first emperor of Ch'in (Qin), Ch'in Si-hwang-ti (Qin Shi-huangdi), dispatched three thousand boys and girls to the Korean Peninsula to obtain a miracle herb root, probably ginseng, to give him perpetual life. But they never returned to China and settled in Korea. True or not, these tales indicate that the ancient Chinese saw Korea as a utopia, where life was far better than in China, with its constant war and turmoil. The Chinese referred to the Koreans as the "gentlemen of the country in the east."

The early Koreans practiced shamanism. Shamanism has been the oldest mode of worship for Koreans, since the time before Buddhism and Christianity were introduced. Koreans may observe all three religions at the same time. For example, one may be married in a Christian ceremony, go to a shaman when one gets sick, and have a Buddhist funeral. In fact, the ultimate god for Koreans in Christianity and shamanism is called by the same word *Ha-na-nim*, which means the "Lord in the Heaven." Kwōn-ung, the father of the founder of the first Korean kingdom, Tan'gun Chosōn, was such Ha-na-nim, who descended upon the sacred mountain Paek-tu-san, or White Head Mountain. The main characteristic of shamanism is ancestor worship. This formed the basis of the family and clan systems which extended into the formation of the society and the nation.

CHINESE HAN PROVINCES

In 194 B.C. the general Wiman established Wiman Chosōn Kingdom around P'yōngyang in the northwestern Korean Peninsula. In 211 B.C., the Chinese emperor Chin Si-hwang-ti (Qin Shi-hwangdi) conquered six other neighboring nations and united China. The Chinese emperor consolidated the Chinese border against the Korean kingdoms in the east by repairing and connecting existing walls into the massive Great Wall, using 500,000 war prisoners. His policy was one of self-containment and defense. However, his empire did not last long. In 206 B.C. the new Han Dynasty of China was established. The Han Dynasty was more centralized and outward-looking and took an offensive posture against neighboring states, including the Korean kingdoms. In 108 B.C., the Han emperor Wu Ti destroyed Wiman and established four Han provinces. One of these provinces was Nang-nang, or Lolang in Chinese. This Han province was established in the area of the capital city of Wiman, Chosōn, and it became the center of Chinese military, civil, cultural, and commercial affairs.

Chinese civilization had started to flow into the Korean Peninsula through Nang-nang. This was the only time in Korean history that China could establish its colonies in the central part of Korea, where occupation forces were stationed. The Han Empire not only occupied Korea, but expanded westward to Persia and Afghanistan. The Chinese are proud of the Han Empire to such a degree that they call themselves sons of Han, and the Chinese race has been referred to as the Han race. The Han emperor appointed governors to the four Korean provinces, and they were directly responsible to the central government of the Han emperors. The Chinese introduced customs, the Chinese writing system, and literature. Commercial exchange took place, but it was largely exploitative, favoring Chinese officials and merchants. Nang-nang had become the trading center of East Asia. By 75 B.C., the four Han provinces in Korea were consolidated into two provinces around Nang-nang. Merchants of Nang-nang traveled to China and Japan and acquired riches.

By 56 B.C. a native Korean kingdom, Koguryō, was established in the north of Nang-nang and expanded in Manchuria. The ruling family of Korean Han went down to the southern part of the Korean Peninsula and established three Han kingdoms. The Nang-nang province of the Chinese Han Empire began to feel pressure from the north and south. In time, Nang-nang's civilization advanced until in some points it surpassed the level of the Chinese Han proper. By this time the Korean Peninsula was solidly in the Iron Age. Ancient Nang-nang artifacts show their refinement. It was the Alexandria of the East Asia.

THREE KOREAN HAN KINGDOMS

Because of the expansion of the Chinese Han Empire in the west-central Korean Peninsula, indigenous Korean tribes were pushed down to the southern part of the peninsula, which was endowed with rich land and plentiful rainfall.

Koreans took up farming, abandoning traditional hunting and livestock raising. However, nomadic characteristics were still present. These restless people were compressed into a small area in the southern half of the Korean Peninsula, and they were ready to look for new land. Accustomed to roaming in the vast central Asian continent, they had a need for a larger territory. Expansion of the Chinese Han Empire in the central part of the peninsula brought a new level of civilization to early Koreans, although they had had contact with the Chinese culture even before that. Nang-nang was a Chinese colony in the beginning; however, gradually it attained self-rule and became more of an independent state. The Chinese Han Empire became weak and Korea was too far away. The new Korean nation in northern Korea produced wise Koguryŏ kings and became stronger, nibbling into the territory of Nang-nang as military help was not readily available to that province from the Chinese mainland.

While the northern kingdom of Koguryŏ was expanding into Manchuria and into Nang-nang territory during the first century B.C., Korean ruling clans of the Han tribes founded three Han kingdoms: Chin Han, Ma Han, and Pyŏn Han. It is believed that rulers of these three small kingdoms were relatives. Chin Han was the northernmost of the three, occupying east-central Korea. Ma Han was in the southwest and Pyŏn Han was in the southeast. All three kingdoms had commercial trade with Nang-nang and thus received news of the latest developments of Chinese civilization.

THREE KINGDOMS: KOGURYŌ, PAEKCHE, AND SILLA

Each of the Han kingdoms was made up of thirty to fifty tribal groups. Eventually, two or three of them acquired predominance. From Chin Han, Paekche Kingdom emerged in 18 B.C. and eventually annexed Ma Han. From Pyŏn Han, Silla Kingdom was founded in 37 B.C. Koguryŏ Kingdom, which was founded in the Amnok (Yalu) River basin in 56 B.C., was still separated from those two newer Korean states by the Chinese province of Nang-nang. The Korean Peninsula was divided into four distinctively different regions for more than three hundred years, until Koguryŏ finally crushed Nang-nang in 313 A.D. Koguryŏ then expanded to the Liaotung Peninsula, thus occupying all of Manchuria and the northern part of Korea. Because Koguryŏ occupied the Chinese province of Nang-nang and the neighboring Chinese border, it had more contact with China, both military and cultural.

Koguryŏ Kingdom

Koguryŏ took over the capital city of Nang-nang, P'yŏngyang, near the Taedong River. On the scenic hills, the new rulers built P'yŏngyang-sŏng castle. They inherited a well-established, rich civilization. They also built two large castles near the Liao River and named them Lyodong-sŏng and Ansi-sŏng. These castles were built to defend Koguryŏ territory against Chinese invasion, and they played an important role in defending the country. The

Koguryō king who was responsible for the greatest expansion of the territory was King Kwang-gae-t'o (375–413 A.D.), who built and consolidated a great empire.

Whenever China became united and was able to exert great power, the Korean kingdoms felt its weight. But after the Han Empire collapsed in 220 A.D., China became divided into several parts, and dynasties rose and fell rapidly for over two centuries. Chinese leaders were too busy with internal struggles to pay attention to the Korean borders. Koguryō enjoyed relative peace with the Chinese, but it had to contend with the rising powers of Paekche and Silla.

Paekche Kingdom

The founder of Paekche was Onjo, who was a descendant of the Puyō kings and second son of the founder of Koguryō. When his older brother became heir apparent to the throne of Koguryō, he immigrated to Chin Han with his followers and set up a tribal domain, which later became predominant. His descendants moved the capital city and named it *Puyō,* after their ancestral kingdom to the north. Paekche Kingdom eventually occupied all of the southwestern part of Korea, south of the Han River basin. Although the founders of Koguryō and Paekche were related, these two kingdoms had become competitors and fought each other often. In 342 A.D., Paekche forces invaded the capital city of Koguryō, set fire to the city, and killed its king, Kogukwon, at P'yōngyang castle. Thereafter, these two states became mortal enemies. After this bitter lesson taught by Paekche, Koguryō greatly increased its military preparedness.

Early Silla Kingdom and Kaya (Imna)

In the southeast of the Korean Peninsula during the first century B.C. was the Pyōn Han Kingdom. It was a loose federation of many tribes, and since it was farthest from Nang-nang, it developed civilization last of the three kingdoms. One of the chieftains of Pyōn Han became dominant and was elected the head of state of Silla, which succeeded the kingdom of Pyōn Han. The first king of Silla was a wise man named Pak Hyōk-kō-se, who was an elder of the Pak family. Several clans, including Pak, Sōk, and Kim, shared kingship on a rotational basis. This governmental system was unique among the three kingdoms. It took several centuries for the Silla Kingdom to adopt a centralized government system, and by the midfourth century A.D. it was able to occupy most of the southeastern part of the Korean Peninsula and exert pressure on the small kingdom of Kaya, later called Imna. Japanese called Korea *Mimana* or *Kara*, a deviant pronunciation from *Imna* and *Kaya*.

Kaya was a maritime kingdom and an offshoot of the Puyō horseriders of Manchuria and the northern Korean regions. The neighboring kingdom to the west of Kaya was Paekche, whose people were descendants of Puyōs who had a more congenial relationship with Kaya. There was constant warfare between Kaya and Silla to the east. The Kaya people, who were excellent warriors, succeeded in forming Tae Kaya (Greater Kaya), occupying a large portion of Silla territory. In general, however, Kaya, which was a much smaller nation than Silla, felt pressure from Silla and sought a new region for expansion. The roaming horseriders of the vast Manchurian plains could not be satisfied with the small area of the southern tip of the peninsula. They began to build large ships capable of navigating the seas. The archaeological findings of ancient ships unearthed in Kaya, southern Silla, and northern Kyushu of Japan resemble the Viking ships of Europe in size and shape. Using these ships, the Kaya established settlements on the Japanese islands of Tsushima, northern Kyushu, and the southern tip of Honshu. Gradually the Kayan kings' domain extended from the southern part of the Korean Peninsula to the southwestern regions of the Japanese islands. Chinese historians called them *Wei* (in Korean *Wae* and in Japanese *Wa*). Later, after the seventh and eighth centuries, the word *Wei* was used to indicate only Japanese. However, before the sixth century, it referred to people who lived in both the southern part of the Korean Peninsula and the southern part of the Japanese islands, because they were one people, the people of Kaya (later called *Imna*).

From the second century B.C. to the fourth century A.D., large-scale immigrations took place from Kaya to the Japanese islands. In the sixth and seventh centuries, people came from Paekche. Although Kaya, on the Korean Peninsula, was smaller than either Silla or Paekche, it had a highly developed civilization. Its pottery and weapons were more refined than those of Silla. These Korean settlers from Kaya (Mimana) created the Iron Age Yayoi culture of Japan and later founded the unified centralized government of the Yamato nation in Japan. The kings of Yamato state, the ancestors of the present-day Japanese emperors, were in fact chieftains of Korean Kaya (Imna) settlers. Other waves of the Korean immigrants from Paekche in the seventh and eighth centuries helped to create a first golden age of the Nara and Heian periods in Japan. These Korean settlers had not had an easy time because they had to battle against the Neolithic indigenous tribes of Kumaso on the island of Kyushu and Ainu on the island of Honshu. History proved the Ainus and Kumaso violent people.

3

Early Korea and China, 100 B.C.–700 A.D.

THE WAR BETWEEN THE CHINESE EMPIRES AND THE KOREAN KINGDOMS

After the Han Empire, three dynasties were established in China: Wei (220 to 265), Shu (221 to 265), and Wu (222 to 280). Among them, Wei was the closest to Korea. With the intention of succeeding the Han Empire in Nangnang, Wei sent military forces to northern and central Korea. However, Wei's attempt was short-lived, as it was itself destroyed by the following dynasty, the Tsin. Tsin then divided into West and East Tsin; it was followed by three northern dynasties and five southern dynasties that lasted to 557 A.D. China's divisions and internal struggles lasted nearly three hundred years, providing relative calm on the Korean–Chinese border. However, almost immediately after the unification of China under Sui Wen-Ti (who was succeeded by his son Yang-ti), in 590 A.D., China set out to conquer the Koguryō kingdom of Korea. The expeditionary force sent out to subdue Korea in 598 A.D. was a failure, the Koguryō forces in Liaotung castle on the border held firm against Yang-ti's Chinese forces, whose food and water supplies became exhausted.[1]

In order to prepare for the second invasion of Korea, Yang-ti built great granaries in the Lok'ou and Loyang areas capable of holding 1,700,000 tons of grain. He then built the Grand Canal stretching twelve hundred miles from south and central China through these great granaries to transport more than a million army troops and supplies to Cho near the Chinese–Korean border. The Grand Canal, which Yang-ti built for war against Korea, was also the largest canal ever built, even to the present day, and served China for fourteen hundred years, connecting the country from south to north (because almost all the rivers in China flow from west to east). Finally Yang-ti was ready to invade Koguryō.

He had stockpiled enough supplies for his army of more than one million men, and the invasion of Korea began in 612 A.D. Koguryō opposed the invasion with an army of three hundred thousand men, which was inferior in number but better trained and more battle-experienced than the Chinese. Ūlji Mundŏk, one of the most celebrated generals in Korean history, defeated the Chinese army in several pitched battles, in Lyodong Sōng (Liao-tung Ch'eng), near present-day Mukden Manchuria; P'yōngyang castle; and finally Ch'ōngch'ōn River. Defeat of the Chinese forces was so complete that one million Chinese were nearly annihilated. Only twenty seven hundred escaped alive.[2] The invading Chinese forces were so completely destroyed that the general's defense plans and ambush tactics became models for military strategy.

THE WAR BETWEEN T'ANG CHINA AND KOGURYŌ KOREA

The great defeat of Sui caused the downfall of the Sui Dynasty in five years. Li Shih-min, who engineered T'ang's takeover of the dynasty from Sui, considered Sui Yang-ti's defeat by Koguryō a disgrace to the Chinese race. But he had to overcome power struggles with his two brothers, and not until 627 A.D. did he formally become Emperor T'ai-tsung of T'ang Dynasty by killing his two brothers and forcing the abdication of his father, Li Yuan. Once he became the T'ang Emperor of China, he set his mind to the conquest of Koguryō. Whenever Korea's neighbors became strong, Korea suffered the consequences, and its people became victims. Again, the aggressor and invader was China, not Korea. In 645, T'ang Tai-tsung mobilized 170,000 men and himself led the army against Koguryō. Anticipating such an invasion, Koguryō had stationed 100,000 troops at two castles, Lyodong sōng and Ansi-sōng. T'ai-tsung was able to capture Lyodong sōng, but not Ansi-sōng. Battles raged every day for more than two months, until mid-September, when the weather became cold. The battle site was too far away from the seat of government at Ch'ang-an (present-day Hsi-an [Xian] in north-central China). T'ai-tsung had to withdraw his forces after much loss, but not without military courtesy. The defending Koguryō general, Yang Man-chun, appeared on the top of the castle and bode farewell to the emperor, and the emperor responded by giving him a present of one hundred large rolls of fine silk and praising him as a fine general. T'ai-tsung could not accomplish his ambition to conquer Koguryō in his lifetime; he died in 649 A.D. He was, however, responsible for building the golden age of the T'ang period in China, which surpassed any other civilization of the world of that time.

THE SECOND WAR BETWEEN T'ANG CHINA AND THE THREE KINGDOMS OF KOREA

T'ang Kao-tsung, the son who succeeded T'ai-tsung, did not abandon his father's ambition toward Korea, but wanted to accomplish it at a slower pace by using diplomacy as well as military power. He began diplomatic exchanges with the southeastern kingdom of Silla. Silla, which was the last founded and smallest of the three kingdoms, somehow managed to seize the Han River valley in the central part of the Korean Peninsula and enlarge its territory. Silla now had access to an excellent waterway into the Yellow Sea, enabling its people to sail to T'ang China. Silla's diplomatic approach offered T'ang Kao-tsung the opportunity to accomplish his father's failed ambition. T'ang and Silla concluded a secret military alliance; neither Koguryō nor Paekche was aware of this event. Victorious Koguryō, which had won several great wars against China, became overly confident and sent its army into northern Silla. Koguryō tried to capture the Han River valley in order to close off Silla's route to China, while Paekche attacked Silla from the west and took some forty castles. The desperate Silla queen sent her royal cousin as emissary to Kao-Tsung and begged China's assistance. China, which had not been able to crush Koguryō with two great military campaigns by two emperors of two dynasties, saw an opportunity that it should not miss.

T'ang and Silla planned a joint military invasion of Paekche. The stage was set, and a date of attack was set. They decided to attack Paekche first because it was the weaker of the two Korean kingdoms. T'ang Kao-tsung sent 130,000 troops over the Yellow Sea and landed them on the western coast of Paekche, while 50,000 Silla forces crossed the Paekche border from the east. King Uija of Paekche, who had fought many wars against Silla and had taken hundreds of towns and castles previously, had become tardy in military and government affairs, indulging his tastes for wine and women. He was totally unprepared for an invasion from the east and west by two great armies. The Paekche general Kae Paek could muster only five thousand soldiers. He fought four battles and won all, but he could not win the war and was killed in battle. The king and crown prince were taken prisoners and sent to T'ang China. The end of Paekche came on July 18, 660 A.D., after 678 years as an independent nation. Paekche enjoyed a civilization smaller but no less brilliant than that of Nangnang or T'ang. Paekche played an important role in transmitting civilization to Japan before it succumbed to allied forces of Silla and T'ang. The Silla general was Kim Yu-sin, one of the most famous generals in Korean history. At that time, Silla also had wise King Kim Ch'un-ch'u, officially known as King Mu-yōl.

King Uija died soon after he arrived in China and the crown prince was given a post in the T'ang government. T'ang established five occupational regions in the Paekche territory and tried to rule Paekche at least for several years. Meanwhile, the remaining forces of Paekche gathered volunteers and their leader Pok-sin invited Prince P'ung, who was visiting Japan, and made him king while seeking military aid from Japan. Japan, whose royal family and more than one-third of whose nobility originated from Paekche and Imna (Kara), tried its best to save Paekche by dispatching an army, but at Paek-chōn River (Kūm River today) its naval forces were defeated by the allied forces of T'ang and Silla. Paekche's stronghold of volunteer forces was taken over by the joint forces of T'ang and Silla in 663 A.D., putting an end to the effort to revive Paekche.

Even before this final stage of Paekche, in 661, T'ang forces, with the aid of Silla forces, encircled the Koguryō capital at P'yōngyang castle for many months, until cold winter weather prevented continuation of the siege. T'ang withdrew its forces from P'yōngyang in February 662. Koguryō survived this attack, but soon after the death of strongman Kae So-mun, the two sons developed a power struggle and the older son voluntarily surrendered to the T'ang emperor. In 668, T'ang again attacked Koguryō, which was weakened by internal strife. This time T'ang captured most of the castles in Manchuria and encircled the capital city of P'yōngyang. Silla's forces joined in also. After 705 years, Koguryō met its final destruction.

Although T'ang China succeeded in destroying two of the Korean kingdoms with the help of Silla, T'ang did not share the fruits of the war with Silla and occupied both Paekche and Koguryō territory. Suddenly realizing T'ang's intentions on the Korean Peninsula, Silla feared for its own existence. Soon yesterday's allies turned to enemies. Silla began to invade Paekche and Koguryō territories on its own. Inevitably, T'ang and Silla forces clashed at the Kūm River, Yesōng River, Yang ju, and finally P'yōngyang sōng. Victorious Silla forces had swept away T'ang from most of the peninsula by 677 A.D. In this way, Silla finally united the Korean Peninsula. Unstable T'ang's occupation of half of the Korean Peninsula lasted only nine years; T'ang Chinese forces could retain some part of the northernmost peninsula and the southern part of Manchuria, but not for long. After the destruction of Koguryō, one of its generals, Tae Cho-yōng, gathered the Koguryō people and established a new kingdom of Palhae in Manchuria in 698 A.D. The territory of Palhae was gradually enlarged to the area of the former Koguryō Kingdom. The people of Korea recovered most of the former regions of the three kingdoms but had to endure prolonged warfare, turmoil, and suffering, which were due to China's hunger for power.

THE LINGERING ILL EFFECTS OF THE T'ANG CHINESE INVASION OF KOREA

Koreans describe war as *Nan-li*: *Nan*, meaning "disorganization" and "disorientation," and *li*, meaning "separation" and "dislocation." Whenever there were large invasions such as those by the Chinese Han, Sui, or T'ang, the Korean people tried to escape from the wars and battlegrounds and became refugees by the millions. Korean families became separated, and quite often they lost their homes. Countless people became sick or died. Each war and invasion caused a large movement of people to other areas. From the time of Puyō back to the tenth century B.C. through the Wiman Chosōn period and then to the Three Kingdoms period of Koguryō, Paekche, and Silla, the people of Korea were almost constantly on the move. The Korean horseriders moved from present-day Manchuria to the Korean Peninsula and then to the Japanese islands. When the Paekche was crushed, another large wave of migration of people from the Korean Peninsula into the Japanese islands occurred.

In addition to the massive movement of refugees caused by the invasions of the T'ang Chinese troops, there were other ill effects on the Korean people and their civilization. With encouragement from the T'ang central government, Chinese generals and troops rounded up men, women, and children from the old Koguryō and Paekche territories, took them to China as war booty, and sold them as slaves. The number of such kidnapped people reached 200,000 in Koguryō territory and 13,000 in the Paekche area.[3] This slave trade became so profitable that even after Silla unified the Korean Peninsula and a new Korean kingdom of Palhae was established in Manchuria and northeastern Korea in 676 and 698 (forcing T'ang Chinese troops from both Korea and Manchuria), the slave trade of Koreans, especially of women, continued in China. To do this, Chinese civilian gangs organized pirate groups and raided the Korean coastline to kidnap people for the slave trade. Such inhumane deeds against the people of Korea expanded to such proportions that both Silla and Palhae had to take major steps to stamp out such illegal activities (see Chapter 6).

THE CHINESE CULTURAL INFLUENCE IN KOREA

Chinese Characters and Literature

A writing system with Chinese characters was introduced to the Koreans even before the period of the Han Dynasty of China in Nang-nang Province in the northern part of Korea. But in the later part of the first century B.C., when the Chinese provincial governments were established, use of Chinese characters and documentation in Chinese writing had become standard. Adoption of Chinese writing was also frequent in Koguryō, Paekche, and Silla. These writings were in Chinese classical writing in the Chinese literary style. One such example was the inscription on the memorial stone of King Kwangket'o of Koguryō, written in Chinese characters. Koreans then began to use the sounds of Chinese characters for writing their native language. Since the Korean language was altogether different from Chinese, it could not be written in the Chinese way. To overcome this problem, Koreans used Chinese characters that had similar syllabic sounds for Korean syllabic sounds to express spoken language for literature (such as poems and songs) in Korean. This system was called *Idu*. Idu employed only the sounds, not the meaning, of the Chinese characters. This was the forerunner of the present-day Japanese kana writing system, which is essentially abbreviated Chinese characters. Koreans dropped this writing system when they invented a true scientific phonetic alphabet in the fifteenth century.

For the education of nobility and scholars, Koguryō established a university, *Taehak*, during the period of King So-su-lim in 372 A.D. The university was modeled after that of the Chinese and taught Chinese philosophy, literature, and literary writing as well as military affairs. About the same time Paekche also adopted the Chinese writing system. History books began to be compiled during King Kun-so-ko's reign. Educational systems flourished in Paekche, which established five Paksa (equal to modern Ph.D.s) systems and taught philosophy, art, literature, poetry, and more. Educated Paekche scholars later introduced the first Chinese books to Japan and taught Japanese royalty. Paekche attained many of the peaks of the highest development of a refined civilization.

Introduction of Confucianism

Confucius was born in 551 B.C. during the Chou Dynasty, at a time when the breakdown of social law and order caused much suffering. Concerned about the suffering, Confucius first tried to get a high government position in several divided regional kingdoms, so that he could implement his governing philosophy in actual practice in a government; however, he failed to attain such a position in any government. Confucius decided to teach his ideals in his later life and opened a school where as many as three thousand students gathered.

After Confucius' death in 479 B.C., his disciples compiled his teachings and talks into the book *Lun-Yu* (Analects). About 150 years later another famous scholar, Mencius, expanded and strengthened Confucianism. The central idea of Confucianism was *Jen* (benevolence or humaneness) of the government toward the people and among the people themselves. Activities of people were to be controlled by five rules of daily conduct and morality: loyalty to the king and state, filiality to the parents, trust between friends, respect for elders among siblings, and love and peace between husband and wife. It was a moral code to rule country and family. The emperors of Han China adopted Confucianism as an official philosophy because it encouraged loyalty to the king as a first principle. The Han provinces were established on the Korean Peninsula in 108 B.C.; Confucianism, the state principle of the Han Empire, came to Korea about 100 B.C. For millennia, this philosophy influenced Koreans, especially during the Li (or Yi) Dynasty (1392–1910). Confucianism became deeply embedded in the fabric of Korean society.

Introduction of Buddhism

Buddhism originated with Siddhartha Gautama, who was born a prince in a small kingdom in India, near Nepal, in 563 B.C. He witnessed the suffering of common people outside his father's palace and desired to learn the cause of human suffering. Subsequently he abandoned his kingdom and family and wandered about from place to place, meditating. After six years of suffering, he became enlightened. He concluded that the causes of all human suffering were greed and desire. Such enlightenment was regarded as the attainment of *nirvana*, the salvation of the soul, which must go through endless cycles of birth, suffering, pain, death, and rebirth through reincarnation, controlled by a relationship of cause and effect. What we had in this life was the result of previous lives, and so on. Until this cycle was broken, it would continue. To break this painful cycle of life, he recommended an eightfold pathway: correct views, thoughts, speech, conduct, livelihood, effort, mind control, and meditation. He reasoned that through meditation, one could control one's mind and be rid of desires, which were the source of all trouble and suffering. This philosophy took several centuries to develop into a form of religion.

Buddhism came to Korea (Koguryō) much later, from India through China in 372 A.D. During the rule of the Chinese Han emperor, Ming-ti (58–76 A.D.), a scholar named Ch'in Ching visited India and returned with monks and Buddhist scriptures loaded on white horses. The emperor became a believer of Buddhism and built the first Buddhist temple in China, the Temple of White Horses. This was the beginning of *Mahayana*, or Greater Vehicle, Buddhism, which was introduced to Korea, and later to Japan, through Korea. During East Tsin of China (317–420), Chinese emperors sent a monk with a statue of Buddha and Buddhist scriptures to the Koguryō king. This was the beginning of Buddhism in Korea. Within three years, a temple was built and the Koguryō king encouraged his people to believe in Buddhism. In 384 A.D. another Buddhist monk traveled to Paekche from China; he, too, was greeted warmly by the Paekche king. A Buddhist temple was built in Hansan, and soon ten more monks arrived from China. This was the missionary period of Buddhism. Buddhism was introduced to Silla from Koguryō between 417 and 458, and Buddhism was adopted as a state religion. King Chinhūng of Silla became a monk himself, and his queen became a nun. Among the three kingdoms of Korea, Silla saw a golden age of Buddhism, which is reflected today in the Pulguksa temple and the Sōkgulam sculptures of Kyōngju. The Buddhist art of Paekche was no less brilliant than that of Silla. Unfortunately, Paekche's temples and Buddhist artifacts were largely destroyed by warfare. However, the world's oldest wooden structure, Horyuji Temple in Nara, Japan, was built between 605 and 680 by Paekche architects and artists and still stands intact today, after more than thirteen hundred years. It is one of the grand masterpieces of world architecture.[4]

Taoism in Korea

Confucianism preached societal order based on certain moral codes. It was supported by emperors of the Chinese Han Dynasty, but as Han power declined, Confucianism also declined. During the T'ang Dynasty period, Taoism gained popularity among scholars. This new trend was also adopted by Koreans as T'ang power increased. It is said that Taoism was started by a mystic person named Li Erh, commonly called Lao-tzu. Lao-tzu opposed any form of organization, including government, and any rules. To him, a government official was worse than a common thief. Although Lao-tzu was born in the sixth century B.C., about the same time as Confucius, his reaction to the lawless society of his time was quite opposite to the Confucian philosophy of law and order: "Do not bind yourself to anyone or any rules; live as you like; do not concern yourself with future or past; live for today" was his basic idea. Constant states of inactivity and formless, shapeless states of being were Taoist ideals. This "nothingness" created a form of "mysticism." Taoists believed that Lao-tzu never really died; thus, Taoism also became a form of religion which let people attain earthly perpetual life.

When Taoism was introduced to Korea, it became quickly combined with traditional shamanism because of their similarity of beliefs. In shamanism, one who reaches a certain spiritual level can turn into *Sansin* or "Mountain God," and attain immortality. Taoism was first introduced to Koguryō in 624 A.D. by the T'ang Emperor Kao-tzung as a form of cultural exchange between China and Korea. It was then introduced to Silla, where it was adopted by the young nobles of Hwa-rang. Hwa-rang was a society of young nobles who enjoyed self-development of body and soul, much like the youth of ancient Greece. Taoist philosophy states "Nature is the only thing you can rely on. Become one with nature." This philosophy agreed with Hwa-rang's ideal, "Enjoy mountains and water." They also liked the Taoist idea "do nothing," because they believed that "It's not far, but need not reach it." They believed in the shaman ideal of becoming a mountain spirit able to live forever on a beautiful mountain with flowing water.

4

Korea and Early Japan, 200 B.C.–700 A.D.

JOMON CULTURE (8000 B.C.–200 B.C.)

Early Japan was divided into distinctly different cultures. The earlier culture was the Jomon, named for the shape of their pottery. Jomon pottery had rope-shaped decorations on the surface and was baked at the relatively low heat of about eight hundred degrees. The people of this culture were essentially a Stone Age cave-dwelling people who hunted and fished for their livelihood. Some of the Jomon were Ainus, a prototype Caucasoid people who split early from the main line of Caucasians and migrated down from the north through Hokkaido to the southern part of Honshu.[1] Others of the Jomon were believed to have come from Southeast Asia, carried by the Black Current through the island chain of Ryukyu to Southern Kyushu and the southern part of Honshu. These two groups of people mixed in the western region of Honshu. They were still so primitive that there were no clear-cut social orders, forms of government, or distinction of rich and poor. They had yet to develop farming.

YAYOI CULTURE BY *TORAI-JIN* (NEW SETTLERS FROM BEYOND THE SEA) (200 B.C.–400 A.D.)

Beginning about the second century B.C., an entirely new culture began to appear in the northern part of Kyushu and the southern tip of the Honshu island, geographically closest to the Korean Peninsula. This new culture was not a development of the Jomon people, but was transported by newcomers from the Korean Peninsula. Archaeological findings have shown that most, if not all, of the newcomers were from Korea.[2] This new Yayoi culture was imported to the Japanese islands by the so-called Torai-jin, or people who "came across the sea." Several points clearly connect the early Koreans with the Yayoi culture of Japan: language similarity; physical/body features; instruments people used; iron tools and pottery; rice cultivation and farming; use of horses for military purposes; seagoing vessels; burial customs; and shamanistic rituals.

Language Similarity

Both Korean and Japanese are Ural–Altaic languages. As noted earlier, the syntactic construction of these two languages is almost identical. This element is the slowest to change. After two thousand years, these two languages have the same syntactical construction even today. Some morphological elements are also similar. For instance, "where to" is expressed with the suffix *-e*. Questions use *-kka?* at the end of sentences, and statements use *-da* or *-ta* in both languages. Sentences ending in *-yo* are also often used in both languages. In both Korean and Japanese, verbs appear at the end of the sentence with endings and tense infixes; nouns can be placed anywhere in the sentence as long as denotative suffixes (postpositions) are attached; honorific forms are used extensively. Thus, the fundamental features of the Korean and Japanese languages are almost identical. Some people point out the difference in nouns, attempting to distinguish Korean and Japanese origins. While syntax and morphological language features were slow to change, lexicons changed readily, especially nouns. This was because loan words could be adopted easily. While Ural–Altaic Korean language structures stayed unchanged, many nouns of the indigenous native languages entered into the Japanese language. Thousands of Chinese words, and in the twentieth century, many English loan words, entered into the Japanese language. Thus, while the Japanese language started from the ancient Korean language, its lexicon gradually changed during two thousand years of history.

Facial and Body Features of the Yayoi People

The excavation of ancient Yayoi period tombs in Japan has revealed that bones found in northern Kyushu and southwestern Honshu, where Koreans migrated from 200 B.C. to 400 A.D., were quite different from bones of the indigenous Jomon people, who lived in Japan before the Yayoi culture. The newcomers were much taller, by an average of several inches, and had higher foreheads than the natives of Japan, and bones were identical to those found in the Kaya (Imna) and Silla areas of the Korean Peninsula.[3]

Instruments People Used: Iron Tools and Pottery

The Yayoi was an Iron Age culture. Iron tools were introduced into the Japanese islands by Koreans. Because of this, there was no Bronze Age in Japan. The newcomers from the Korean Peninsula used iron weapons and horses against the Stone Age people. Many iron spears, long, straight two-edged swords, and knives found in Yayoi tombs were identical to those found in tombs of the Four Kingdoms period on the Korean Peninsula.[4] Iron weapons were instrumental in winning protracted wars by the new settler–warriors against the fierce native Ainus and Kumasos.

The Yayoi people used distinctly different pottery. Their highly refined, decorated pottery was baked in twelve hundred degree heat and was much harder than the Jomon pottery (which was baked at eight hundred degrees and crumbled easily). Yayoi pottery was identical to pottery from Kaya, Silla, and Paekche of the 200 B.C. to 400 A.D. period. These stoneware products were used as utensils and for decoration in shapes of ships, birds, horses, and so on.

Rice Cultivation and Farming

The Yayoi culture practiced rice cultivation, and its farming methods were the same as those of the Koreans in the southern Korean Peninsula. The growing of rice was first introduced to northern Kyushu and spread onto Honshu.[5] Korean Torai-jin, the newcomers, carried rice seeds with them. The Jomon culture people had been primarily engaged in fishing and hunting, and this was one of the major differences between the Yayoi and Jomon people.

Use of Horses for Military Purposes

Many archaeological findings indicate that the Yayoi people were horseriders and mounted cavalry warriors. The indigenous Japanese Jomon people never saw horses before the Koreans moved into Japan with horses. The settlers were also invaders. The use of horses in battle together with iron armor and weapons was instrumental in winning the battles against the Jomon people. Although numerically superior, the Stone Age Jomon people were no match for the newcomers, who were well organized, well armed with iron weapons, and mounted on horses. These features were characteristic of the Puyō people, who came through Koguryō and Paekche and settled in Imna and Kaya. By the fourth century A.D., these conquerors pushed the native tribes to the central Honshu region, occupied the Kinki region of Japan (Osaka, Nara, and Kyoto regions), and established the Yamato state.

In 1958, the noted Japanese historians Ishida Eiichiro, Oka Masao, Kawakami Namio, and Hachiman Ichiro coauthored *Nihon-minzoku-no Kigen* (Origin of the Japanese Nation), in which they stated that the founders of the Japanese imperial family were Koreans.[6] As noted earlier, the Japanese called the imperial family *Mimana*, after a kingdom in the southernmost part of the Korean Peninsula.[7] The people of Imna were originally from the Puyō Kingdom in Manchuria, the ancestors of the Paekche Kingdom. But as Paekche and Silla became stronger, Mimana was pushed down to the southernmost coast of the Korean Peninsula. The hard-pressed people of Imna had to cross the China Sea and Japan Sea to the Japanese island of Kyushu. The squeezed Imna

(Kaya) territory was too small for these descendants of the Puyō people, who were used to wandering on horseback on the great plains of the central and eastern Asian continent. Thus, they had to find new, and larger, territory.

Seagoing Vessels

The remains of Yayoi ships have been unearthed in recent years, including some in the Shizuoka and Nigata areas of Japan. Drawings of the ships on pottery of the Yayoi period and decorations of ships on copper plate also have been found. The ships were of similar design to Italian gondolas or Viking ships, which curved up high at the front and back, marked with high posts. This type of ship has also been found in the southern part of the Korean Peninsula in the area of Ulsan, Kyōngju, and Kaya (Mimana), and the ships were made by the same people.[8] The ships were capable of ocean navigation. Although the distance between the Korean Peninsula and the northernmost coast of Kyushu is only about one hundred miles, it would have been formidable to navigate. However, the two large islands of Tsushima lay in between. It was not difficult for early Koreans to arrive in Kyushu by way of these islands. Japanese mythology indicates the interaction of early Koreans with the people of Japan, in the story of Susano-o, the younger brother of the sun-goddess Amaterasu, who misbehaved and was exiled back to Mimana. However, the main flow of people was from the Korean Peninsula to the Japanese islands. This flow continued into the eighth century, until the early Koreans occupied most of what we now call Japan.[9]

Burial Customs

As more people migrated to Japan from Korea, they formed not only the ruling imperial family but the majority of the nobility. With them came the old burial customs of the Korean Peninsula. Tomb construction was similar in the Koguryō, Paekche, and Silla Kingdoms. The tombs had large chambers, sometimes decorated with wall paintings, and belongings were buried with the deceased. Some of the wall paintings are magnificent, and are still intact in the P'yōngyang area. The old Silla capital of Kyōngju was called the City of Tombs. The city contains giant tombs of the Silla kings and queens, and their golden crown jewels are still being unearthed today. The early Japanese emperors built tombs similar to the Korean tombs. The tomb of the Japanese Emperor Nintoku is considered to be the largest in the world.

Shamanistic Rituals

Koreans believed in shamanism, the worship of ancestral spirits believed to have attained immortality. Japan's earliest mythological ruler, Amaterasu Omikami, the great sun goddess, was believed to be a shaman ruler. Queen Mimeko of the Japanese country called Yamatai was also a shamanistic ruler, during the third century A.D. The early Japanese rulers had a dual function, to govern the people and to function as the medium between the human and spirit worlds.

Japanese shaman rulers used Sanshu-no Jingi, or the Three Divine Instruments: a long, straight double-edged sword, identical to the type used by Koguryō and Paekche warriors; a necklace made with carved bear-claw-shaped jade; and a polished copper mirror.[10] These three instruments were handed down from emperor to emperor for nearly two thousand years and constituted proof of imperial legitimacy. These were identical to instruments used on the Korean Peninsula by the upper class in the early Four Kingdom period and used by shamans. Even today, Korean shamans use a sword and a mirror for their religious rituals.

The founder of the Korean kingdom of Chosōn, Tangun, was half divine and half human according to the mythological tales, and the Japanese Tenno (imperial) clan also claimed to be, up until the midtwentieth century. In order to keep the lineage pure, members of the Tenno clan were strictly forbidden to marry outside the clan and usually married cousins. After the Second World War, Akihito was permitted to marry a commoner. In this way, the Tenno clan was able to maintain unbroken rule over Japan for nearly two thousand years, the longest imperial lineage in the world. By the sixth century, the Tenno clan secured the Kanto region (Tokyo area) to the east and continued to push forward to the northern extreme of Honshu. This movement took nine centuries to complete. By the tenth and eleventh centuries, the Ainus had either become mixed or were pushed up to Hokkaido, which was called *Ebisu Kuni*, or Country of Barbarians. Hokkaido was not assimilated by the Japanese until the mid-nineteenth century.

KIKA-JIN (NATURALIZED IMMIGRANTS)

By the end of the fourth century, continuous waves of settlers had established the economic, political, and military foundations of a new country in Japan. By the seventh century, new immigrants began to arrive, most from the Paekche Kingdom. They were no longer military people, but artisans and scholars. The small state of Mimana (*Imna* in Korean), in the southernmost section of the Korean Peninsula, provided people and a new civilization to Japan; however, Imna became increasingly weaker, and by 562 A.D., it was annexed by Silla. This caused a flow of more people and materials to Japan. Silla, in the southeast section of the peninsula, was closest to Japan geographically but was farthest from Japan culturally. Paekche, in the west, had closer ties with Japan, during the period when Imna had frequent contact with Japan. But when Imna fell, Paekche became the main provider of new people, technology, and arts to Japan. The new Yamato government welcomed the newcomers from Paekche, awarding them high posts, wealth, and social standing. The next wave of immigrants were from the higher social classes of Paekche. They were scholars, architects, and artisans of the highest order, and some were members of the royalty and nobility. Paekche so influenced Japan that the Japanese culture of the sixth and seventh centuries may be considered an extension of the Paekche culture. Chinese classics, Buddhism, agricultural techniques, weaving, medicine, architecture, music, arts, and crafts were major Paekche introductions to Japan. Japan encouraged people who had expertise in these fields to stay in Japan and gave them positions which were inherited by their descendants for many generations. Those who specialized in writing and literature were called *Kuhito*, artisans were called *Hehito*. Such encouragement and special treatment caused a flood of immigration from Paekche to Japan, which represented the fourth and fifth major waves of immigrants to Japan from Korea. These new naturalized Japanese citizens were called *Kika-jin*.

Among the most noteworthy events of that time were the introduction of Confucius' *Analects*, and *Ch'ŏnja Mun*, the book of one thousand Chinese characters by the Paekche scholars Wani and Ajiki. Wani was later invited into the Japanese imperial court; he tutored the Crown Prince Shotoku, who established a new Japanese government modeled on those of continental Asia with new laws. Other major events were the introduction of Buddhism in 538 and the construction of magnificent temples such as Horyuji and Hokoji (*Asuka tera*) by the Paekche people. Sculptures produced by Koreans and preserved in these Buddhist temples are the finest art products in Japan of any age. Early Japanese called Paekche *Kudara*, an alteration of the Korean word *Ku-nara* or *K'ŭn-nara*, which means "home country" or "motherland." This relationship illustrates Japan's relationship to Paekche in the early ages.

After the destruction of Paekche by the allied forces of Silla and T'ang China in 660, the flow of Paekche immigrants to Japan increased greatly. At the same time, unified Silla took up and maintained commercial trade with Japan. The Japanese government established trade centers in several Japanese ports close to Silla and provided language interpreters to promote trade.

The Korean kingdoms provided their people and civilization to Japan continuously in different ways for nine hundred years, nearly half the history of Japan. These developments were recorded in the oldest Japanese history books, *Nihon Shoki* (720) and *Kojiki* (712). The flow of people and culture was from the Korean Peninsula to Japan, not from Japan to Korea. Some minor Wai (Japanese) pirate activities were recorded in Korean history books, involving no more than a few hundred, and they were quickly subdued. The beneficial role of Koreans was acknowledged by Japanese historians and government officials, including the Japanese Emperor Hirohito. Historically, Koreans were very good neighbors to the Japanese.

The waves of Korean immigrants to Japan can be divided into roughly four periods: The first wave started about 200 B.C., during the Yayoi period in Japan; it was the beginning of the introduction of continental civilizations through the Korean Peninsula. By the third century Korean influence was in full swing, but the newcomers could not yet establish a strong centralized government in Japan. The founders of the new Yamato state, including the imperial family, emerged from this group.

The second wave occurred from the end of the fourth to the beginning of the fifth century, when the Yamato government had been firmly established and interaction with the southern part of the Korean Peninsula was very active. This was the period of the Emperors Ojin and Nintoku, and the period of the Great Tombs in Japan modeled after the Korean tombs.

The third wave was from the middle of the fifth to the first part of the sixth century. Silla and Koguryō powers became stronger and Paekche was hard-pressed. Consequently, many Paekche scholars, artists, and craftsmen migrated to Japan, seeking safety from the never-ending warfare and responding to the Japanese government's welcome.

The fourth and final wave was in the second half of the seventh century, en masse from Paekche, when it was destroyed by the joint forces of Silla and T'ang China. Eventually these people became involved in Japanese politics, government, and the military and became powerful forces in Japanese society. Many became nobility in the central Japanese court as well as powerful regional lords with military power, especially in the Kanto area.[11] The last Korean settlers were sent out to the undeveloped forest regions of Kanto (Tokyo and surrounding areas today), because the central region of Kinki (the Kyoto, Osaka, and Nagoya areas today) was already settled.[12] The newcomers were told to cultivate new territory and subdue the still fiercely resisting Ainu tribes in that area. With these newcomers came prominent clan members such as Genji, who was also descended from early Korean settlers. They moved on to the central virgin land of Honshu, as their ancestors had for millennia. The Kanto area was still untamed Ainu territory, and these newcomers to the area had two tasks: to defend themselves from native attacks, and to develop the vast uncultivated lands. They were successful in creating new irrigation systems to new farmlands after clearing forests. They also started to raise horses, an age-old tradition, as they were descendants of the horseriders of the Puyō people of Korea and Manchuria. Horses and iron weapons were very effective against the Ainus. After several generations of hard work, the Korean settlers developed vast manors with rich farmlands. By the tenth to eleventh century, these manorial regional lords organized self-sustaining military forces which were able to subdue and assimilate many of the Ainus. Those Ainus who were not ready to subordinate themselves to the new settlers were pushed farther up to the north, to Tohoku, in the extreme north of Honshu.

Rise of Military Clans in Japan

Most of the manorial lords who were descended from Korean settlers were first called *Chito* ("Head of the Land"). They governed their lands without much help from the central government in Kyoto. These lords were the forerunners of the *Daimyos* (regional military lords) of Japan, who started the

Bushi (Samurai) rules. One clan gathered such military power that it took possession of political power over all of Japan and established a shogunate government in Kamakura, near Tokyo today.[13] Minamoto Yoritomo, the first shogun of Japan, who established the Kamakura Shogunate government in 1185, was a Genji and a descendent of Korean settlers. Some of the Genji clan became so rich that their wealth overshadowed that of nobles in the central government in Kyoto. It is said that Minamoto Yorimitsu (948–1021), who was the lord of three regional countries, made a "simple" present for the open-house party of his friend Fujiwara in Kyoto of thirty fine horses and a house full of expensive furniture for the entire mansion.[14] The first Shogunate of Kamakura lasted until 1333. The second Shogunate was the Muromachi Shogunate (1336–1573), ruled by the Ashikaga clan in Kyoto. This clan was also a Genji clan and a descendent of the early Korean settlers. In this manner, descendants of Korean settlers almost monopolized Japanese political and military power for many centuries.

Takeda Shingen, one of the most powerful warlords in Japan (1521–1573), also was descended from the Genji clans and proudly proclaimed this lineage in public. Takeda changed his surname to *Siragi* (*Silla* in Korean) and called himself Siragi Saburo to show his ancestry.[15] Thus Korean settlers and their descendants dominated the central government as well as regional areas of Japan. As we have seen, such power began when the Korean settlers Imna, Paekche, and Silla formed tribal kingdoms in Kyushu and the southern part of Honshu from the second century B.C. to the second and third centuries A.D. This power was transformed into the Kamakura Shogunate and then into the Muromachi Shogunate, which lasted until the mid-sixteenth century. The continuous domination lasted for seventeen centuries. The Japanese revered the Korean settlers until the late nineteenth century, when Japanese military expansion instilled discriminatory attitudes toward Koreans and Chinese alike to justify Japanese aggression against mainland Asia.

The Korean settlers were revered to such an extent that some were worshipped as gods in Japanese Shinto shrines (a practice that continues even today). One good example is Ameno Hi-boko, a prince of Silla who settled in Japan with his followers during the reign of Emperor Suinin. He left Silla with his men to search for his lover, who had gone to Japan several years earlier with her parents. He skipped the coast of Kyushu and sailed through the inner sea of Seto Nai-kai, going directly to the Kinki region. He became an important government official and settled eventually in the Hyoko area. He was established in Japan's Izushi Shrine as a Shinto god. His grandson Tajimamori was sent back to Korea to obtain a miracle medicine for long life for the Japanese emperor Suinin, who is said to have lived to be 140 years. This was one of many stories of Koreans who became well established in Japan. Early Japanese society did not exclude Koreans, as has twentieth-century Japan. Today, in the Tokyo area alone, there are 130 Japanese shrines and temples which worship the spirits of Korean ancestors.[16] Several hundred other shrines in Japan also worship the spirits of early Korean settlers.

Dubious Japanese Historical Records of Early Korean–Japanese Relationships Used by the Twentieth-Century Japanese Imperialists

There is no record of discrimination against Koreans in early Japan. In fact, Japanese society welcomed Koreans, offering special privileges, incentives, and high positions, because Koreans possessed high levels of knowledge and skill in literature, technology, arts, and architecture. Not only that, as most Japanese historians now admit, the Japanese royal family and the majority of the nobility in early Japan were of Korean origin in the sixth century. Naturally they welcomed people from their homeland.

The discrimination against Koreans in Japan today is the product of twentieth-century Japanese imperialists and military expansionists who were ignorant of the origins of their ancestry. Before and during the Second World War, these extremists advocated the supremacy of the Japanese "Yamato race," just as Nazi Germany preached the supremacy of the "Aryan race" to justify aggression against their neighbors.

Some Japanese historians were no less irresponsible, contributing to nationalist expansionism by quoting fictitious tales of ancient Japanese conquests of Korea. Some of these tales were quoted from *Nihon Shoki*, which was used by the Japanese ultranationalist and imperialists as a Bible. During the eighth century, when *Nihon Shoki* was written, Japan was in an inferior position in East Asia. In order to enhance the national image, the Japanese historians inserted fictitious tales. According to these tales, Japan dominated mainland East Asia in the fourth century, when the Korean settlers from Imna had barely started to take a foothold in northern Kyushu and south Honshu. Three tales were most common.

The Fictitious Story of Jin-gu

The first such fictional story is the tale of the fourth-century Japanese queen Jin-gu, who led an army; crossed the formidable sea in a great fleet of ships; conquered Silla, which was well established with a strong army by that time; and made Silla a subject of Japan. Today this story is all but dismissed by Japanese historians as a fiction, but it was quoted often in the late nineteenth and early twentieth centuries.

The middle of the fourth century was an unsettled period in Japan, and central government was not yet established. There were some two hundred tribal areas, all battling each other. The Korean settlements in northern Kyushu and southern Honshu were barely taking shape. The Jin-gu story could not have been based on fact. If it was a historical fact that Japan conquered Silla and subjugated it, it should have been recorded in the extensive history books of the History of Three Kingdoms of Korea, *Sam-kuk Sa-ki*, and *Sam-kuk Yu-sa*.

There is no trace of such a record. This kind of fictitious tale emphasized by historians officially, even in high school textbooks published by the Japanese Government Ministry of Education (Mombu-sho), boosted common Japanese peoples' arrogance and contempt toward their neighbors. This belittling discriminatory attitude became firmly entrenched in the minds of the Japanese. The false history produced countless victims in the neighboring state of Korea in modern times.

The Japanese government and its hired historians claimed not only to their own people, but to the world that the Koreans were an inferior race unfit for self-determination and self-government. For this reason, they argued, Japan must occupy and govern Korea. Yet, they were talking about a people who had a high level of civilization and more than five thousand years of continuous independence, more than twice as long as Japanese history. Throughout history and up to modern times, Japanese have learned from Koreans practically every aspect of civilization, because Korea had attained higher levels.

The Jin-gu story is today rejected not only by most of the younger generation of Japanese historians, but also by Western historians. The American historians Jon Carter Covell and Alan Covell, in their book *Korean Impact on Japanese Culture*, assert that the Jin-gu story was twisted around 180 degrees by the Japanese historians. They argue that Jin-gu was a Korean princess, the last of the Puyō Kingdom, who left the central Manchurian and northern Korean region in 346 A.D. because her homeland was destroyed by Hsienbi. The remaining Puyō people protected the young princess and went south to Paekche. The Paekche people, who themselves had originated in Puyō, received Jin-gu warmly. She later married the Kayan king Chuai. King Chuai already had a foothold in northern Kyushu and battled the Kumaso tribes of southern Kyushu. Kaya (Imna) was a maritime kingdom whose ships frequently carried settlers to Japan. When the king died suddenly, the young Queen Jin-gu who was now pregnant, took the throne. She organized a greater armed force, conquered Silla, and then went over the sea to northern Kyushu from Silla in order to carry out her husband's unfinished task of conquering the Kumaso of southern Kyushu tribes.[17] The Kumasos were the dark-skinned Neolithic era aborigines who settled on Kyushu, possibly after migration over the southern seas to Japan. They were thought to be a violent people. Jin-gu's troops were Puyō horseriders armed with iron weapons and armor. Jin-gu went from Korea to Japan, not from Japan to Korea. By virtue of marriage to the Kayan king, she ruled Kaya and part of Silla and Japan. The Covells' argument is generally in agreement with archaeological findings regarding linguistic linkage, level of civilization, and technological development of Japan and Korea of that period.

The "Nihon-Fu" (Japanese Office) Story

A second example, often quoted by Japanese historians who supported Japanese conquest of Korea, was the mention of "Nihon-Fu" in the book *Nihon Shoki* (Records of Japan, 720), which briefly stated that a Japanese office existed in Kaya or Mimana. *Fu* indicates that it was some kind of government office. But the book did not describe its function, nor did it say that it was a governing organization. The brevity of this one mention in thirty volumes of a history indicates its insignificance. Certainly it was not the Japanese colonial government which ruled the Korean Peninsula, as some Japanese historians claim. If it was, at least one volume of *Nihon Shoki* would have been allocated for it. Also, there is no mention of a Japanese governing body anywhere on the Korean Peninsula in extensive Korean history books such as *Sam-kuk Sa-ki* or *Sam-kuk Yu-sa* of the Korean Three Kingdom period. If there was an important Japanese government office with military forces which ruled the Imna, Silla, and Paekche Kingdoms, there should have been extensive descriptions of it in these books.

Imna, or Kaya, was an independent state with its own kings and government, but it also was the ancestral home of the Japanese imperial family; therefore, they could have maintained an official diplomatic liaison legation in Imna and nothing more. If Japan had a strong military force which could conquer two kingdoms, Imna would not have been so easily annexed into Silla in 562. *Nihon Shoki*, a collection of centuries' worth of orally transmitted Japanese history, is essentially unreliable. At any rate, the "Nihon-Fu" story was written for the first time in 720, nearly two hundred years after Imna was annexed by Silla, and has no historical value. Postwar Japanese historians also reject this story.

An Ambiguous Stone Inscription

The third example is the inscription on a stone monument of the Koguryō King Kwang-gae-t'o (375–413). The inscription was partially destroyed and was incomplete, but the Japanese historians who advocated conquest of the Korean Peninsula interpreted it to say that Wae (meaning ancient Japanese or South Koreans, but not necessarily an official government) traveled over the sea, conquered something (which cannot be read, but was assumed to be Silla and Paekche), and made them subjects of "something." King Kwang-gae-t'o was the Koguryō king who attacked Silla and Paekche, took their territories in border areas, and subjugated people in these occupied territories. Why would Koguryō erect a monument to Japanese conquest in a place of the achievements of their own king? The inscription lacks clear divisions between the sentences, leaving the inscription open to interpretation: "The Wae came over the sea [end sentence here]. King Kwang-gae-t'o [abbreviated] conquered Silla and Paekche and made them subjects." This interpretation agrees with historical facts. In the later part of the fourth century, the Japanese Yamato state was just beginning to consolidate its new territory of the Kinki region of Japan. It is a farfetched idea that Japan, at that unsettled stage, was able to mobilize a great army, cross a formidable sea with a great fleet, and conquer two well-established countries which had strong armies. There is no trace of such a large undertaking in official Japanese history books, nor any trace of archaeological remains.

At that time Paekche and Silla had formed an alliance, successfully defending themselves against the Koguryō king's continuous attacks. Only a few years earlier, Paekche forces had attacked the capital city of Koguryō (P'yōngyang) and killed the king of Koguryō, and Koguryō's resentment of Paekche was still fresh. For this reason, they called Paekche *Paek-Jan* in the inscription. It was an abbreviation of *Paekche Janak* or *Janjae*, a derogatory characterization referring to Paekche's vicious gangs or stragglers. If Koguryō could not destroy Paekche itself, it wished for someone else to do so. Thus, in another sense, the inscription may have been wishful thinking. At any rate, Wae denoted both southern Koreans and people who lived on the southwest Japanese islands, the same Kaya people who had ruled both regions in ancient times. Wae did not denote Japan alone, as was the case later.

In addition, other evidence has surfaced recently which questions the validity of the inscription. The Korean historian Li Chin-hi has argued that the Kwang-gae-t'o memorial was a politically motivated forgery by Sakou, a Japanese spy during the early Meiji period (1880–1900). Sakou worked directly for the Japanese army staff headquarters, which was planning to invade Korea and Manchuria. The spy fabricated a false clay stub, supposedly a duplicate of part of the memorial of King Kwang-gae-t'o, and distributed it to the community of Japanese historians who enthusiastically supported Japanese imperial expansion into Korea and Manchuria during the 1880–1910 period.[18] This stimulated the Japanese desire to "retake" the Korean Peninsula and "repeat" history.

Such manipulations of history were common during the first half of the twentieth century in Japan. If these stories of Japanese conquests of Silla and Paekche were accurate, there would be no need to deny them, because such events took place so often in world history. However, a fabricated history for political and military purposes requires a thorough critical review. Japanese nationalist historians not only manufactured and exaggerated stories of Japanese conquests of Korea, but also completely hid or distorted historical facts about Korean contributions to early Japan. It was unthinkable for these Japanese historians that Koreans could have played such an important role in Japanese history. To these imperialists, Korea and its people existed for the purpose of Japanese conquest and exploitation. Japanese who knew the facts did not talk about them, or they would be purged from Japanese society. This attitude dies hard. High school history books sponsored by the Japanese Ministry of Education still contain this type of fictional story of Japanese conquests and minimize the Korean origins of Japanese history, even in the 1990s.

Recent Historical Publications in Japan on the Korean Origin of the Japanese Nation

However, after World War II, some academic-minded historians started to describe the origins of the Japanese people and culture in ways that were profoundly tied to the people and culture of Korea. *Nihon-minzoku-no-Kigen* (Origin of the Japanese Race), written by Ishida Aiichiro, Oka Masao, Kawaue Yamio, and Hachiman Ichiro, describes the Korean origins of the Japanese and of the Japanese imperial Tenno clan who established the Yamato state of Japan. *Nihon-no Chosen Bunka* (Korean Culture in Japan), written by Ryutaro Shiba, Masa-aki Ueda, and Tatsu-shu Kin (Kim, Tal-su), describes Korean and Japanese similarities and the predominance of Korean settlers in early Japanese history. *Chosen* (Korea), by Tatsu-shu Kin, adds important information about the roles played by Koreans in the early history of Japan, including the history of the Japanese rulers descended from the Korean settlers. *Wai Koku-no Sekai* (World of Wai, Ancient Japan), by Ueda Masa-aki, describes in detail how ancient Japan was developed and how Korean settlers who traveled over the sea introduced the first civilization to Japan. He also expresses his anger over the Japanese treatment of Koreans and the way historical materials were manipulated by Japanese historians to satisfy Japanese military aggression on the Korean Peninsula during the period 1910–1945.[19] *Nihon-no Rekishi* (History of Japan), by Inokami Kiyoshi, is an honest historical account of the Japanese–Korean relationship. *Chosen shi* (History of Korea), by Kajimura Hideki, emphasizes the uniqueness of Korean culture apart from Chinese culture, and its closeness to Japanese culture, which originated on the Korean Peninsula.

These are just a few of the many books on this subject. They are all in the Japanese language and written by noted Japanese scholars, most of whom are university professors. It is encouraging to see that after World War II, these younger scholars emerged as true historians, not as hired "mouthpieces" for nationalist politicians and military expansionists. There are also many non-Japanese historians, such as the Korean scholar Kim Tal-su and the American scholar–statesman Edwin O. Reischauer, who support the theory.

The new historians agree that Korean pioneer settlers in Japan, in the period from the second century B.C. to the eighth century A.D., settled in the Japanese islands in several large waves and played a central role in the founding of the Japanese government, political and military establishments, and developments of society, technology, and arts. The younger scholars unanimously reject the theory that the early Japanese Yamato state sent an army to Korea and conquered and occupied the Korean Peninsula at any time. They all agree that the flow was from Korea to Japan and that it continued for many centuries.

The history of the inflow of Koreans into Japan was similar to the history of European settlers in America. In both cases the settlers won their new lands with determination, hard work, courage, and ingenuity. Both gradually moved inland over the centuries, exploring and cultivating new lands. Both had to become militarily strong as they constantly faced indigenous native attacks. Koreans were vastly outnumbered by the natives in the beginning; however, they were better organized and had the advantage of Iron Age technology. Subsequent waves of immigrants enabled them to control all of the Japanese islands. Koreans not only brought a new higher civilization and organized government to Japan, but also opened up new virgin lands, cleared forests, introduced effective irrigation systems, and created vast farmlands. After several centuries, they could claim great riches. However, regionalization of wealth and military power gradually led Japan into the rise of regional lords, internal struggles, and a feudal society similar to that in Europe in the Middle Ages. Until then, Japanese society rewarded Korean settlers and their descendants with the pinnacle of political and military power and wealth, including the lineage of the imperial throne that has endured to this day.

Supporting this history of Korean penetration of Japanese society is the register of families compiled by the Japanese government in 815 A.D. Over one-third of the nobles listed in this official register were of Korean descent.[20] However, it should be noted that this first official register was compiled after considerable racial mixing had already occurred. If such a register had been compiled during the period of the founding of the Yamato state in the third to fourth centuries, the proportion of Korean family origin may have increased to over two-thirds (if not almost all) of the nobles.

Today the majority of Japanese historians state that Koreans composed the conquering forces of the Tenno clan, who introduced new civilization, governmental systems, technology, religion, arts, and literature into the Japanese islands in the early historical period of Japan. However, Koreans were still an elite minority of the population, and the majority of the people were descendants of the indigenous Ainu and Kumaso. Gradually these three distinctively different peoples became mixed to form the present-day Japanese society. There is no written record or archaeological finding that indicates any atrocities were perpetrated by ancient Korean settlers and rulers against the indigenous natives of Japan. They were gradually and gently assimilated into the new civilization which Koreans introduced. Such an assimilation process was beneficial to everybody.

Notes to Part I

CHAPTER 1

1. Vreeland, R. Shinn, P. Just, and P. Moeller, *North Korea* (Washington, D.C.: American University, 1976), 45.

2. Ibid.

3. *A Handbook of Korea* (Seoul, Korea: Korean Overseas Information Service, Government of the Republic of Korea, 1990), 57.

4. Ibid.

5. Ibid., 58.

6. Edward Kim, "Focus on News: North Korea." *Seoul Magazine* (Seoul, Korea: Samsung Moon-Hwa Printing Co., November 1993), 29.

7. *Handbook of Korea*, 62.

8. Ibid.

9. Ralph Gray (ed.), "The Ainu of Japan." *National Geographic*, December 1969, vol. 48. no. 13, 198.

10. Ibid., 199.

11. Li P'yōng-do, *Kuksa Taekwan* (Overview of the History of Korea) (Seoul, Korea: Bo Mun Kak, 1975), 13.

CHAPTER 3

1. Dun J. Li, *The Ageless Chinese* (New York: Charles Scribner's Sons, 1971), 168.

2. Headquarters, Department of the Army, *U.S. Government: United States Army Handbook for Korea*, 1958, 12.

3. Tatsu-shu Kin, *Chosen* (Korea) (Japan: Iwanami Shin-Sho, 1990), 55.

4. Ienaga Suburo, *Nihon Bunkasi* (Cultural History of Japan) (Tokyo: Iwanami Bunko, 1982), 60.

CHAPTER 4

1. Edwin O. Reischauer, *Japan: The Story of a Nation* (New York: Alfred A Knopf, 1970), 9–10.

2. Ibid.

3. Ienaga Suburo, *Nihon Bunka-Shi* (History of Japanese Culture) (Tokyo: Iwanami Shisho, 1982), 17.

4. Masa-aki Ueda, *Waikokuno Sekai* (The World of Wai: The Early Japan) (Tokyo: Kodansha, 1989), 60.

5. Ibid., 48–49.

6. Tatsu-shu Kin, *Chosen* (Korea) (Tokyo: Iwanami Shin-sho, 1990),3.

7. Ibid.

8. Masa-aki Ueda, *Waikokuno Sekai* (The World of Wai: Early Japan) (Tokyo: Kodansha, 1976), 62.

9. Edwin O. Reischauer, *Japan: The Story of a Nation* (New York: Alfred Knopf, Inc., 1970), 10.

10. Shiba, Ueda and Kin, *Nihon-no Chosen-Bunka* (Korean Culture in Japan) (Tokyo: Chuko Bunko, 1990), 52.

11. Ibid., 32, 72.

12. Ibid., 72–75.

13. Ibid.

14. Taro Sakamoto, *Nihonshi Shojiden* (Encyclopedia of Japanese History) (Tokyo: Yamakawa Publishing Co., 1970), 667.

15. Shiba Ryutaro, *Nihon-no Chosen-Bunka*, 75.

16. Tatsu-shu Kin, *Chosen*, 13.

17. Jon Carter Covell and Alan Covell, *Korean Impact on Japanese Culture* (Elizabeth, NJ: Hollym International Corp., 1984), 12–25.

18. Kajimura Hideki, *Chosenshi* (History of Korea) (Tokyo: Kodansha Co., 1989), 52, Li chin Hi, *Kokaito-O Oryuhi-no Kenkyu* (Research on Memorial Stone of King Kwang-kae-t'o), (Tokyo: Yoshikawa Kobunsha, 1972).

19. Masa-aki Ueda, *Waikokuno Sekai* (World of Wai; Ancient Japan) (Tokyo: Kodansha, 1989), 13–15.

20. Hans Johanees Hoefer, *Korea* (Hong Kong: Apa Productions Ltd., 1981), 34.

Part II

The Early Middle Period: Unified Silla, Palhae, and Koryŏ Kingdoms, 668–1392

5

Unified Silla and Palhae (P'o-hai)

T'ANG CHINA AND SILLA

The major aim of Chinese policy toward Korea through two dynasties of Sui and T'ang was to destroy the Korean Three Kingdoms, especially Koguryŏ. After more than a half century of repeated invasions of Korea, after the annihilation of Chinese forces of more than one million men led by Emperor Yang-ti himself, and after another humiliating loss by the Chinese forces led by the T'ang Emperor T'ai-tsung, China realized that it could not conquer Korea alone. China therefore enlisted the help of Silla. It could finally destroy Koguryŏ and Paekche, but its ambition to conquer all of the Korean Peninsula had not ended. China not only was not willing to share the spoils of war with Silla, who contributed the major effort, but also occupied all of the Koguryŏ and Paekche territories without the consent of Silla. China then sent large forces into Korea and attacked Silla. War broke out between T'ang of China and Silla of Korea. Silla was fortunate to have an outstanding general, Kim Yusin, an able prince, Kim Ch'unch'u (later King Muyŏl), and a well-trained army. After numerous battles, at P'yŏngyang castle, Kŭm River, and Yangju near Seoul, Silla won significant victories and was able to cleanse T'ang forces from the Korean Peninsula. A small country, Silla could not occupy all of Koguryŏ's territory; it could, however, occupy P'yŏngyang, the capital of Koguryŏ, and earlier Nang-nang (Loyoung). Silla's new territory could not quite reach the Amnok (Yalu) River, which is the border between Korea and China today. Silla accomplished this by 676.

Palhae Kingdom

The old territory of Koguryŏ in Manchuria was lost temporarily until a new Korean kingdom was established by a Koguryŏ general, Tae Cho-yŏng, in 698. T'ang China, which had exerted great power in the beginning of the dynasty, began to wane by this time. Empress Wu (685–705), the onetime consort of T'ang Emperor Kao-tsung, who engineered the takeover of more than half of the Korean Peninsula, was too busy consolidating her own power through struggles in which she removed her own sons from the imperial throne on two occasions. She therefore could not pay much attention to the affairs of Korea. After Palhae Kingdom was established, its rulers and people took a cool attitude toward Silla, as their resentment was still fresh and they could not forgive Silla for siding with T'ang China to destroy their country. From that time on the two countries went separate ways. Many people of Koguryŏ, however, became displaced by wars and went south to join Silla because the southern part of the Korean Peninsula had a warmer climate, rich farmland, and a higher standard of living. Some stayed on in the northeastern part of the Korean Peninsula, which is the Ham-kyŏng Province of Korea today, and the eastern part of Manchuria. Once the Korean nation, although divided, dominated all of the Korean Peninsula and Manchuria, and even early Japan. It had all the makings of a great nation but is now more or less shrunk down to a small part of the Korean Peninsula. From that time on, although Koreans maintained prolonged independence and sporadic sparkling civilizations, they could not escape the sad fate of being a small country located among big nations. On many occasions, whatever they produced was rooted out from the country and taken away to be replanted elsewhere. However, descendants of the Koreans were not always meek. One of the subtribes of the Koguryŏ Kingdom, the Chins (*Nuchens* or *Jurchens* in Chinese) from the old Korean Palhae territory, rose again in the middle of the seventeenth century; called themselves *Manchus*; created the Ch'ing dynasty; occupied all of Manchuria, China, Tibet, Turkestan, Mongolia, Vietnam, and Burma; and created and ruled one of the largest empires the world has ever known, continuing until 1911. During this creation of the Manchu dynasty of Ch'ing, Koreans on the Korean Peninsula suffered again, but were permitted to maintain independence as "brothers" of the Manchus. More detailed observations are reserved for a later chapter (see Chapter 8, the section *Rise of the Chin Nation [Nuchens]*, and Chapter 10, the section *Chin [Nuchen] Invasions of 1627 and 1636*).

A GOLDEN AGE OF SILLA

From 676 to 935, Silla enjoyed relative peace, insulated by Palhae to the north from the turmoil of whatever was happening on the mainland continent of Asia. Japan was undergoing war against Ainu tribes for many centuries and left Silla alone. There were some disturbances by Chinese pirates along the seacoasts, but these were not severe enough to endanger the country. This peaceful period gave Silla a chance to cultivate its civilization and develop a golden age, the second after the Three Kingdoms period.

Unified Silla organized new political administrative divisions and created nine provinces. In addition to the three provinces for the old Silla territory, Silla created three provinces for the old Paekche territory, and three more in the old Koguryō territory. This gave them better control of political administration. The people in old Paekche and Koguryō were not easy to handle and there were often rebellions. In order to lessen this problem, Silla took in the old Koguryō king as one of its nobility. Basically, Silla was under a system of nobility rule while having a centralized government. Silla failed to move its capital city to a more centralized location by maintaining Kyōngju as the capital city. Silla instituted land reforms modeled after T'ang China's land distribution system; like that of T'ang, the principle was that all the lands were state-owned. Whenever a child was born, it was given a certain plot of land. When that person died, the land was returned to the state. While the farmer cultivated the land, the state derived about ten percent of its crops as tax. But a farmer was permitted to substitute the farm product with labor, wood, or silk for tax. Greater landholdings were allocated to nobility and government officials. This system worked for a while although it was not equitable. The system started to break down as the population increased, and the farmland could not keep up with it. More powerful nobility acquired greater land by forcible seizures. Power and wealth concentrated in the capital city, which enjoyed such prosperity that the population consisted of 160,000 households, or close to one million people. It was one of the largest cities in the world at that time.

CULTURE OF THE NOBILITY OF SILLA

Silla had a strict caste system even among the nobility. The highest rank was Sōng-gol, held by a person both parents of whose came from the royal family; the second highest was Chin-gol, that of a person with one parent from the royal family. These people had vast palaces surrounded by huge gardens with lakes, trees, and flowers. Some of them owned as many as three thousand slaves, and the same number of cattle, horses, and pigs. Slaves were traded as any other commodity. Their children formed associations called Hwa-rang, something similar to the Boy Scouts of America today, but the membership was reserved to nobility. Members of Hwa-rang had to go through strict military training together with literary studies. They valued physical beauty, believing that a beautiful person also had a superior soul. They annually selected the best-looking man and woman and held a huge party attended by all the members.

Silla royal families and rich nobles adorned themselves with glittering jewelry made of pure gold and jade, and such jewelry is still unearthed today from Silla royal tombs. These products included the gold crowns of kings, queens, and princes. They wore jewel necklaces, bracelets, and pendants which hung from the waist to the feet. These luxurious artworks had no rival in their scale and beauty anywhere in Asia. Perhaps they can only be compared to the jewels of ancient Egypt or Rome, or to some of the European crown jewels. They were preserved intact for an average of fifteen hundred years in more than seven hundred giant tombs (fewer than half a dozen tombs have been excavated to this date). It was the Korean custom to bury belongings with the deceased in elaborately decorated chambers within tombs. This custom of all three kingdoms was also transferred to early Japan. This glimpse at the past shows how rich the early Korean societies were.

One such example is *ch'ŏnma-ch'ong*, or Flying Horse Tomb, in Kyŏngju. This tomb was excavated in 1973, revealing more than ten thousand artifacts that had been buried with a member of the Silla royal family. Among the more important objects were a beautiful gold crown with fifty-eight jade pieces, a solid gold belt with many dangling gold and jade pendants, gold and jade tiger-claw-shaped earrings, pottery, and a painting of a flying horse. The flying horse painting, for which the tomb was named, depicts the Silla belief that their shaman king, half divine and half human, was capable of flying, mounted on a heavenly horse which had wings on each of the four legs. The crown also had two gold wings, attached on each side. The artifacts showed that the descendants of the Puyŏ horseriders of the north carried the same customs many centuries later in Silla.

The artifacts were evidence of the Korean nation, their customs and culture, and the high level of civilization the Silla people attained. These artifacts were valuable not just because they were made of precious jewels and gold, but because their exquisite workmanship was almost unparalleled anywhere in the world. Since the discovery of these Silla items, many art authorities have become convinced these items deserve a prominent place in the history of art of the world. It also showed the uniqueness of Korean culture compared to that of the Chinese. Koreans adopted many things Chinese; however, they always maintained unique Korean characteristics. Silla gold crowns and pendants, for example, bore no resemblance to anything Chinese.

SILLA ARTS, ARCHITECTURE, AND SCIENCE

The Silla people's artistry was demonstrated in excavated artifacts; however, Silla reached an artistic zenith in its sculptures and architecture. These beautiful artworks have been noted the world over. The U.S. Federal Research Division, Library of Congress, book *South Korea, A Country Study*, notes that "Koreans have a highly developed aesthetic sense and over the centuries have created a great number of paintings, sculptures, and handicrafts of extraordinary beauty." The book says of the Buddhist arts of the Silla period, "A number of bronze images of Buddha and Buddhisattvas were made during the sixth, seventh, and eighth centuries. The images are not mere copies of Indian or North Chinese models, possess a distinctly 'Korean' spirit that one critic has described 'as indifference to sophistication and artificiality and a predisposition toward nature.'"[1]

The most outstanding sculptures are the stone images found in the Sŏkkuram Grotto Shrine, a manmade stone cave built ground-up, located near the city of Kyŏngju. These peerless sculptures are considered to be far more refined and lifelike than any others in Asia. The central stone sculpture in the rotunda of the grotto is the culmination of Silla sculpture, a magnificent rendering of a beautiful face and lifelike body clad in a thin robe that falls in shallow folds. This superb sculpture was carved from one piece of hard granite, which, unlike softer marble, would break away at the slightest mistake by the artist. This perfectly balanced artwork has been preserved intact for over twelve hundred years. Perhaps the only comparable sculpture is that of ancient Greece. (It has even been speculated that a lost tribe of Greeks immigrated to Silla or that a Silla artist traveled all the way to Greece and learned to create such beauty. However, this is no more than fanciful speculation.) If Sui and T'ang China had any influence on Silla art, it was in the early Silla period, where many other such Buddhist sculptures were found throughout Silla territory. However, the Sŏkkuram sculpture and several dozen other sculptures surrounding it in the same grotto prove that Silla artworks far surpass the level of the Chinese in beauty and perfection.

About the same time as Sŏkkuram Grotto was built, in 751, construction of the Pulkuksa Temple began. At that time, unified Silla enjoyed a peak of power, wealth, and artistic achievement. This temple of great scale is one of the oldest wooden structures of the world, together with Horyuji Temple of Japan (built by Paekche architects). It is considered a masterpiece of architecture in its symmetry and beauty. Two beautiful stone pagodas and a giant bell were also built at the same time.

FIRST PRINTED MATERIAL IN THE WORLD

Discovered at Pulkuksa Temple in 1966 was the world's oldest printed material, believed to have been printed in the mideighth century or earlier. There were two famous stone pagodas in the central courtyard of this temple, and legend held that within one pagoda was a box of pure gold holding a *sari* (bone of the highest Buddhist priest) of the Silla period. Nobody dared to break the pagoda apart. One midnight in 1966, all the monks in the temple heard a loud explosion. Several hundred monks poured out from their quarters and saw thieves scurrying away from the pagodas. The thieves had dynamited a pagoda in order to steal the golden box but had not had time to look inside it. While the pagoda was being repaired, authorities decided to open it up, and they found, indeed, a box made of gold. However, its contents were not the bone but an old scroll of Buddhist Dharani scripture. To everyone's surprise, it was a scroll printed with a wooden block which predated such Chinese or Japanese materials by more than two hundred years. It turned out to be the oldest printed material ever found. Koreans were pioneers in the science of printing throughout the ages. The world's first printed material with metal type was produced by Korean inventors in 1234, ahead of Gutenberg by some 220 years. Descriptions of this invention are reserved for a later chapter in this book. Following the discovery of Pulkuksa Temple, credit for the invention of the first wooden block printing, as well as the first movable type, was granted to the Koreans. The discovery of the world's oldest known printed material made front-page headlines all over the world in 1966. Printing technology was surely a mark of the highest civilization.

FIRST ASTRONOMICAL OBSERVATORY IN ASIA

Along with mathematics, astronomy was an important part of the study of science in Silla. Star charts were made by observation of the night skies. These charts are still preserved today. The study of astronomy was probably tied to astrology. To observe the stars, Silla astronomers built an observatory in 647 in the city of Kyōngju. The observatory was built with 365 carved stones, the number of days in a calendar year, and there are twelve rectangular base stones, plus twelve separate levels of stones above and below a central window. This milk-bottle-shaped or telescope-shaped tall observatory was taller than most buildings in the city at that time and served scientists very well. They could chart the heavens in detail, a capacity which surprises even astronomers today. Silla scientists named this fourteen-hundred-year-old stone structure Chōmsōng-dae, which means star-gazing platform.

6

Silla and Palhae: Relations with China and Japan (680–940)

SILLA AND T'ANG CHINA

After Korea and China battled for domination of the Korean Peninsula, their relationship became cool for a few years, but then both countries started to exchange people, culture, religion, and merchandise. The exchange of people took place in the form of exchange students and Buddhist monks. The first hundred years of the T'ang period was perhaps the best period in Chinese history. It is safe to say that T'ang China was the biggest, wealthiest, most advanced, and most cosmopolitan nation of that period in the world. Students from many nations went to T'ang China to learn philosophy, literature, science, and religion. Silla was no exception. Some of these Korean students became famous in China, but most returned home and introduced new Chinese culture. Many of them became professors (Paksa, or Ph.D.) in the national university (Kuk-hak) established in 682. This national university taught ethics of Confucianism, Iching, poetry, literature, and mathematics. Students at the Silla national university were children of nobility and the term of study was nine years. Those who could not keep up with the pace of learning were expelled from the school. There were other schools for astronomy and medicine. The purpose of these schools was to educate national leaders.

Exchange of Buddhist Monks

Even before the unification of Korea, Silla had already adopted Buddhism as the national religion. This happened after the Silla king overcame the resistance of some of the powerful nobles. With increasing cultural exchange between Silla and T'ang China, Buddhist missionary monks from T'ang were welcomed by the Silla kings and many temples were built at the expense of the state. The famous Silla monk Sung-jon, who studied in T'ang, returned to Silla, built a temple called Kal-hang-sa, and began a lecture series. There were five sects of traditional Mahayana Buddhism (Great Vehicles) in Silla. These were formed under the influence of Pure Land sects and relied on the power of Amitabha, the Buddha of Infinite Light, who presides over the Pure Land, the true paradise. The believers of these sects not only had to perform good Buddhist deeds, but also invoked the help of Amitabha by calling Amitabha continuously. These sects believed that the salvation of one's soul depended on the external power of Amitabha. They encouraged people to chant the god's name millions of times until Amitabha would bestow his help upon them.

This variant Buddhism did not satisfy all Buddhists. T'ang dynasty scholars believed in the philosophy of Taoism, which encourages self-determination of thoughts, rejecting control by any outside forces, including gods. Their ideas were incorporated into Buddhist doctrine. They rejected the assistance of Amitabha for the enlightenment of their own souls and believed that enlightenment had to come from within one's own consciousness. This was the birth of Chan Buddhist sects, which started in China during the T'ang dynasty. The idea of the Chan sect was introduced to Korea, where it was called Sōn; later, when it was introduced to Japan, it was called Zen. Sōn advocated reliance on one's own power for salvation of the soul. To do this, they reasoned that concentration of mind, meditation, and absolute quietness were of primary importance. In order to achieve these goals, Sōn Buddhists in Silla built their temples in remote mountains, where the scenery was beautiful and quiet, away from mundane human society and city life. Because of this, Sōn Buddhist sects were known as *San* (mountains). There were nine Buddhist sects in Silla, most of whose founders had studied in T'ang China. One famous monk was Hejo, who studied in T'ang China, went to India to visit Buddha's birthplace, and later wrote a travelogue of India which became an important travel reference book (727). There were so many Silla Buddhists living in T'ang China that they built a temple called Silla Wōn in the Shiantung area, which became a center of Korean social activities.

THE MARITIME EMPIRE OF SILLA

Trade with China and Japan

There were two types of trade between Silla and T'ang China, one official and the other private. Because Silla defeated T'ang forces militarily and forced T'ang to pull out of the Korean Peninsula, there was no reason for Silla to subjugate itself to T'ang. However, traditionally Chinese emperors considered any official commercial exchange as a tribute, and to show the emperor's generosity, China provided a generous amount of commodities for whatever goods that were brought into China. That was very agreeable to Silla. In reality, it was just another form of foreign trade, and it took place on a large scale. Silla brought gold, silver, ginseng, cotton products, gold and silver artifacts, horses, seal skins, and so on, to China, and received tea, clothes, silverware, books, and so on, in return.

Silla ships practically monopolized trade with China and Japan because Silla was located between those countries. Silla's ship-building industry had developed considerably in respect to ocean-going vessels. There were two routes to China from Korea, one from the Inchon area of central Korea to the Shiantung Peninsula of China, the other route from the coast of Chōnla province to the Shanghai area. There was frequent trade between Silla and Japan. Silla ships arrived at Chomon and Chikujen in Japan, carrying silk and cotton goods. Because trade was frequent, the Japanese government hired language interpreters and stationed them in Tsukushi.

Because of the extensive trade between Silla and China and the many Silla students in T'ang, a Korean town called Silla Pang, or Silla community, was established in Shiantung, China. As mentioned earlier, when Koguryō and Paekche kingdoms were defeated, T'ang military rounded up civilian men, women, and children in those countries and took them as slaves to China. There were as many as two hundred thousand from Koguryō and thirteen thousand from Paekche, and many were sold as slaves. The slave trade in China became very profitable business, and Chinese "slave pirates" raided Silla coastal areas to capture slaves.

A Silla monk called Boko (or Kungbok) who lived in the Shiantung area witnessed the slave trade and became angry. He went back to Silla in 828 A.D. and asked the Silla King Hūng-dōk for an army of ten thousand men and ships, which was granted. He set up headquarters in the Chōnghae area and was able to wipe out the Chinese pirates. His power grew after that event. He built a great commercial fleet, traded with China and Japan, and, in time, was able to monopolize trade. Thus he established a maritime empire and accumulated great power and wealth.[1] He was ranked among the Silla nobility and was powerful enough to attempt to marry a Silla princess, the king's daughter. His sudden attainment of power aroused the jealousy of other nobles, and eventually he was killed. However, the maritime empire and naval power he built for Silla remained.[2] From the time of Silla, for many centuries, Korea maintained ship-building technology, maritime leadership, and the strongest naval power in East Asia. This was demonstrated on several occasions. In 1274, when Kublai Khan of China invaded Japan, he had to rely on Korea's ship-building industry and naval power. In 1592, when Japan invaded Korea with an army of 150,000 troops, the Korean navy destroyed the Japanese fleet and saved Korea from Japanese conquest.

RELATIONSHIPS OF THE KOREAN PALHAE KINGDOM WITH JAPAN AND CHINA

Twenty-two years after Silla's unification of Korea, in 698, a new nation was founded by a Korean general in Manchuria and the extreme northeastern part of the Korean Peninsula. At first called Chin (or Jin), the country was later called Palhae. The king and all the nobles of Palhae were Koreans from Koguryō. Eventually the territory of Palhae extended to about two-thirds of the present Manchuria in the east, and also included territory north and east of the Amur River of Russia today and the eastern portion of the northern Korean Peninsula.

Because its rulers were Koreans from Koguryō, they were familiar with the highly developed civilization of the past and set out to recreate the glory of the P'yōngyang region. Tae Cho-yōng, founder of Palhae, called himself King Ko and set up a government modeled after the old Koguryō Kingdom. Because of the inhumane treatment of the Koguryō people by the T'ang Chinese after the Koguryō Kingdom's defeat, Palhae bore deep resentment against T'ang. Palhae's ill feeling toward T'ang culminated in a direct military attack on China's Shiantung Peninsula and an occupation of the region in the guise of private pirate forces.[3] The historical evidence indicates that this military action was carried out on the Shiantung Peninsula of China to recover and take home some of the Koguryō people who were kidnapped by T'ang forces when Koguryō lost independence; some two hundred thousand had been taken and traded as slaves. The Shiantung Peninsula was a slave trade center. Palhae forces returned many of these people home to Palhae in the 720s during the rule of the second king of Palhae, King Mu.

The T'ang emperor, angered by this Palhae action, solicited the help of the Silla King Sōng-dōk to punish Palhae, and the armies of T'ang and Silla landed on the coast of Palhae. However, their effort could not accomplish anything, as T'ang became weak and Palhae's strength was growing. They soon withdrew their troops. About the same time, while the antagonism of Palhae was still fresh toward T'ang and Silla, Palhae's King Mu sent a diplomatic delegation to the Japanese court of Emperor Seimu and requested the opening of diplomatic relations. King Mu stated in his letter to Seimu, "We have recovered the lost land of Koguryō, and we intend to guard our old traditions of Puyō." The Japanese emperor himself was a descendent of the horseriders of Puyō and therefore welcomed such a proposal from the Palhae king.[4] After this Palhae delegation's visit to Japan in 720, diplomatic, trade, and cultural exchanges started immediately and continued for several centuries.

King Mu's son, King Mun of Palhae, three generations removed from the Koguryō era, felt less animosity toward T'ang. He realized that it was important to resume relations with T'ang China and began to exchange diplomatic representation with China. King Mun ruled Palhae wisely for fifty-seven years, and during his rule Palhae reached a zenith of its civilization. He adopted many T'ang systems, including governmental organizations. He moved his capital city in 756 then again in 786 to Tong-kyōng. Although Palhae territory did not include the P'yōngyang region of the old Koguryō capital and the cultural center of northern Korea, Palhae strove to maintain Koguryō civilization and traditions. Archaeological remains from Tong-kyōng indicate the massive scale of its buildings, castles, walls, and the city as a whole. To the end, Palhae never forgave Silla for siding with a foreign nation, China, for the destruction of the same Korean nation Koguryō. The Palhae Kingdom never exchanged diplomatic representatives, or even recognized Silla's existence, for the entire 228 years of its rule, although it shared a common border with Silla. Palhae's resentment of Silla was very deep.

WOMEN'S EARLY SOCIAL AND FAMILY POSITIONS IN KOREA, AND THE NEIGHBORING STATES OF CHINA AND JAPAN

Chinese piracy was the result of Chinese social structure and custom. The pirates were groups of gangsters who engaged in cruel kidnapping of young healthy people, especially women, at sword point before their parents' eyes. Organized Chinese pirates raided coastal villages for human "treasures," because a young woman could fetch a handsome price in slave markets in China, which had a severe shortage of females. Whenever there was any opportunity, even Chinese troops engaged in similar acts, on a larger scale.

For millennia, Chinese society considered women inferior to men, almost nonpersons. A reflection of this age-old Chinese custom was female infanticide. Females were considered to be nonproductive, unable to work as men did in the field producing farm products. When parents became old, daughters did not support them, because they were married and had become members of other families. When daughters married, parents had to provide an expensive dowry which became the property of other people. A daughter meant a lifelong financial burden for a Chinese family. It had become a widespread Chinese custom to kill a female infant as soon as it was born. Often they were buried alive. This custom was so widespread that China developed a chronic critical shortage of women, a condition that continued for a millennium. To make this situation worse, Chinese society and governmental law permitted a rich man to keep many wives at any given time.

The Chinese custom of binding female feet was developed as a way to control women. When a girl was only a few years old, parents would start to bind her feet in such a way that the still soft young feet would bend over downward and could not grow larger. This would force the female to tiptoe around the house on the back of the feet, unable to walk very far. Rather than the aesthetic reasons often emphasized by Chinese writers, this custom was actually designed to prevent women from escaping, a loss of property men could not afford. Chinese women had to suffer lifelong pain and inconvenience. The foot-binding custom lasted for a thousand years, from the tenth century until the first part of the twentieth. With this kind of social practice in China, it was no wonder that Chinese pirates would abduct Korean women for profit, especially when they were highly prized for their reputation of being beautiful. However, this Chinese effort to supplement the shortage of women in their society met an abrupt end by 826, because Silla had grown into a great maritime power and took actions to stop it.

Except that Chinese imported their social problems to Korea by raids of pirates which caused temporary problems to Korean women, females in Korea did not face the serious troubles suffered by Chinese women. Women of Silla enjoyed social status equal to that of men, including several thrones occupied by reigning queens. This kind of ultimate power was seldom given to women in other East Asian countries. If women acquired political power in Japan or China, it was mostly through positions of regency. Silla had three reigning queens, Sōn-dōk, Chin-dōk, and Chin-sōng. In shamanistic societies of the Three Kingdom period of Korea, women controlled religious services and the healing of the sick, therefore enjoying greater social standing. There is no record of Korean society's engaging in infanticide of girl babies; it was simply unthinkable for a Korean to engage in such cruel activities. In families, although Koreans outwardly adhered to the Chinese Confucian philosophy of subordinating women to father and then to husband, in actual social practice Korean women were given status equal to husbands. Women's voices on family matters were heard with respect in Korean society. Korean sons usually obeyed their mothers, because of Korean custom, not philosophy. The position of Korean women was unique in this regard. This was the legacy of a matriarchal society in early Korean history.

As noted, Chinese women endured lifelong suffering for ages. Japanese women, as dictated by Japanese social custom, had to obey unconditionally three men in their lives: first their fathers, next their husbands, and, when they were old, their sons. Japanese women were completely subservient to men for life. However, Korean women never were. In the early age of Japanese history, from the first to third centuries, when Korean settlers were steadily moving into the Japanese islands, even Japanese women seem to have enjoyed power and influence.

The Chinese *Book of Wei* tells the story of the Japanese queen Himiko in Yamadai tribal country. She was a shaman queen who controlled her people with shamanistic practices when there were great disturbances in the society. This was also the way of Korean rulers in Korea in the same period of 230–250. Her domain was the Tsushima, Ito (Hakata), and Matsura (Matsubo) regions, closest to the Korean Peninsula. When she died, a male succeeded, but because of domestic disturbances, the kingdom made a thirteen-year-old girl named Toyo queen.[5] Thus, when Korean customs were predominant in Japan, Japanese women also enjoyed equal social status and power. The mythological founder of Japan, Amaterasu Omikami, or Sun Goddess, was a shamanistic female ruler who had the combined powers of religion and government. When

Korean customs prevailed, Japanese ancient society gave women equality. However, as the wave of Korean settlers to Japan lessened after the eighth century, the position of Japanese women declined gradually over the centuries. A masterpiece novel by Lady Murasaki Shikibu, *Story of Genji* (1001–5), depicted the lives of Japanese court ladies from the tenth to the eleventh century, when court ladies still enjoyed relative equality and free love. And the lives of Japanese women in the nineteenth and the first half of the twentieth centuries have been far removed from the eleventh century of Shikibu's time, when women were treated as men's equals.

THE DECLINE OF THE SILLA AND PALHAE KINGDOMS

The Silla and Palhae kingdoms both enjoyed prosperity and a high level of civilization; however, their ends came at about the same time, in the first half of the tenth century. Silla's decline originated within the country, caused by corruption of the central court and ensuing rebellions. Palhae's fall was caused by external force, the expanding military might of Khitan (Qitan), later called Liao.

Silla's Downfall

Korean society was based on a clan system for many millennia. The clan was responsible for each of its members. If any member of the clan committed a crime, the society punished the clan as well as that particular individual. When there was an honor, the entire clan shared its glory. Koreans called this custom *Shijok*. The custom was also transported to Japan by Korean settlers, and there it was called *Uji*. Clans kept detailed family histories, going back over a thousand years. This tightly knit greater family system exerted tremendous power and influence in the society; the society of the Silla kingdom was in fact a gathering of such clans. There were three major clans which shared the kingship of Silla on a rotational basis. These families were Pak, Sōk, and Kim. The power and wealth of the society were shared equally.

Silla experienced no internal struggles for power in the early period. However, after the fourteenth ruler of Silla, the Kim family held a monopoly of power and ruled until 936. When the Kim clan monopolized power, the power struggle was not checked by the clan system, but rather on an individual basis. The powerful nobles of the Kim family often murdered rulers and set themselves up as kings. When some of them did not succeed, they went to their own stronghold and raised an army of rebellion. Such power struggles at the center were felt at localities, which had become accustomed to continuous rebellions. The locally powerful clans gradually acquired more power than the central government in Kyōngju.

To make matters worse, toward the end of Silla, Queen Chinsōng indulged in luxury which she could no longer afford and exhausted the Silla court's financial resources. She was also very promiscuous. She would engage in lewd activities with several men at any given time and favor them with high government posts. When the court's financial resources became exhausted, she raised taxes so high that people no longer could pay them. Rebellions broke out all over Silla. It was her eleventh year of rule, but she had to abdicate.[6] Her nephew succeeded to the Silla throne but rebel strongholds were firmly established, and the king's domain had shrunk to a small area around Kyōngju.

Kyōn-hwōn in old Paekche territory and Kung-ye in the central Korean Peninsula were the strongest rebels. Kyōn-hwōn established a kingdom for himself in 892 in the old Paekche territory in the southwest of the peninsula and called it the Later Paekche Kingdom. Kung-ye claimed the central region of the Korean Peninsula and named it the Late Ko-(gu)-ryō in 901. He also called his kingdom Ma-jin. Kung-ye was successful in the beginning; however, he lacked kingly virtues and executed many of his subordinates over the slightest matters. He was eventually killed, and Wang-kōn, second in command, was elected to be king. Wang-kōn renamed his kingdom Koryō and selected his birthplace as the capital. The city was called Song-ak (present-day Kaesōng), and it was the year 918. This was the beginning of the Koryō (Korea) dynasty.

A few years later, in 935, the Silla king abdicated his throne in favor of Wang kōn. The Silla Kingdom finally met an end after 993 years, from 57 B.C. to 935. Wang-kōn took the Silla king into his court and made him a noble. Wang-kōn still had Kyōn-hwōn to contend with; however, fortunately for him, Kyōn-hwōn's family developed a feud among themselves, and Kyōn-hwōn surrendered to Wang-kōn. In this easy way, all of the Korean Peninsula came under his rule. Fundamentally, it was due to his reputation as a benevolent man who had true leadership qualities. Wang-kōn became the founder and first king of the Koryō dynasty, called *Koryō T'ae-jo*. He began his rule of the entire Korean Peninsula in 935.

TEMPORARY SETBACK OF THE KOREAN CHIN NATION: PALHAE'S DOWNFALL

The Palhae Kingdom established by the Koguryō people in 698 A.D. came to an end in 926 A.D. Unlike that of Silla, which had crumbled as a result of internal corruption, Palhae's fall was due to external conquest by another nation, Khitan (Qitan). A Mongolian tribe near the Liao River became strong under the able military leader Apochi, began to conquer neighboring tribes of Mongolia, and had secured most of Mongolia by early 920. Once this was done, he turned his forces toward the east and crushed Palhae's forces in 926. Khitans burnt the capital city of Palhae, which was almost totally destroyed. Palhae had enjoyed relative peace for 228 years and had a high level of civilization, but because of this peaceful existence, her military preparedness became lax. The Korean sister nation Silla never attacked Palhae, and vice versa; there was not a single war between them for more than two hundred years. By the early tenth century, Silla was weak and unable to control most of the country. In the northern sector of the Silla territory, the new nation of Koryō was born by 918, but had yet to control all of the Korean Peninsula. Only eight years after the founding of Koryō, Palhae was destroyed by Khitan.

As Khitans burnt and looted towns and villages of the Chins, the displaced people of Palhae fled from their land onto the Korean Peninsula by the hundreds of thousands. Koryō was barely established when this happened. Chins told the new king of Koryō that they had the same ancestors, that now Koryō was their father, and they would be Koryō's sons, and they begged him to accept them. The king, a compassionate man, permitted them to stay. Chins always described international relationships in terms of family relationships: father to son, brother to brother, elder uncle to nephew, younger uncle to nephew, or elder brother to younger brother. This was the clan system, the Korean social fabric. When they said they were the sons, they meant complete subjugation. The Koryō king, T'ae-jo, was able to expand his territory to the north as far as the Amnok (Yalu) River, as Palhae was gone. The new border was several hundred miles farther to the north, covering most of P'yōngan Province and about half of Hamkyōng Province; however, it faced the hostile Khitan Empire across the Amnok (Yalu) River. The Chins, who lost their country temporarily, survived as a nation under Koryō stewardship, most of them remaining in the region of Manchuria. The Chins, in a century or so, would bounce back and completely destroy the Khitans, who changed their name to Liao Empire in 1125 and created a vast empire of their own. Until then, Koryō was vulnerable to numerous attacks by Khitan.

7

First Half of Koryō: To the Twelfth Century

ESTABLISHMENT OF THE NEW KINGDOM OF KORYŌ

The name *Koryō* is derived from *Koguryō*, and was adopted by Western nations as *Korea*. The first king of Koryō, Wang-kōn (also known by his official name Koryō T'ae-jo), annexed Silla and later Paekche, and when Palhae was felled by Khitan, he occupied some of the Palhae territory to the north reaching the Amnok River in the western sector. But Koryō could not quite reach the Tuman River, today the boundary with Russia. The new territory of Koryō was much larger than unified Silla ever was. The ruling class of Palhae, who were descended from the Koguryō ruling class, escaped from the pursuing Khitan forces and moved south to Koryō, where they were welcomed by T'ae-jo. They were given positions of nobility in the new government of Koryō.[1] The Chin nationals north of the Amnok River became disorganized and formed a separate tribal state. Koryō T'ae-jo became very angry about the way the Chin people were treated by the Khitans. When the emperor of Khitan sent an emissary to Koryō with fifty camels as a present to T'ae-jo, he angrily locked up the Khitan's emissary on a small island and sent back the camels to Khitan. He was a compassionate man and had no stomach to receive gifts from the harsh, cruel Khitans, who treated people of the sister state of Palhae in such an inhumane manner.

Koryō inherited a highly developed civilization intact from unified Silla and added the best of Palhae. This was a marvelous beginning. Koryō eliminated the corruption and social ills of Silla, reorganized governmental systems, and redistributed lands in a more equitable way. However, as always in Korean history, her neighbors did not leave Korea alone to enjoy the fruits of civilization. To the north, on the central continent of Asia, military and political conflicts arose which Koryŏ was unable to escape. Invading forces swept across the Korean Peninsula, destroying everything in their path. But however precarious the situation was, Koryŏ managed to hang on to independence and self-rule by whatever means possible, using on some occasions military force, at other times, diplomacy. Koryŏ not only maintained independence during these difficult times, but also achieved another pinnacle of civilization unseen anywhere in the world at that time in the arts, science, and technology.

CONSOLIDATION OF THE FOUNDATION OF KORYŌ

The first one hundred and twenty years was the first period of Koryŏ, when major efforts of the state were devoted to consolidation of the government of Koryŏ. In the beginning, the old Silla system, which was modeled after the Chinese Han and T'ang systems, was adopted. Koryŏ established a centralized government with three divisions and six departments in the government to oversee various aspects of governmental affairs. There were one prime minister, two deputy prime ministers, and six ministers of the departments of civil service, treasury, education and examination, defense, justice, and engineering. In addition, there were nine smaller departments which controlled various other government affairs. Greater importance was placed on the civil service system of government, which was based on the selection of government officials according to ability as judged by civil service examinations. This was a radical departure from the Silla system of government, which selected officials on the basis of family background. In addition to the centralized government in the capital city, Koryŏ established ten provincial governments.

Koryŏ established a national university which taught many different subjects. In addition, twelve colleges were built in the provincial areas, teaching such subjects as government, philosophy, medicine, mathematics, accounting, and astronomy. The professors were given the titles of doctors of literature, doctors of medicine, and associate professors, and they were all government officials. Usually students studied under private tutors, and when they reached a given level they were allowed to enter the government universities and colleges. They then took civil service examinations in two areas, literature and science. The education and examination systems were completed by 958. Koryŏ also established national libraries and archives, and the king's library, Susŏwŏn (Academy of Books and Records), boasted many hundreds of thousands of books.[2]

Land reform took place at the same time as establishment of the civil service system. Instead of paying government officials with money or regular pay, a set amount of land was given to them for life, according to the person's rank. The land was to be returned to the government after death. The man was free to cultivate his land any way he wanted, including with the use of tenant farmers. It was a kind of feudalistic organization. However, this system prevented a single family from owning vast farmlands as had happened during the Silla period. After a century or so, the lands were inherited by the descendants, and the reformed land system started to break down. Buddhist temples in particular accumulated vast lands and behaved as feudal lords.

MILITARY PREPAREDNESS OF KORYŌ

As Koryō witnessed the fall and destruction of Palhae by Khitans, they began to feel very insecure. Even the Sung Empire of China was invaded by Khitans and lost sixteen Yen-Yun Districts, including Peking (Beijing), in 947. Khitan began to call the country the Liao Empire in 947 and became more aggressive toward Koryō and the Chins.

Three Major Invasions of Liao and the Great Victory of Koryō

In order to prepare for an eventual conflict with Liao, Koryō began to organize and train about three hundred thousand troops. As expected, Liao invaded northern Koryō in 993 but was repulsed by the Koryō forces. Koryō began to build castles in the northeast area against future border violations. In the meantime, Liao enlarged its territory and became a mighty empire controlling northern China north of the Yellow River, all of Mongolia, and almost all of present-day Manchuria. It was waiting for a chance to pounce on Koryō. After the withdrawal of Liao troops from the Korean Peninsula, the Koryō government sent troops north to the region of the Amnok River, secured the region, and built castles in strategic points. It also repaired and strengthened the walls of the old capital city of P'yōngyang of Koguryō and Nang-nang, which had fallen into disuse. P'yōngyang was made the western capital (Sōkyōng) of Koryō. By 1009, the time of Koryō's seventh king, Mok-jong, there were corruption and disorder at court, caused by the king's in-laws and mother. The king and his in-laws were purged by an army general, Kang Cho. Some of Koryō's officials and people did not quite agree with Kang Cho's extreme measures, but most felt good about cleaning the corruption within the court.

The conflict in the Koryō court gave Liao the pretext to invade Koryō again. The Liao emperor, Shen-tsung (Sheng-zong), personally led four hundred thousand troops across the Amnok River and invaded Koryō territory. The new Koryō king, Hyōng-jong, gave a three-hundred-thousand-man army to Kang Cho to defend the country; however, he was defeated in battle and captured. The Liao emperor invited Kang Cho to become his subject, but he chose to die. Liao troops invaded the Koryō capital city of Kae-sōng and burnt it to the ground, but the western capital of P'yōngyang castle held. Koryō suffered initial losses, but won other battles. The war continued to the following year, 1010. P'yōngyang castle was still threatening the rear of the Liao forces, and the Liao emperor decided to withdraw his troops. After the withdrawal, Liao still claimed suzerainty over Koryō and the return of six counties east of the

Amnok River which were Chin territories. Koryŏ flatly refused Liao's demands. Liao never owned the six-county region at any time and had no right to demand it. In fact, the previous Liao emperor had agreed to Koryŏ occupation of that territory because Liao had a difficult time controlling the Chins.

Subsequently Liao invaded Koryŏ for the third time. In 1014, Liao built a bridge across the Amnok River and began to construct military bases along the river. There were constant skirmishes with the Koryŏ forces. In 1018, Liao massed two hundred thousand troops and struck south toward the capital city of Koryŏ. The Koryŏ general and leader of the defense forces was Kang Han-ch'an, one of Korea's most celebrated generals, perhaps only next to Ŭlji Mundŏk of Koguryŏ, who annihilated Sui China's army of one million troops led by Emperor Yang-ti himself, and Admiral Li Sun-sin, who crushed the invading fleet of Japanese forces in 1592–98. Koryŏ forces built a dam with a floodgate in the Tae-chŏn River, and twelve thousand cavalry forces waited to ambush the approaching enemy forces. When those forces were halfway across the river, Kang's forces released the flood water. With the enemy thus disorganized, Koryŏ infantry and cavalry struck Liao's army in force. The result was a complete rout of the Liaos. Out of two hundred thousand, only a few thousand escaped alive.[3] The battle is known as the great victory of Kwiju of Koryŏ.[4] After this crushing defeat, Liao never again violated Koryŏ territory. Exhausted, Liao sought peace with Koryŏ. The two countries exchanged missions and agreed not to violate each other's territories again.

The warfare between Koryŏ and Liao and the defeat of the Liao forces gave the Chins a chance to regroup and strengthen their power to the north. In order to prepare against Liao and the Chins, Koryŏ mobilized 350,000 men and built the outer castle wall to the capital city and a one-thousand-li- (about three-hundred-miles) long defense wall in the Chin country in Ham-kyŏng Province.

EARLY KORYŎ'S ACHIEVEMENTS

Great national crises created national unity and extra effort of the nation. As had happened on many occasions in Korean history, foreign invasion produced destruction of cities, buildings, arts, and other treasures. This time it was the destruction of the king's library, which housed hundreds of thousands of rare books. The Liaos burned the library as well as the king's palaces and government buildings. Like the phoenix that rises from the ashes, Korea made an extra effort to rebuild what was lost in the war. King Hyŏn-jong ordered a group of scholars to rebuild the library, collecting and reprinting books. Not only did the scholars succeed in rebuilding the library, they also safeguarded the books from further destruction by making duplicates with wooden block printing. Wooden block printing developed into wooden-type printing, and as noted earlier, Koryŏ scholars and engineers invented the world's first metal type on record in 1234 A.D., ahead of Johannes Gutenburg of Germany by 220 years. Koreans resurrected themselves from destruction by neighboring states, and used adversity as a springboard to new heights of civilization. This was a recurring pattern in the history of Korea. Koryō people printed thousands of books in the 1100s with wooden plates, including the *Great Tae-jang-kyōng* (Great Collections of Buddhist Scriptures) with more than eighty thousand plates. Another achievement was the publication of detailed historical records of the Koryō period.

KOREA'S THIRD GOLDEN AGE DURING KORYŌ

After the Koryō forces' resounding victories over Liao, Korea enjoyed relative peace for a hundred years or so. This gave Korea the chance to build a third golden age. Koryō Korea's golden age was marked by developments in book printing, publication, and dispersal of knowledge on philosophy, literature, religion, and science. Private and public printing agencies printed and distributed tens of thousands of books throughout the country. Books were also exported to China and Japan. Handwritten copies of books were no longer commonly used. Learning was encouraged by the Koryō government. In fact, extensive learning had become mandatory for anyone who aspired to a higher social position, because he had to pass competitive civil service examinations implemented by the central and local governments. As a greater number of people studied harder, it had become more difficult to pass the examinations, because they were competitive with only a given number of slots available. This situation increased demand for more printed books and for the opening of public and private institutions of learning. By 1100, there were twelve universities and colleges operating in Koryō, teaching many different subjects. These schools produced well-known scholars and scientists. Special mention must be reserved for the printing art of Koryō, because, as mentioned previously, that art had developed in Korea before any other country. In use of materials and clarity of characters, Korean printing was unmatched anywhere else in the world.

INVENTION OF THE WORLD'S FIRST MOVABLE METAL TYPE BY KOREANS AND ITS USE IN PRINTING

During the rule of Mun-chong (1047–1083), Koryō had already developed the necessary scientific technology and metallurgy skills to make coins that had names on them with well-designed convex characters. These coins were marked *Hae-tong T'ong-bo*, *Sam-han T'ong-bo*, *Tong-kuk T'ong-bo*, and so on. Together with the large silver coin *En-byōn*, these coins were widely used. The technology of making these coins was quite similar to that for casting movable metal type for printing, because both coins and type required the same kind of metal and casting of convex characters. It is believed that casting of movable type was done as early as the eleventh century in Korea, although there was no definite mention of it in the history books. The first record of using metal type appears in the preface of the fifty-volume *Kogŭm Sangjŏng Yemun* (Old and New Details of Governmental Ethics and Laws), written by the famous poet Li Kyubo for the prime minister Chae Wu. He specifically noted that the entire book was printed with movable metal type. The book was published by the Koryŏ government by 1241, but work started in 1234.[5] The author did not say that this book was the first to use metal type, and scholars think that the use of metal type must go back two hundred years to the 1050s, because Koryŏ had the technology to do so and there was tremendous demand for printed books.

The invention of printing required an accompanying highly developed technology, metallurgy, and science. Korean technology was ahead of Johannes Gutenberg, who "invented" movable type in the 1450s , by 220 years. Banall in *History of Science* acknowledged that movable metal type was first invented in Korea centuries earlier and introduced to Europe in the fifteenth century for printing Bibles.[6] Mongols are thought to have taken information about movable metal type to Europe. They invaded Koryŏ in 1231–32; during 1235–40, they turned westward to Europe, led by Batu, grandson of Genghis Khan, who had already occupied Russia. The Mongol general Batu invaded Poland, Bohemia, Hungary, and the Danube Valley, reaching Germany and Austria in 1240–42. There, Batu crushed the allied forces of Europe. The stage was set for him to occupy all of Europe with his army of two hundred thousand troops, when the Great Mongol Khan Ogodei passed away. Batu was in line to inherit the Mongol Empire, so he quickly moved away from Europe, and Europe was saved. The Mongols, during this period, conveyed much new technology from East to West, including gunpowder and cannon. The introduction of movable metal type was another, according to Banall, although it took two centuries actually to produce usable metal type in Germany, because Europe did not have the casting technology to make large quantities of metal type in the thirteenth century. An even greater lapse of time occurred with the introduction of paper with wooden fiber, which took one thousand years to travel to Europe from East Asia.

By 1403, during the Li Dynasty, Korea used movable metal type to such an extent that the king's type casting center was established and printing tens of thousands of books (see Chapter 9).

KORYŌ CELADON ART AND ITS NEW TECHNOLOGY

Pottery making was closely associated with Koreans for millennia. It was part of their everyday life. From the time of the Puyŏ Kingdom of horseriders of the pre-Christian era to the Three Kingdoms period of the descendants of the Puyŏ people on the Korean Peninsula, pottery was a central part of shamanistic religious ceremonies as well as daily life. In the ancient tombs of nobles of Silla, Paekche, Imna (Kaya), and Koguryŏ, modern archaeologists have found pottery preserved intact. All of these Korean states had a highly developed art of pottery. By the tenth and eleventh centuries, pottery began to take shape as celadon, made not only for utensils, but also as art objects. Such pottery showed the figures of mounted cavalry warriors, animals, human figures, and others. Koreans also used decorative celadon roof tiles for their buildings. They valued art products of celadon to such an extent that they gave it equal value to gold and silver.

Korean pottery production influenced Korea's neighbors as well. When Koreans moved into Japan, they created the new culture called Yayoi. Historians divide the Japanese into two distinctively different cultures based on their pottery. The new Yayoi pottery brought in by the Koreans was far superior to the old Jomon pottery. From the first century B.C. down to modern times, the love affair of Japanese society and Korean pottery continued. At times this created misfortunes for Koreans, especially during the Japanese invasion of the 1590s. The Chinese were influenced by the Korean pottery industry as well. During the Silla period, Silla created a maritime empire and controlled trade in East Asia. The Shiantung Peninsula of China, which juts out several hundred miles into the Yellow Sea, is separated from the Korean Peninsula by only about one hundred miles. It was a trade center and the center for Silla people in China. The peninsula, unlike any other place in China, had become a center of the pottery industry from the T'ang down to the Sung period. By the eleventh century, China's celadon making was well under way. However, in the level of refinement and art, the Chinese never reached the level of Koryŏ celadons.

There are two well-known critiques of Koryŏ celadon by noted historians of Asian art. In *Arts of Korea*, Evelyn McCune states, "During the twelfth century the production of ceramic ware reached its highest refinement. Several new varieties appeared simultaneously in the quarter of a century, one of which, the inlaid ware must be considered a Korean invention."[7] Neither the Chinese nor the Japanese had produced inlaid celadon, which was unique to Koryŏ wares. McCune quotes Mr. Honey of the Victoria and Albert Museum of England, who after World War II wrote "The best Corean (Korean) wares were not only original, they are the most gracious and unaffected pottery ever made. They have every virtue that pottery can have. This Corean pottery, in fact, reaches heights hardly attained even by the Chinese."[8] No wonder that Koryŏ celadons are highly valued the world over, held in the major museums as national treasures.

Unfortunately, during and after the repeated invasions and warfare on the Korean Peninsula, much pottery was destroyed; however, the few pieces remaining show Koryŏ's unparalleled artistic refinement. Koryŏ celadon was one more example of Korean inventive genius. Celadon production technology advanced until Koryŏ artisans could not only make inlaid celadons, but also could bake them in thirteen-hundred-degree fires and produce jewels of celadon in a beautiful greenish hue, resembling jade, the jewel of East Asia. This was never duplicated in any other country, and the technology of Koryŏ celadon has been lost even in Korea since the sixteenth century. Modern researchers and artists have been trying to recreate it for many years now, without much success. Imitations never even approach the beauty and perfection of Koryō celadon. The Chinese seldom admitted non-Chinese products were superior to theirs, but a Sung master in T'ao P'ing Lao Jen, wrote, "Secret color of celadon of Koryō ranked as First under Heaven."[9] This superb color was believed to have come from the natural baking of the pottery with some ingredients mixed in the clay, and not from painting. In addition to this beautiful light greenish blue background, the decorative motifs were done with engraved inlay with unpainted hard white clay or copper. The most popular motifs were flowers, birds (especially cranes), trees, and human figures.

KORYŌ ARCHITECTURE AND CONSTRUCTION OF NEW CAPITALS AND TEMPLES

After the Koryō army defeated the Liao Empire, the ensuing peace agreement between the two nations gave Koryō a chance to devote more energy to domestic affairs. Farmlands produced higher yields and large regional landowners accumulated greater wealth. From the second half of the eleventh century for the next hundred years, Koryō undertook great building projects. First, Koryō selected two more capitals and gave them the same status as Kae-kyōng, Koryō's main capital. Kae-kyōng was the birthplace of the first King T'ae-jo, hence the reason for its selection. However, its natural setting was not suitable for defense; nevertheless, its walls were reinforced at great expense.

The second capital was Sō-kyōng, the western capital, of P'yōngyang. P'yōngyang was one of the most beautiful cities in the world. Not only had it a scenic setting with beautiful mountains and rivers, it also was a formidable natural fortress. The city was encircled by two rivers, and along the Tae-dong River for more than ten miles there was, and still is, a several hundred foot high sheer cliff at the river's edge. On top of the cliff was the castle, a picturesque as well as solid defensive fortress. Tens of thousands of cherry blossom trees bloom in springtime, lighting up the whole mountainside in pink, and many love stories originated in this romantic city. Numerous great battles were fought around P'yōngyang. In the Koryō period P'yōngyang Sōng castle held against Khitan attack and thus saved the nation. The Koryō king wanted to make P'yōngyang one of the three capitals of the kingdom and often resided in the palace in P'yōngyang.

Another capital the Koryō king designated was Nam-kyōng, the southern capital, present-day Seoul. For defense, Seoul has the Han River to the south and rugged mountains to the north. Until the Koryō period, that region did not have the significant historical role of P'yōngyang. When it was selected as one of the three capitals, new palaces and walls were built around the city. Later, the first king of the Li Dynasty moved its capital there in 1395 and made it a primary capital. *Seoul* actually means, in the Korean language, "capital city." Much construction and building took place, but perhaps most significant was the construction of Hūng-wang-sa Buddhist temple. As Buddhism became the national religion of the Koryō Kingdom, greater numbers of temples were built. There were seventy temples in Kae-kyōng alone, and it looked as if the whole city were one temple city. In 1056, new construction began and it took twelve years and national financing to build a massive temple of 100,800 square feet. The king and nobles believed that the power of Buddha would protect the nation.

Another major achievement of the Koryō period was the printing of the Buddhist scriptures by wooden block printing board. In times of invasion such as by Liaos (Khitans) or Mongols, Buddhist temples undertook major printing projects of publishing the Buddhist scriptures, in order to elicit Buddha's help in the national crisis. One such project required eighty thousand printing plates. Koryō invented movable metal type and used it in 1234, but for such a massive project the wooden plates were still used by the Buddhist temples. By 1392, the Koryō government established the Library Institute and placed matters concerning casting and printing books with movable metal type under its jurisdiction, according to available government documents.[10] The stage was set for a new era on the Korean Peninsula.

8

Second Half of Koryō: Warring Period

RISE OF THE CHIN NATION (NUCHENS OR JURCHENS)

A part of the Korean nation that ruled the northern Korean Peninsula and east of the Liao River for over fifteen hundred years, through the Puyō, Koguryō, and Palhae kingdoms, had lost its nationhood in the middle of the tenth century. The people of this region called themselves Chins. This was the name of the tribal nation, not the official title of the country. As noted in the previous chapter, the Korean word *Chin* or *Jin* could be expressed with several different Chinese characters. The Chinese called them *Nuchen* (Jurchen), which means "women Chen." Koryō adopted the Chinese name *Nuchen* and began to call them *Yōjin*. Whatever outsiders called them, the Chin tribes, who were hard pressed by Liao (Khitan), began to have breathing room when the Liao met the crushing defeat by Koryō and became more or less docile in the mideleventh century. The chieftains of the Chin tribal nations paid regular visits to the king of Koryō with annual tributes and called Koryō "the father nation." One time Koryō took six regions of northeastern Chin territory north of the Hamhūng area, but these territories were returned to the Chins at their fervent request. In general, the relationship of Koryō with the Chins was a friendly one. There were two groups of Chins, western and eastern. The western Chins were more Sinicized and paid homage to Liao, while the eastern Chins were more independent of Liao, keeping close contact with Koryō.

The eastern Chins became more organized, and in the first part of the twelfth century, they began to invade Liao territories toward the west. These were the Chins' lost territories of Palhae, which Liao had taken from them little more than one hundred years before. Throughout this time the Chins maintained their way of life. Kinship among clan members was the main social foundation, and they shared awards and punishments. They were still horseriders like their ancestors and engaged in periodic group hunting and livestock raising. The eastern Chins produced a great military leader, Wenyen Akuta, who changed the whole structure of the East Asian mainland. Previously the Liao Empire had occupied sixteen Yen-Yun Districts of Sung China. Sung, unable to dislodge Liao from northern China, had been sending emissaries to Koryŏ asking its king to cooperate with Sung to attack Liao from the east and west. Koryŏ, which had a peace agreement with Liao, did not agree to Sung's requests. By 1115, Akuta occupied most of present-day Manchuria and declared his nation the *Chin* (*Jin*) Empire. He adopted the Chinese character "gold," which was pronounced the same as the Korean word *Chin* or *Jin*. By this time the Liao court became corrupt and militarily weak. Sung saw an opportunity to recover lost territory in northern China from Liao. As Sung had been requesting the Koryŏ Kingdom for years, Sung turned to Chin for help in attacking Liao. Chin forces, which won battle after battle, accepted Sung's invitation and concluded an alliance in 1122. While Chin was again victorious against Liao forces, Sung could not even capture Peking (Beijing). The Chin forces had to help Sung occupy the city, thus crossing deep into Chinese territory. In 1125, Chin forces captured the Liao emperor, ending Liao rule after 210 years. Liao had invaded the Chin territory of Palhae Kingdom in 926 and burned its capital city and looted the country, but the situation was now completely reversed. The entire Liao territory was taken by Chin, and Sung China faced stronger Chin forces. Sung was too weak to honor her side of the agreement; therefore Chin had no obligation to honor it. It had been foolish for Sung to ask help from Chin. Chins still remembered that when their ancestors' kingdom Koguryŏ was defeated by the allied forces of Silla and T'ang China, the Chinese forces rounded up their ancestors by the hundreds of thousands to be taken to China. And then the Chinese called them Nuchens, an insult.

The following year, the Chins sent down a two-pronged invasion army across the Yellow River and surrounded the Sung's capital city of Kaifeng. The Sung emperor Hui-tsung abdicated in favor of his son and begged for peace. The Chin emperor demanded indemnity of ten million taels of gold, twenty million taels of silver, and twenty million bolts of silk. There was no way the Sung emperors could meet this demand, and therefore the capital city fell to the hands of the Chin in 1126. Two Sung emperors, Hui-tsung and Ch'in-tsung, were captured. Akuta held a victory celebration party and ordered the two Sung emperors to attend dressed in blue, the servants' color. Akuta forced them to address him as "elder uncle," a title of greater power and authority than father in the Korean clan system. Upon hearing the two emperors addressing him as "elder uncle," Akuta bestowed new titles on the two Sung emperors, for the father "Duke of Confused Virtues" and for the son "Marquis of Recurrent Confusions."[1] Akuta settled down in Zhongdu (Peking or Beijing) and made it a capital city of the Chin Empire, which now contained all of northern China, Mongolia, and present-day Manchuria. The Chins' rather humorous treatment of the Sung was far more lenient than what T'ang China had done to Akuta's ancestors of Koguryō.

In the following year, 1127, Akuta sent an emissary to the Koryō king and requested that Chin and Koryō be brother–brother and prosper together in the future. Koryō was accustomed to being called father. Now that the Chin state had become stronger it demanded to be called brother, with equal status. That angered some Koryō officials, but they could not do much against the mighty empire in the north. Koryō accepted the new family relationship. This was all based on the traditional Korean clan system. The Chin Empire never invaded Koryō by force. Like Palhae Kingdom before it, the Chin Empire respected clan kinship. The present-day Korean leaders of North and South should learn from their ancestors' tradition of respecting each others' integrity and cease hostility to each other: It is not the Korean way. Akuta was a wise leader in many respects. He warned his people never to become Sinicized because the Chins would lose their fighting ability and become too soft to maintain their traditions. He told them if Chins became too assimilated into the Chinese culture, China would engulf the Chins, and they would lose without a single battle. He told them that was exactly what happened with the Khitans. During his dynasty, his people heeded his advice and maintained their identity. Several centuries later their descendants, Later Chins or *Ch'ings* (*Qings*), newly called *Manchus*, again conquered China in the early seventeenth century; however, they had forgotten his wise advice. Akuta, as conqueror of China, had the power to do whatever he wanted. However, he treated the Chinese people leniently except for keeping the two Sung emperors and a few nobles as "guests" for political reasons. The Chinese characterized the Chins as "barbarians" and had called them derogatory names for many ages. When the T'ang Chinese had had the opportunity, they committed immeasurable atrocities against Akuta's ancestors. Akuta would have none of these things. He showed the Chinese who really were the civilized, and who truly were the "barbarians." When Akuta's descendants, the Ch'ing, again ruled all of China, they also treated the Chinese people with compassion. Similar generosity by conquerors was repeated in history after World War II by the victorious Americans toward their former enemies, Japan and Germany. Restraining their power and treating the vanquished enemy as humans were marks of civilized people.

MILITARY DICTATORSHIP IN THE KORYŌ KINGDOM

After a diplomatic peace settlement was established with the Chin Empire, Koryō did not have to be concerned about foreign invasion for a while, but it began to develop power struggles internally. The Koryō's class division was well established by the beginning of the twelfth century. It was almost similar to a caste system. These class divisions and the struggle between ruling classes of civil and military officials were the main cause of internal unrest. The

Koryō's classes were roughly four: the upper, middle, lower, and humble classes. Unlike in a modern Western society, these class divisions were so rigid that nobody could move up or down from inherited social positions.

The upper class was the ruling class of gentry, consisting of scholars, government officials, military officers. One had to be born into this class, who were usually rich landowners. The family registers were kept for each of the families belonging to this class by the family as well as by the state. Only the members of this gentry class, called *Yangban*, were allowed to attend universities or take civil service examinations leading to high positions in the government. Usually civil officials excelled in this examination, and hence they could attain higher positions, more power, and wealth. Military officials, although they contributed to the security of the nation by defeating the Liao and Chins of the northeast, were left behind in social standing within the ruling class. *Yang* [both]–*ban* [sector] designated both civil and military officials; however, later it designated the gentry (upper) class in general. The middle class was composed primarily of lower level government officials and their descendants, and they had good education and manners. The lower class was the most numerous, consisting of soldiers, tenant farmers, merchants, and artisans. These people were the main providers of the society. Although they did not have very high social standing, this class included artists such as porcelain makers who produced art objects of unparalleled beauty. The *Ch'ōn-in*, which may be translated as "humble class," consisted of station keepers, butchers, public or private slaves, and their descendants.

All of these class positions were inherited from generation to generation. One did not have the freedom to leave one's class. This class structure provided some stability to the society. However, the underlying unfair arrangements kept people angry and dissatisfied. Personal talents were ignored except in rare instances.

In the later part of the twelfth century several rebellions broke out. King Injong's in-law acquired power and revolted against the young king and was crushed. A man called Myochōng advocated moving the capital to P'yōngyang, and when the king refused him, he revolted. This revolt was also put down. With each revolt the military had to be called in. Regardless of what the soldiers did, they were always looked down on by civil officials and were treated almost as slaves. For example, a civil official once burned a general's eyebrow as a prank. Finally the military generals staged a coup d'etat and seized power from the civil officials. The situation remained unsettled, with power transferred from one general to another, until finally the general Ch'ae Ch'ung-hōn seized power and established a dictatorship of the Koryō government. In order to consolidate his power he purged everybody, including kings. He built a private army and killed off his political enemies. During his lifetime, he set up four kings and eliminated two kings. He was the most ruthless dictator. His power structure was similar to the shogunate system of Japan. His family held power for four generations, the longest rule of any one family. This military dictatorship produced great disruption and uneasiness within society. As it was a time of national crisis, with Mongols under Genghis Khan moving toward Koryō, such an unusual power structure was also useful to Koryō from a defensive point of view.

THE RISE OF THE MONGOLS AND KORYŌ'S RESISTANCE

While Koryō was undergoing internal political change by the establishment of a military dictatorship, an unprecedented military conflict was brewing in north-central Asia. A man named Temujin in Mongolia succeeded in conquering the neighboring tribes of Mongolia, and in 1206 he proclaimed himself *Genghis Khan*, or Almighty Emperor. He was a military and political genius. He also truly enjoyed military conquests, conquering other tribes and nations for the joy of the conquest itself. To support his personal ambitions, he maintained troops of hardy nomadic Mongolians who practically lived on horseback. They could sleep on horseback, shoot down animal game or the enemy with ease, and even ride horses upside-down. The Mongol forces moved so fast that they could usually strike an enemy's forces even before those enemies were informed of the Mongol invasion. Mighty empires fell one after another to the swift Mongol cavalry. Genghis Khan invaded southern Russia, the Ukraine, northern China including Peking, and the western Manchurian region. He died of battle wounds suffered when he invaded West Hsia (Xia). His third son, Ogodei, succeeded his father and continued to expand the empire.

The Chin Empire, which formed a shield for Korea against the Mongols, fell in 1233. Now the Mongols were at Koryō's doorstep. They wasted no time. That same year Ogodei dispatched an army into Koryō under the command of Salledei. There were severe battles in the northern region of Koryō; as usual P'yōngyang became a battleground. Koryō forces put up strong resistance at P'yōngyang and Kwiju and refused to surrender. Historical records showed that both sides used cannons and gunpowder. The Koreans poured molten iron liquid on the Mongol forces. The Mongols were forced to withdraw toward the Manchurian region, but they received a promise that the Koryō king would eventually travel to see the Mongol emperor. Not only did Koryō not keep that promise, it also took up a stronger defensive posture by moving its capital to the large Kangwha Island fortress. Kangwha Island had a large area near the central west coast, separated by several hundred yards of waterway from the mainland Korean Peninsula. The Koryō government moved one hundred thousand residents of the capital city of Kae-kyōng to the island and built high defensive walls along the coast of the island facing the mainland. The government also built palaces, government buildings, and houses, in preparation for protracted war against the Mongols. In a few years the fortification of Kangwha Island was completed.

The Mongols did not like this new Koryō defensive posture. The Mongol general received orders again from Emperor Ogodei to invade Koryō. Salledei did so and captured the empty city of Kae-kyōng; however, he could not touch Kangwha Island, the new capital of Koryō, because it was protected by the strong Koryō navy and the high castle walls. The Mongols crossed the Han River and continued the invasion of the southern Korean Peninsula, but at Ch'o-in castle the Mongol general Salledei was shot to death by a Korean archer. His army became disorganized and had to withdraw again. The Mongols burnt cities everywhere they went and destroyed buildings and temples, leaving nothing but ashes. Once again Korea met destruction at the hands of a neighbor, this time the Mongols. The Golden Age of Koryō was left in ashes. However, the phoenix Korea would rise again from the ashes, to build another Golden Age in the early fifteenth century. This cycle seemed to be the fate of the Korean people. The Mongols, however destructive they were, could not do anything to the Koryō king and his government in the Kangwha Island capital. The Koryō people formed a *ūibyōng*, or volunteer army, commanded by regional strongmen or Buddhist monks who fought the Mongols, quite often successfully. This state of battle continued and the Mongols withdrew completely, while still demanding Koryō's allegiance. Koryō resisted this demand until 1259 then decided to seek a diplomatic solution with the Mongols. Probably because Koryō never surrendered to the Mongol Empire it was allowed to maintain independence while all of the mainland Asian nations from the China Sea to the Mediterranean Sea lost theirs.

In 1259 King Ko-jong sent the crown prince with forty attendants to the Mongol capital, where he met Emperor Mangu. A year later he met Kublai Khan, when he became the emperor of the mighty Mongol Empire. By this time, Kublai Khan had conquered South Sung and his domain reached to Persia, Mesopotamia, Syria, China, and all of Russia. Kublai Khan took a liking to the Koryō crown prince (later King Wōn-jong), gave him the prettiest of his daughters, and made him his son-in-law. Thus Koryō was linked to the Mongol Empire through marriage. King Wōn-jong made the Mongol princess his queen, and the historical record indicates that he truly loved her. Thereafter it became standard procedure for Korean kings to marry Yüan (Mongolian) emperors' daughters. From Kublai Khan's view, it was a political marriage that assisted his ambition to conquer Japan. Kublai Khan needed Korean shipbuilding technology and industry and the Korean navy. As noted in the previous chapter, the earlier kingdom of Korea, Silla, had created a maritime empire and controlled East Asian commercial trade and naval affairs. The Koryō Kingdom, having inherited this tradition, was still unmatched by other nations in commercial trade and shipbuilding. Consequently, the Mongols in China asked Koryō to contribute ships and naval forces to invade Japan.

MONGOLS AND KOREAN WOMEN: KOREAN EMPRESSES IN CHINA

For over a millennium Korean women had the reputation of being beautiful. Whenever Korea's neighbor nations invaded or occupied Korea, women were hunted by foreign troops. They were not only violated by these foreign troops, but also taken away. This happened from T'ang troops of the seventh century down to the Japanese forces of the twentieth century. Korean women were on average several inches taller than their counterparts in China or Japan. Consequently, they were slimmer looking, and, having a higher forehead, their faces looked more oval rather than round and flat. Even in modern-day Japan, beautiful women are considered to be *chosen-gata*, or of the Korean type, and most well-known Japanese actresses fit this type, according to several scholars of "Korean Culture in Japan."[2] This attitude toward Korean women among neighboring nations was of course unwelcome to the women and their families. This reputation in fact caused disasters of historic proportion on many occasions. The T'ang Chinese invasion of the seventh century and the Japanese occupation of the twentieth century were the most cruel and inhumane events for Korean women, who were used primarily for the sexual satisfaction of men, a true degradation.

The Mongols treated women somewhat differently. In Mongol society, as in Korean society, women enjoyed relatively equal status with men. Women's social standing in the family and society in Korea and Mongolia was far different from that in China and Japan, where they were treated as almost equal to animals. The Mongols did look for Korean beauties in cities and villages, forcing Korean families to dress young women in men's clothes in order to hide them. However, once the Mongols took these young women in, they gave them respectable places. The Korean women who willingly or unwillingly went to Mongol China usually ended up in the higher echelon of Mongol society among nobles, high officials, or rich men, and some even in royal families as wives. One such example was the consort of the Mongol Emperor Shun-ti (Shun-di) of Yüan China. This Korean empress bore him a son who became the next emperor of the Yüan Dynasty, Chao-tsung.[3]

KORYŎ'S FORCED PARTICIPATION IN THE MONGOL INVASION OF JAPAN

The new capital of the Koryŏ Kingdom on Kangwha Island was still secure from the Mongol forces, but Kublai Khan managed to put Koryŏ under his influence through marriage. His next step was the conquest of the Japanese islands. Although the Mongol forces excelled in land warfare, they had little experience in naval war. They also lacked the technology for building vessels large enough to carry a great armed force. First, Kublai sent envoys numerous times to Japan and tried to subjugate Japan by diplomatic means. These attempts were not successful. Koryŏ tried to mediate between the two parties, for Koryō suffered from long warfare with the Mongols and did not want another war with Japan. The king of Koryō tried to convince Kublai that such a war would bring little benefit. Kublai was adamant; he ordered Koryō to build warships. Koryō shipbuilders worked on the project, however reluctantly. Korean shipbuilders from the time of Silla were known for building solid ships; however, this kind of great building project that was rushed under orders of the Mongol invaders could not possibly produce good quality ships.

In 1274, a forty-thousand-man army left the Korean port of Hap-p'o for Japan. Koryō provided most of the nine hundred ships and eight thousand men, scant lip-service, and the rest was made up with Mongol Chinese army. This allied force first occupied the Tsushima islands, and then landed on Hakata, Kyushu. Japan was under the rule of the Kamakura Shogunate, and their soldiers were battle experienced by prolonged internal wars. The number of Japanese forces was also greater than that of the invading forces. Gunpowder explosives startled the Japanese soldiers but produced few other results. While the battle was raging on the shoreline, a typhoon struck. Most of the ships capsized, and many soldiers were drowned. The Japanese called this wind *Kamikaze*, a wind of god.

Having failed in this first invasion of Japan, Kublai became even more aggressive and demanded that Koryō build more ships. Koryō's King Ch'ung-yōl dispatched a mission to Kublai and explained that Koryō could not afford another invasion of Japan. Kublai was not moved by Koryō's advice and sent missions to Japan with threatening letters. Japan beheaded Kublai's delegate and built stone walls along the coast of Kyushu. Kublai was very angry and demanded that Koryō speed up preparations for a second invasion of Japan. He established headquarters in Koryō and gathered all the military resources of East Asia under his command. The total invasion force numbered 150,000 troops, consisting of Mongol, Chinese, Korean, and Vietnamese, and five thousand warships. Koryō contributed ten thousand men and nine hundred vessels.[4] The Koryō force formed a very minor portion of the total force. Some Japanese historians have viewed this invasion as a Mongol–Korean invasion, but in fact the Korean force was only six percent and Korea was reluctant to participate. By this time, Kublai had conquered South Sung also and could use its naval fleet.

In 1281, the great invasion force sailed toward Japan. They struck Hakata beach, but the Japanese forces were well prepared and put up fierce resistance. The Mongol soldiers, who were not accustomed to sea battles, became seasick and could not fight well. They tied their ships with iron chains to stabilize them and lessen their movement, a grave mistake. When one ship was sunk it pulled down the rest of the ships chained with it. When a typhoon struck a few day later, it was a total disaster for the Mongols and their allies. Many drowned. Koryō's historical record indicated that 19,397 returned alive of the eastern invading force of forty thousand.[5]

Despite such a great failure, Kublai did not abandon his plan for a third invasion of Japan. By this time, all of Asia (except India and Japan) and part of Europe were under Mongol command, the largest empire the world has known. The unfinished business of conquering Japan was a small matter involving a culturally backward country; however, in the conqueror's mind, whatever remained unconquered had to be conquered. Nevertheless, Koryō could not continue to support Kublai's unreasonable demands. Kublai kept a large horse ranch on Cheju Island for his army to invade Japan; the Koryō king requested that it be withdrawn.

The Mongol Empire of Yüan was a cosmopolitan state, and people from all over the world gathered there. There were thousands of Europeans and Arabs engaging in commerce. Korean scholars were welcomed to Yüan, because they had been well educated at Korean universities and colleges, and many could write classical Chinese better than the Chinese. The Mongol rulers classified the Westerners and Koreans as above the Chinese in social status. Korean scholars were given equal opportunity to take the civil service examinations in Yüan. Many of them fared quite well and became high-ranking officials. One such Korean scholar was Li Kok, who had the pen name *Kajŏng*. He wrote to Kublai Khan that Koryō had become exhausted and could not participate in Kublai's third invasion of Japan, and that even if Kublai succeeded, he could draw little benefit from such a victory. Kublai finally gave up that ambition and never again attempted to invade Japan. Li Kok's son was Li Saek, whose pen name was *Mok-ūn*. Li Mok-ūn also passed the Yüan empire's civil service examination with top rank and was appointed as a high government official in Yüan. He later returned to Koryō and became the prime minister. He was one of the three most famous philosophers and scholars of Koryō, called *Sam ūn*, or the Three Ūns.

YÜAN (CHINA) AND KORYŌ (KOREA) TOWARD THE END

The Mongol Empire, which put most of the world under its domain, began to wither as soon as the fire of conquest was extinguished. From Genghis Khan down to his grandson Kublai Khan, the rulers were all military conquerors. South Sung came under Mongol rule during the time of Kublai Khan, who conquered almost every place he could reach, short of Western Europe, India, and Japan. However, to conquer lands with military power was one thing, and to hold and rule such vast territory a totally different matter. After Kublai's death in 1294, Mongol rulers degenerated quickly; with no more wars to be fought, they became soft and corrupt. They started to behave like the Chinese rulers before them. The only difference was that the Chinese rulers ruled their own people, whereas Mongols were foreigners to the Chinese.

Within half a century after Kublai, rebellions broke out all over China. The new Mongol rulers were not as tough as their forefathers. In the 1360s, the lack of leadership became worse during the rule of Emperor Shun-ti, a fun-loving, indecisive individual who would rather engage in activities of Lamaism than state affairs. While the whole of China was embroiled in serious rebellions, especially the one in southern China led by Chu Yüan-chang, Yüan Shun-ti totally neglected the affairs of state. In order to save the empire of Yüan, some nobles rallied around the Korean Empress Chi, whose son was the crown prince of Yüan. Because of the emperor's lack of interest in state affairs, Empress Chi had taken an active role in governance and had already become a power in the Yüan court. She had been an effective leader for some years. Many nobles started a movement to unseat Emperor Shun-ti and install the crown prince as emperor with Empress Chi as regent.[6] They insisted that it was the only way to save the Yüan Empire, which was not even one hundred years old. Normally that period was the golden age of any empire or kingdom, as exemplified by the examples of the Han, T'ang, Silla, Koryō, and even Japan's Heian period. The Yüan Empire could have been saved if proper measures had been taken. However, some Mongol nobles objected to the idea of a foreign-born empress sitting in the center of power.[7] It was a silly notion; it was a matter of survival. The birthplace of the empress should not have mattered so much. For example, the latter-day Russian empress Catherine the Great was a German, a foreigner to Russians, but she was a great ruler. Thus, the Yüan court became divided.

Sensing this, Chu Yüan-chang, who controlled most of southern China by this time, dispatched an army of 250,000 to Peking (Beijing), the capital of Yüan, in 1368. The Yüan Emperor Shun-ti had no army to oppose them and quickly vacated the city and escaped to Inner Mongolia, K'aip'ing. He died there soon after, and his crown prince succeeded him. This was Chao-tsung, who named his new empire the North Yüan.[8] He ruled Inner and Outer Mongolia, Lingpei, Kansu, northwest Manchuria, and part of Russia. He still ruled a large empire and he owed that to his able empress mother. Chu Yüan-chang, who had risen from a class of poor peasant farmers and joined in a band of roving bandits, gathered enough forces to expel the foreign Mongols and established himself as a new emperor of the Ming Dynasty in 1368. He was an uneducated man but was able to do the right things at the right times; for example, he struck when the Yüan princes were corrupt and divided.

Upon learning the Yüan emperor was ousted from China, the Koryō king severed diplomatic relations with Yüan and took measures to open relations with Ming. However, at the urging of the prime minister, Koryō reopened relations with North Yüan. In the meantime, the Koryō king Kong-min appointed General Li Sōng-ge as field marshal of the Koryō forces, gave him an army of twenty thousand troops, and ordered him to march north into the Manchurian region and recapture the lost land of Koguryō, Palhae, and the Chin Empires. It was the Koreans' long wish to recreate the great empire in the north. It was an opportunity that could be found once in a millennium. The able General Li Sōng-ge marched into the Manchurian region in 1370, took numerous castles, and finally took Liao-yang Castle, the major stronghold of the remaining Mongol forces, in present-day Manchuria east of the Liao River.

General Li recorded in his battle diary that he had occupied all the territory east of the Liao River and tamed the tribes within it. However, such occupation did not last long. In the middle of winter in severe cold the Korean forces did not have enough clothes and provisions remaining. General Li received a pledge of loyalty to Koryō from the tribes and withdrew. It was a hastily organized undertaking with insufficient support from the king. Furthermore, General Li was more interested in the Korean Peninsula than the Manchurian region.

While this was going on, the Koryō King Kong-min was engaged in dubious activities himself. To leave an heir to succeed his throne, he had an illicit affair with the concubine of his trusted subject, the former monk Sin Tun, with Sin's tacit approval. Later the king adopted Sin's son as his child, saying that the child was really his own. However, such a claim was unlikely. Later King Kong-min was killed by one of his male lovers. This messy situation in the Koryō court created great difficulty, because there was no rightful heir to the throne. After much discussion, high-ranking officials decided to install the adopted son of the king as the new king and named him King Wu, because the late king had willed it. King Wu was only ten years old. Many people opposed this act, including General Li Sōng-ge.

DEMANDS OF MING CHINA AND RESULTING POLITICAL CHANGES IN KORYŌ

Ming China, after capturing Peking (Beijing), gradually expanded into the southern Manchurian region. After this region was held by the T'ang Empire for about forty years in the seventh century, no other Chinese empires could hold it. In fact, the warlike people of this region were the source of the destruction of Chinese empires. Liao, the Chin empires, and then finally the Mongol Empire contributed to the downfall of Chinese empires. This domination lasted for six centuries. The vacuum created by the fall of the Mongol Empire in the region east and south of the Liao River was temporarily filled by the Koryō forces under General Li, but he could not hold the region because his forces lacked resources. He even helped eliminate the Mongol forces there. After his withdrawal, the Ming forces moved into the Liao River basin. It was a serious mistake for Li to withdraw. After the Ming Chinese forces occupied the southern Manchurian region, Ming shared the border with Koryō across the Amnok River. Present-day Manchuria east of the Liao was the home of the Korean nations. Koreans had lived there for millennia. The Chinese had never lived there, although they occupied it from time to time. Why would anyone let someone else occupy his home?

After occupying the land north of Amnok River, Manchuria, Ming sent a letter to the Korean king and demanded the "return" of territory north of P'yōngyang because it was once occupied by the Mongols. This infuriated the Koryō court. In 1388, Koryō mobilized a force of about forty thousand and ordered General Li Sōng-ge and others to move into the Manchurian region and cleanse the Ming army from there. This time it was rather too late. Li and the other general did not cross the Amnok River, but stationed their troops on Wui-hwa-to Island in the river. They requested King Wu and Prime Minister Ch'ae Yōng to withdraw Korean troops from the border area but were refused. Finally Li and the other generals turned back to P'yōngyang, where the king and prime minister were staying, and staged a coup d'etat. They deposed the king, saying that he was not the true heir but the son of the monk Sin. The prime minister was exiled. Later both of them were killed. Chōng mongju, a famous scholar and opposition leader, was also murdered. Li removed or exiled many old-line aristocrats from the Koryō court and consolidated his power. He was an excellent horseman, a dead-shot archer, and an outstanding military strategist. He was a Chin from Hamhūng, the border area of the Chin territory and Koryō. His father was the governor, who administered that region with a private army. Li was responsible for eliminating the Japanese pirates who raided the Korean coast for more than a century. Thus the stage was set for a new era on the Korean Peninsula.

Notes to Part II

CHAPTER 5

1. Federal Research Division, Library of Congress, *South Korea* (Washington, D.C.: U.S. Government Printing Office, 1992), 5.

CHAPTER 6

1. Li Pyōng-do, *Kuksa Taekwan* (Overview of National History) (Seoul: Po MunGak Co., 1985), 154.
2. Ibid.
3. Ibid., 138.
4. Ibid., 137.
5. Tanaami Hiroshi, *Shin-Nihonshi-no Kenkyu* (New Research on Japanese History) (Tokyo: Obunsha Co., 1967), 30.
6. Li Pyōng do, *Kuksa Taekwan*, 159.

CHAPTER 7

1. Li Pyōng do, *Kuksa Taekwan*, 168.
2. Ibid., 186.
3. Kin Tatsu-shu, *Chosen* (Korea) (Tokyo: Iwanami Shin-sho, n.d.), 72.
4. Li Pyōng do, *Kuksa Taekwan*, 201–202.
5. Kin Tatsu-shu, *Chosen*, 160–161.
6. Ibid.
7. Evelyn McCune, *The Arts of Korea* (Rutland, VT: Charles E. Tuttle Co. Publishers, 1962), 174.
8. Ibid.

9. Jon and Alan Covell, *The World of Korean Ceramics* (Seoul: Si-sa-yong-o-sa, Inc., 1986), 46.

10. Li Pyōng do, *Kuksa Taekwan*, 310.

CHAPTER 8

1. Dun J. Li, *The Ageless Chinese* (New York: Charles Scribner's, 1971), 126.
2. Shima Ryutaro, Yamata Masateru, Kin Tatsu-shu, *Nihonno Chosen Bunka* (Korean Culture in Japan) (Tokyo: Chuko Bunko, 1983), 59.
3. Li Pyōng do, *Kuksa Taekwan*, 271.
4. Ibid., 259.
5. Ibid., 260.
6. Dun J. Li, *The Ageless Chinese*, 271.
7. Li Pyōng do, *Kuksa Taekwan*, 270.
8. Ibid., 279.

Part III

The First Half of the Chosōn Kingdom—Li Dynasty, 1392–1650

9

Early Chosōn and Korea's Fourth Golden Age

The first two hundred years of the Li (or Yi) Dynasty was relatively peaceful. Korea had no major conflict with its neighbors, although there were some power struggles among the royalty and nobles. From 1392, when Li Sōng-ge founded the Chosōn Kingdom, to 1592, when Japan invaded Korea with an army of 150,000 troops, Koreans created one of the world's most highly developed civilizations. To be sure, the Li (spelling based on the McCune–Reischauer system) Dynasty Chosōn Kingdom inherited the Koryō civilization, which was already more sophisticated than those of China, Japan, or even Europe. China, which built a sparkling civilization during the T'ang period, had been occupied by the foreign powers of the Khitan, Chin (Manchus), and Mongols for more than four centuries, from the middle of the tenth century to the latter part of the fourteenth century, and its culture had more or less regressed. And Japan was in the midst of two centuries of civil war. Nothing mattered to the Japanese except war and survival during that prolonged period, until Hideyoshi unified Japan in 1590. During those two hundred years, Korea maintained peaceful relationships with China, while the Japanese were busy fighting themselves. Koreans were able to build a fourth golden age during this period.

UNSETTLED BEGINNING OF THE CHOSŌN KINGDOM

The transition of power from the Koryō Kingdom to the Chosōn was peaceful for the nation and the people. There was little damage to property or life. Most elements of Koryō society were inherited by the new rulers with little change. However, there was a power struggle within the Li royal family, reminiscent of the beginning period of T'ang China when the T'ang Emperor

Li Shih-min (T'ang T'ai-tsung) killed his two brothers and forced the abdication of his father. In Chosōn Korea, Li Pang-wōn was the fifth son of Li Sōng-ge, the founder of the Chosōn Kingdom. Li Pang-wōn was the driving force of most of the plots and undertakings which had made his father the first king of Chosōn. To do this, Pang-wōn undertook extraordinary measures, including the assassination of political foes. When he personally led a gang of assassins and beat the opposition leader, the scholar–statesman Chōng Mong-ju, to death at Sōnch'uk Bridge, Pang-wōn's father became very angry, to him such action was simply unacceptable, but his son's deed could not be reversed. Through this act, Li Sōng-ge assumed kingship. However, he never approved Pang-wōn's aggressiveness and sometimes cruel behavior.

As soon as Li Sōng-ge ascended the throne, he named the youngest of his eight sons the crown prince, bypassing Pang-wōn. Pang-wōn's anger was beyond description. To make the situation worse, each of the eight sons had a private army of his own, in the Chin tribal tradition. Within six years, Pang-wōn's private army attacked and killed two of the king's youngest sons, including the crown prince. Li Sōng-ge, fearing for his own life, abdicated, and the second son, Pang-hwa, was made king. Pang-hwa was only a puppet of Pang-wōn, who watched every move of his older brother. Pang-hwa was named King Ko-jong, but was not much of a king as Pang-wōn controlled every little affair. The fourth son of Li Sōng-ge, the first king (whose official name was T'ae-jo), Li Bang-gan, who was angry at this situation, attacked Pang-wōn with his private army but was defeated. Pang-wōn now exiled his brother Pang-gan.

King Ko-jong, fearing for his life, abdicated in favor of his brother, Pang-wōn. He became the third king of the Chosōn Kingdom, King T'ae-jong. His father, King T'ae-jo, was given the title of "Senior King." T'ae-jo was so disheartened that he went back to his birthplace, Hamhūng. This was primarily a power struggle within the royal family, scarcely noticed by the commoners. Once he became king, as also happened with Li Sheh-min of T'ang, King T'ae-jong became an effective ruler who did much to consolidate Chosōn Kingdom. However, his actions had set a precedent of bloody purges among the royalty and nobility which continued throughout the Li Dynasty and contributed significantly to the weakening of Korea.

DEVELOPMENT OF NEW SOCIOPOLITICAL TRENDS

Downgrading of the Military

The first new trend was the downgrading of the military. During the Koryō period the governmental system was developed to give equal standing and prestige to the military. The high-ranking governmental officials were called *Yangban*, designating both sectors, the civil and military; later the word was used to indicate the ruling class or gentry. The military of the Koryō era had enough power to crush the invading Khitan force of two hundred thousand men and resist the Mongols for forty years. In the beginning of the Chosōn Kingdom the princes had had private armies and had used them to gain personal power; hence a deep-seated distrust of the military had developed. All the private armies were disbanded by the king's decree. Military and civil officials were rotated around the country regularly, so that no official stayed in one place for more than three or four years. Military officials could almost never reach high-ranking positions as cabinet ministers or above. To make matters worse, Chosōn Korea became dominated by Confucian scholars, who in general despised the military. This situation became worse as peace continued. When Japan invaded Korea in 1592, the Chosōn government could barely muster ten thousand defenders against one hundred fifty thousand invading enemy troops. What saved Korea at that time was Ūibyōng, or volunteer militia, that sprang up all over Korea, not the regular government troops. This weakness in national defense eventually made the country vulnerable to foreign occupation in the twentieth century, at the end of the Chosōn Kingdom.

Rigid, Dogmatic Social Order

The Koryō Kingdom was a Buddhist nation. So many Buddhist temples were built in the capital city of Kae-kyōng that the whole city looked like a temple town, and there were thousands of temples in the country. The power of the Buddhist temples, in great land ownership, followings, and even military power, was so extensive that even the king could not ignore it. Li Pang-wōn, later officially called King T'ae-jong, took control as a dictator and set out to diminish the influence of Buddhism in the Chosōn Kingdom. He ordered that most of the Buddhist temples be closed, except for a dozen large ones. In place of Buddhism he instituted Confucianism, especially Neo-Confucianism of the Chu Hsi doctrine, as the national philosophical principle. The new emphasis on Confucianism was carried too far, to the extent that social behavior became rigid and dogmatic.

Confucianism advocates five principles of human behavior for social law and order. Such law and order was to be enforced by individuals' value systems and not by the government or police. These five principles were loyalty to the king; filiality to the parents; respect for older brothers; harmony between husband and wife; and trust between friends. These doctrines suited King T'ae-jong, because the first principle was the subjects' loyalty to the king. In his life he violated all of these principles, because he betrayed his king, forced his father to leave the capital city, and killed and displaced all of his brothers. However, now that he was king, he demanded that everybody obey the Confucian principles. He passed a law forbidding remarriage of women because he reasoned that it would violate women's faithfulness to their husbands even after their death. The idea of loyalty to the king was enforced to the extent that it was used often as justification for recurring bloody purges and cruel executions of political opponents, involving several dozen people at any given time. These were the long-term trends which were established in the beginning period of the Li Dynasty, and they did not all come about overnight during T'ae-jong's rule.

KOREA'S FOURTH GOLDEN AGE

Korea's fourth Golden Age occurred during the period from 1392 to 1592. At this time, the Chosōn Kingdom had several kings who were concerned about the welfare of the people, strove to be benevolent rulers, and promoted education and science. King Se-jong (1419–1450), in particular, was a great king unmatched in the long history of Korea through many different dynasties. He was the second son of T'ae-jong, Li Pang-wōn. Se-jong was very intelligent, studious, kind, and benevolent from early childhood, so that his father loved him greatly. He was made crown prince when Se-jong's older brother became a monk. Despite his unsettled beginning, T'ae-jong was an effective king, whose major contribution was in education and science. His rule was the beginning of Korea's fourth Golden Age. However, its true flowering, unmatched in East Asian history, occurred during the rule of Se-jong the Great. He was not only a wise, benevolent king, but also a great scholar, scientist, and inventor who was able to organize the best talent of the land and achieve unheard-of accomplishments for his country and people.

Newer Philosophy of Learning, Propagation of Knowledge and Research and Experimentation

The great Chinese philosopher of the Sung period, Chu-Hsi (1130–1200), was the initiator of Neo-Confucianist philosophy, whose influence on East Asian philosophy, especially in China, Korea, and Japan, has been felt for the last five hundred years. His philosophy came to fruition in Korea in the form of scientific developments in the fifteenth and sixteenth centuries. He was a Confucianist but freed himself from axiological study, the study of human value systems which deals with "what is good," and delved into the sphere of epistemology, the study to find truth about the universe. He reasoned that the foundation for finding truth about matters was broad knowledge. He said that such knowledge could be obtained through broad reading or observations. However, he failed to indicate the link between such a foundation, the raw materials, and the goals of finding truth and enlightenment.[1]

Chu-Hsi's new philosophical idea was taken up by three Korean philosophers toward the end of the Koryō Kingdom, Li Saek, Li Sung-in, and Chōng Mong-ju. The new philosophy of learning, which emphasized the broadening of knowledge and reading, increased the demand for books in Korea. With the technology of movable metal type already in use, the new Chosōn Kingdom was ready for large-scale publishing enterprises. King T'ae-jong belonged to the Neo-Confucian school and provided financial backing for the nationwide publishing of tens of thousands of books using movable type made of copper. Two hundred thousand types were cast in 1403 for this purpose. Some of the books produced are still in existence today. This massive publishing project during the King T'ae-jong period was half a century ahead of the work of Gutenberg, whose accomplishment could not approach in scale the Koreans. King T'ae-jong believed in the propagation of knowledge for national advancement of Korean civilization. Nevertheless, it was only a foundation for the progress of science in the search for truth about the universe.

The genius of T'ae-jong's son, King Se-jong, was to gather the nation's most brilliant minds to discover the link between knowledge, the foundation, and the goal, finding truth, and the solution to the problem by research, investigation, and experimentation. This was very similar to John Dewey's experimentalism. However, Se-jong of Korea was ahead of John Dewey by some five hundred years. This scientific method culminated in the creation of the world's most comprehensive, scientific alphabetic spelling system, along with numerous other major inventions. What the Chinese had left as an initial philosophical theory, Koreans completed as new scientific methods which produced magnificent results for the progress of civilization.

New Heights in Science and Increasing Wealth

Under the rule of King Se-jong, Korea attained the highest living standard in East Asia. Korea implemented many new farming methods and irrigation systems throughout the country. To promote these, the king and his subjects invented the world's first rainfall gauge in 1442. Thousands were made and distributed to every locality in the country. By king's decree, every locality had to maintain daily rainfall records. This network of meteorological recordkeeping continued into the twentieth century, producing the world's oldest such record, which was essential for the Korean agricultural industry, because Korea was a rice growing nation. Rice grows in water, hence the emphasis on rainfall. The king himself became a part-time farmer and personally planted and harvested rice on his own plot of land. With rich coastal farmlands, bountiful fisheries, and rich mines, including gold and silver, Korea enjoyed the highest living standard in East Asia. China's living standards, after four centuries of foreign occupation with continued exploitation, together with a population explosion, had fallen drastically from the time of the T'ang period. Japan, after three centuries of civil war, dissipated its resources, and became impoverished by the fifteenth century. Many Japanese coastal farmers turned pirates, and bands of Japanese pirates made their living by raiding the Korean coastline, because they had nothing to eat. Korea was still the center of international trade in East Asia and reaped profits. All these conditions raised Korea's standard of living, setting the stage for another golden age of prosperity.

Invention of Korea's Alphabets Through Linguistic Research and Experimentation

Perhaps the greatest accomplishments of King Se-jong were the invention and promulgation of alphabets. Years of research by a committee of linguistic scholars headed by the king himself concluded in the king's twenty-fifth year of rule, in 1443. King Se-jong proclaimed that the Korean and Chinese languages were altogether different, and using Chinese characters for writing the Korean language was unsuitable and difficult. Therefore, he had twenty-eight alphabetic letters developed, a simple system that common people could learn easily and use without much difficulty in daily life. This alphabet consisted of eleven vowels and seventeen consonants. The letters were initially called *ūnmun*, but are called *Hangūl* today. This alphabet was promulgated to the public in 1446.

These researchers first had to separate vowels and consonant sounds and conduct experiments to find what oral sound organ was involved in what way for each sound. They classified each sound as dental, labial, palatal, vocal, apical, aspirated, glottal, or fricative, and so on. These linguistic descriptions were almost identical to the modern descriptive linguistics studies that first appeared in the West in the 1950s; Korean scientific linguistics of the 1440s was thus ahead of the rest of the world by 510 years. European alphabets, including the English, came about by usage over many centuries. Therefore European spelling systems are complicated and confusing. One sound can be spelled in many different ways. There are so many variations for each word that learning to read and write can be extremely difficult. This is not true of the Korean alphabetic spelling system. There is only one letter for one sound with only a few exceptions. Usually an average foreign student with no Korean language background can learn to use the alphabet in about ten days. Korean students can learn to read and write in one week. This was a great advancement over systems based on Chinese characters (fifty thousand or more pictographs) and Japanese kanas, ideographs in few letters, that are difficult to use without additional Chinese characters.

Invention of Advanced Movable Metal Type

In previous chapters, printing and publishing of books with copper type were mentioned. This technology was further developed during the Se-jong period. In 1436, thousands of books which used lead type were published. By this time, type holders which kept type in place without using wax were also invented. Lead type was easier to make and melt down. It was in fact as modern a printing type as today's.

Other Inventions

There were numerous other significant inventions in Korea in the fifteenth and sixteenth centuries. Gerald Leinwand in *The Pageant of World History* points out, "Korea made contributions to the civilization of the world which were quite independent of Chinese. Koreans are credited with the invention of spinning wheel, movable metal type, the compass, the observation balloon, a metal-clad ship, an instrument to measure rainfall, and development of the Korean alphabet. The Li (Yi) Palace Orchestra, founded five hundred years ago, still performs music of the old."[2] He does not mention the precise clock powered by water flow, the sundial, or other Korean inventions. But he continues, "Korean scholars compiled a 112 volume encyclopedia, an original printed copy of which is in the United States Library of Congress."[3] Needless to say, it was the world's first encyclopedia printed with the new lead type. This Korean encyclopedia contained every conceivable scholarly description of the universe and the world of that time and was ahead of other nations by several centuries.

The invention and development of movable metal type, printing, and the publication of books (1234–1436) over two hundred years have been described. The invention and use of the world's first iron-clad battleship will be explained in the following chapter, in the discussion of the Japanese invasion of Korea in 1592. The rain gauge was invented in Korea in 1442; the first rain gauge in the West was made by Bendetta Casteli of Italy in 1639. Korea's invention preceded the West's by about two hundred years. The king ordered a central meteorological station to be set up in Seoul, and the depth of water in the steel rain gauge was measured daily. Copies of this instrument were made by the thousands with porcelain and distributed all over Korea in order to keep the record.

The sundial was invented to measure time by changes in shade. A more precise time instrument was the water-powered clock. Water flowed in precise amounts to move parts of the clock, turning them to indicate the precise time of day.[4] Research in astronomy progressed in earnest; scholars reviewed and researched all the available writings of astronomical findings and records and consolidated them into a new astronomical map. This was inscribed on a stone tablet.[5] In the previous chapter, it was noted that Korea built Asia's first astronomical observatory, which is still standing in Kyōng-ju after thirteen hundred years. Korea's interest in and research on heavenly bodies were strong then, and in the fifteenth century Korea continued to carry out astronomical research.

This scientific progress Korea achieved in the fifteenth and sixteenth centuries may seem elementary by today's standards. However, such attainments were not even dreamed of in other countries at that time. Korea was far advanced in practically every field by several centuries and was far ahead of China and Japan during this period. China was no longer a provider of new civilization to Korea.

Organization of the Government and Civil Service Examination System

The organization of government was similar to that of Koryō. The head of the government was the prime minister with two deputy prime ministers. Under them, there were six ministries: Interior, Treasury, Education, Army and Navy, Judiciary, and Agriculture and Commerce. There were three other independent offices: the Office of Propagation of Thoughts and Literature, the Office of the Overseer of Government Officials, and the Office of the Advisory Council for the King. All of these were designed to promote freedom of thought and speech and were based on democratic ideals to encourage the best ideas to benefit the nation and the people. This system of government worked well in the beginning and contributed to the development of the Golden Age. However, these consultation centers were transformed into battlegrounds of nobles and high government officials. Political infighting and factional struggles led to continuing vicious bloodlettings. Nevertheless, for about one hundred years, the policy of encouraging Neo-Confucian philosophical and political thought produced numerous scholars. The famous scholars Li Hwang (Toe-ge, 1501–1570) and Li I (Yulgok, 1536–1584) consolidated Neo-Confucianist thoughts, and their philosophies were widely accepted by Japanese scholars of the Edo period after 1600.[6] To support its educational policy, the Chosōn government established universities, one in Seoul and four others in the provinces. Sōng-kyun-kwan University in Seoul is still in existence today. These universities were mostly for the nobility and were closely tied with the civil service examinations, which had become even more rigid than in the Koryō period.

Literature and Arts

After the invention of the Korean alphabet and wide use of movable metal type, all kinds of books were published, including novels, philosophical books, medical encyclopedias, geographical notes, and general encyclopedias. Novels were usually in Hangūl (the Korean alphabet) and commoners with little formal education could read and enjoy the stories. Among the most popular books were *Ch'un-hyang Jōn* (a sad love story of a noble and a Kie-saeng girl entertainer), *Sim-ch'ōng Jōn* (a beautiful daughter of a blind man goes through fairylands in order to give her father eyesight), *Hong Kil-dong Jōn* (a magician fights evil officials to save people), and *Hūng bu* (a poor brother story), just to name a few. There were dozens of stories of fantasy to amuse the people. The fifteenth and sixteenth centuries truly constituted a golden age of literature for the common people.

More scholarly books were written in classical Chinese. In 1445, a medical encyclopedia in 365 volumes was published. At that time, there was no comparable medical book anywhere in the world: not in East Asia, and not in Europe. This was the culmination of five thousand years of medical knowledge and experience in East Asia, including Korea, China, and Japan. Modern medicine of today could definitely use such knowledge. A general encyclopedia in 112 volumes was published (and is in the collection of the U.S. Library of Congress). The philosopher Li Toe-ge published a Neo-Confucianist book, *Chu-ja Se Kan-yo* (Analysis of Chu-Hsi's Writings), which became a textbook of East Asian philosophy, not only in Korea, but also in Japan until modern times. *History of the Koryō Kingdom*, in 139 volumes, and *Overview of Eastern Country*, in fifty-seven volumes, were published in 1451 and 1484. A geography book which described eight provinces and three hundred counties in detail, including topography, people, customs, products, and buildings, was published in 1480.

Music developed and enriched the existing Koryō court symphony orchestra. More musical instruments were added. A one-hundred-piece orchestra with court musicians wearing the colorful court musicians' uniform has been, up to today, a grand sight for five hundred years. Its beautiful classical melody has never been altered. Porcelain arts changed somewhat from Koryō porcelains, which had no peer. The color changed to white from light blue-greens and was less refined. Nevertheless, porcelain of the Li Dynasty was still far more artistic than one could find anywhere else in East Asia. While traditional landscape painting was still popular, a new dimension was added to the art of painting. This was the new school of *P'ung-sok Hwa* (painting of people and customs). This style of painting was introduced to Japan, where it became *Ukiyo-e* (picture of mundane worlds).

There were also unique architectural developments in Korea. Kyōng-bok Palace, the second largest in Asia (second only to the Forbidden City Palace of China in its scale), had a unique design not found in China or Japan. The massive Kyōng-hae-ru banquet hall with its enormous stone columns resembled Greek structures more than other Asian structures. Castle walls were also unique, not resembling the Chinese or Japanese. Massive Nam-dae-mun Gate, which guarded Seoul for six hundred years, still stands today and has been classified National Treasure Number One by the government of the Republic of Korea.

The Fourth Golden Age of Korea, in the fifteenth and sixteenth centuries, imbued every aspect of civilization. In many fields, Korea was far more advanced than any country of that time. Korea's inventive genius had still not waned. It progressed to the creation of the world's first iron-clad battleship in the sixteenth century and geographic survey of the eighteenth century. No longer a minor civilization, Korea became the prime mover of East Asian civilization.

POWER STRUGGLES BETWEEN KINGS AND NOBLES

When Li Sōng-ge, the first king of Chosōn Kingdom, took power from the old line of nobles of Koryō with a military coup largely engineered by his fifth son, Li Pang-wōn, most of the nobles were opposed to it. However, they could not do much because they lacked military power. Pang-wōn ruled Korea with a dictatorship for nineteen years. He was succeeded by Se-jong, who reigned for thirty-one years. The leadership and scholarship of Se-jong were such that he virtually mesmerized the scholar–statesmen nobles to cooperate with him fully. As long as the kings were benevolent and scholarly, nobles worked diligently for them regardless of their origin. However, as soon as kings showed an evil side, they moved to destroy them. The nobles were descendants of the old line of Koryō gentry, whose origins were in the central and southern parts of the Korean Peninsula. Few northern Koreans ranked as influential nobles of the newer kingdom. An exception was the Li clan, from the northeastern border area.

After the reign of the two able kings T'ae-jong and Se-jong, trouble developed between the king and nobles. The first son of Se-jong, Mun-jong, became king but was ill and died after two years. His son Tan-jong was only twelve years old when he became king. Seizing this opportunity, his uncle Duke Su-yang set himself up as the prime minister and began to control the government. He removed opposition by killing his own younger brother and a minister. When Su-yang finally seized the throne three years later and sent his young nephew into exile, the nobles became angry. Twelve of the most prominent gathered secretly and plotted to depose Su-yang, who had proclaimed himself *Se-jo*, the seventh king. Unfortunately the plan came out and King Se-jo struck first, before the nobles were ready. Six of the twelve chose to die rather than submit to the illegal king. Six others yielded to Se-jo but refused to serve in his government. This happened in 1455, and was the first of a series of open power struggles. The nobles failed in this first attempt.

In 1494, the great grandson of Se-jo became king, but he was deposed by the nobles. Historians call him Duke Yōn-san, not king. He was extremely corrupt and debauched, hated scholars, and indulged in lewd activities. He collected fine horses and beautiful women. He closed Sōng-kyun-kwan University, the highest learning institution; used its buildings to hold his women; and indulged in orgies. He closed the largest temple in Seoul and made it a stable for his horses. He set out to undo what his ancestors had done, and this included the banning of the Korean alphabet for men. He said the alphabet was too simple and easy to learn; therefore, it was for only fools and women. He had the king's power, and could do such things. But when he began to molest nobles' wives, the angry nobles' patience became exhausted. He became bolder and began to do unthinkable things. For example, he would hide behind a large screen with a peephole and view nobles' wives when they visited to offer new years' greetings to the queen. He earmarked the most beautiful lady and proceeded to summon her to the court in the queen's name. He raped one such lady, who committed suicide. Her husband was so outraged that he recruited nobles willing to overthrow Yōn-san. This time the nobles' plot was successful. Yōn-san was dethroned and exiled to Kang-hwa Island in 1506. He died within a year.[7]

This event was the beginning of the nobles' domination in Chosōn Kingdom. About one century later another king was deposed from the throne.

He was no longer called king, but Duke Kwang-hae. This occurred in 1623.[8] He made the mistake of overestimating the king's power, which no longer really existed. He was exiled to Kang-hwa Island, then transferred to Cheju Island. Kings were no longer the dominant power in Korea from the sixteenth century on. Dominance of nobles continued until the twentieth century, although the Li kings' lineage remained intact.

Now that the nobles had power, however, there was no one person who had the ability to lead them all. The country became an oligarchy in which power was shared by a few influential nobles and high government officials. There was no democratic elective system. Power belonged to factions of nobles, and there were usually rival factions who would oppose each other on every affair. This caused great problems, especially when foreign nations invaded Korea. In the beginning there were two factions, the East Faction and West Faction (which had nothing to do with where they came from). These two factions then splintered into many smaller factions. Li I, the distinguished scholar–statesman of the sixteenth century, became concerned about these rival factions' struggles and tried to mediate between them, to no avail. He advocated the creation of a one-hundred thousand man standing army for the defense of the country against possible foreign invasions, but these political factions could not agree to maintain such an army. Thus Korea was left defenseless. As expected, when the Japanese invasion came a few years later, Korea had no army to defend itself.

10

Chosōn Kingdom's Foreign Relations and Invasions

CHOSŌN KOREA'S RELATIONSHIP WITH CHINA

Korea's ruling class was composed of scholars who were proficient in classical Chinese literature, just as European scholars were proficient in ancient Greek or Latin. Korean scholars were so well versed in the ancient Chinese classics that even contemporary Chinese scholars had a difficult time competing with them. Korean scholars and students no longer traveled to Ming China to learn as they had during the T'ang period. In fact, printed books from Korea were among the major items exported to China, along with gold and ginseng herb. Under these circumstances cultural exchange took place easily. Korea had become technologically very advanced in many aspects, and the Chinese respected this. The dominant Korean attitude toward China was the idea of *Sadae-juūi*, yield to the big ones. High-ranking Korean officials reasoned that since China was larger than Korea in population and territory, there was no sense in offending such a nation. With this in mind, the Korean government sent Ming missions and gifts regularly and received the same generous treatment. The relationship between Korea and China was quite amicable. Unlike the Mongol Empire of Yüan China, Ming respected the independence of Korea and never interfered with Korean politics. They never violated each other's borders. Ming controlled the western part of the Manchurian region, but it could not quite reach the eastern region. The Chins (Nuchens), who had lost the vast empire of Chin but were still independent, were now divided into small tribal states.

Chosōn Korea and Ming China had official exchanges of "gifts," but they in fact constituted official foreign trade. They were large-scale exchanges. Ginseng, an herbal medicine which the Chinese believed to be a panacea, was in such demand that it was far more valuable than gold by weight. Ginseng was a rare commodity found only in deep mountains, but by the sixteenth century, Koreans had learned to cultivate it. Gold was in such huge demand in China that the Korean government had to set an annual limit to the amount it exported to China. The exchange of culture and people took place broadly. As Yüan Chinese and Mongols had, Ming Chinese men welcomed Korean women. Many Korean women became the wives of Ming nobles and one became an empress of Ming, just as one had become an empress of Yüan during the Mongol period.[1] Such intermarriage contributed to the goodwill of the two nations. When Japan invaded Korea, Ming dispatched an army to help in that critical time, assisting greatly. In the seventeenth century, when Ming was attacked by Chins from eastern Manchuria, Korea dispatched an army to help its ally, although it was too late to do any good. It is rare in history that two nations which share a border never fought each other for nearly three hundred years (1368–1644).

KOREA'S RELATIONSHIP WITH JAPAN PRIOR TO 1250

Previous chapter have discussed the pivotal role Korean settlers and warriors played in creating Japanese society. Korean immigrants who moved into the Japanese islands from Imna (Mimana) and later from Paekche had faced the violent indigenous tribesmen of the Ainu and Kumaso people. They were hairy people, shorter than Koreans by an average of several inches. They used stone tools and weapons, together with deadly poison. They had no knowledge of farming or livestock raising. When food was in short supply, history showed that they would raid neighboring villages and engage in cannibalism. Early Japanese history was full of fierce fighting between Korean settlers and the aborigine Ainus and Kumasos. It was recorded that the older brother of Japan's first emperor, Jimmu, was killed by an Ainu's poison arrow. Headhunting, which Koreans never practiced at any time in history, was probably practiced by the Japanese aborigines. Korean settlers introduced rice farming, the Iron Age, the first unified state, and even the Golden Age of the Heian period to the Japanese islands. This took ten centuries, and the Koreans fought the fierce Ainus every inch of the way up to the north of Honshu Island. Gradually the Ainus were subjugated and assimilated. While Korean descendants formed the upper class of Japanese society, their number still remained smaller than that of the indigenous Japanese population. Archaeological findings have proved this fact.[2] While Korean descendants held centralized political and military power through the Yamato State, the Heian period, and the Kamakura Shogunate, the old Ainu ways were dormant. As long as the Korean descendants were in power, the Korean–Japanese relationship was amicable. However, once the Korean descendants began losing power in Japan during the late Muromachi Shogunate in the fourteenth century, relations took a turn for the worse. Japan took up piracy and gradually reverted to the old aboriginal ways of a violent society.

JAPANESE PIRATES IN KOREA, 1223–1592

Japanese history records that the Warring period in Japan officially started in 1467 after the Onin Civil War. However, the actual splintering of Japan into more than two hundred power blocs began a century earlier. Local lords called *Chito Daimyos* actually ruled their lands as little kings. They attacked each other, and the losers and their families would meet death and destruction without fail. It was a matter of survival for them to stay militarily strong. In order to support their goal, they squeezed their farmers and peasants dry. Impoverished peasants in Tsushima Island, northern Kyushu, and southern Honshu and along the Sedo-naikai seacoast began to raid coastal areas of Korea. This Japanese piracy began as early as 1223. By 1353, piracy was severe and had become an annual occurrence. They would move about in bands of forty to fifty armed men, forcibly taking materials and sometimes people. It became so severe that people vacated the seacoast areas of Korea for many miles inland, and the whole region turned into a no-man's-land. They began raids on the Korean coast and later extended them to the China coast.

These small bands of seagoing bandits increased in number to five to six hundred at a time, a small army. They became bolder and attacked towns located thirty to forty miles inland. They would attack and loot and quickly withdraw before government troops arrived. Damage from such raids was so severe that the nation itself was endangered. In 1389, Li Sōng-ge attacked Tsushima Island with his troops to destroy the stronghold of the Japanese pirates. This did some good but failed to stamp out piracy altogether, because the Japanese pirates were coming from all over the southern part of Japan. And the impetus for the piracy, the poverty of the Japanese peasants, continued. Korea tried again in 1419 to end the piracy by attacking the Sho clan in Tsushima with fourteen thousand troops and 227 ships.[3] The Sho clan was the kingpin of the Japanese pirates. Li Jong-mo and his Korean attacking force punished the Sho clan, but it had only a temporary effect.

The Korean government permitted and encouraged trade with Japan in order to solve the basic cause of Japanese piracy, poverty. The government opened the ports of Pusan-po, Chae-po, and Yon-po to the Japanese traders and showed the Japanese that they could enrich themselves without resorting to piracy. This worked for a while. However, in 1510 a dispute developed between the Japanese Sho clan and the Korean local magistrate. The Japanese sent in troops, which created great commotion. This was called the *Sam-po* (Three po) Disturbance. Still Japanese piracy continued. In 1555, a large band of Japanese pirates attacked the Chōlla coast again. Still to come was the greatest piracy of all, the invasion of Korea by 150,000 Japanese government troops which looted and destroyed the entire peninsula.

During the more than two centuries that Japanese pirates ran rampant, a gradual transformation was taking place in Japan itself. Bigger and stronger warlords gradually conquered the smaller ones. Among the few remaining strong warlords, those who had the greatest influence by 1580 were Ota Nobunaga, Tokugawa Ieyasu, and Hashiba (later Toyotomi) Hideyoshi, who was Ota's general. Ota had the advantage of the Japanese emperor's official endorsement. However, he was killed by his own retainer, Akeichi Mitsuhide, at Honganji Temple in 1582. This opened up the opportunity for Toyotomi Hideyoshi to take control of Japan. Ota's murder was not an isolated incident. The practice was known as *Ke Koku Jo* (killing or eliminating one's own master). It was a society in which nobody could be trusted.

Another custom widely practiced by the Japanese was headhunting. Whenever Japanese soldiers went to battle and killed an enemy, they beheaded him and carried the head to their chief to claim credit. During the Warring period of Japan, a soldier with two or three heads strung around his waist was a common sight. This was a custom Koreans never practiced at any time in history. This custom victimized Koreans immeasurably when Japan invaded Korea in the last years of the sixteenth century. Men, women, and children were beheaded. As late as the twentieth century, Japanese occupation forces beheaded Korean freedom fighters. This practice is noted again in later chapters

JAPANESE SOCIETY PRIOR TO THE INVASION OF KOREA

A man named Hideyoshi was born to a poor peasant family. He joined Ota Nobunaga's army as *Ashigaru*, equivalent to a private, the lowest rank. He was in charge of Ota's *zori* (Japanese shoes). One cold winter day, Ota wanted to go out to the yard and summoned Hideyoshi for his zori. When Ota put them on, they were warm, so Ota asked whether the private had been sitting on his zori. Hideyoshi opened his clothes and showed Ota his dirt-smeared chest, saying that he was keeping Ota's zori on his stomach to keep them warm for his master. It was the period when killings and taking over of a master's position were rampant in Japan, and nobody could really be trusted. This event impressed Ota with the loyalty of Hideyoshi. Thereafter, he was rapidly promoted to the rank of general. When Ota was killed by a retainer in 1582, Hideyoshi was in a position to inherit Ota's power. It took several more years of battles and political compromises and the Japanese emperor's backing, which came with the title of the prime minister and the regent. The Emperor Koyosai gave him the family name of Toyotomi in 1588. Toyotomi provided the impoverished Japanese imperial family with generous financial support, when the family could not pay expenses for maintaining a residence or even conducting a funeral. By 1590, he had all of Japan under his command. He decided to invade Korea and China.

As Toyotomi and his subordinate *daimyos*' territorial expansion reached the maximum, they wanted to expand onto the Korean Peninsula and conceived a secret plan to divide up the Korean Peninsula for themselves.[4] Toyotomi sent arrogant letters to the Korean government with unreasonable demands. The Korean King Sōn-jo did not know what the true intentions of Toyotomi were; therefore, he sent two emissaries, one from each of the two political factions, East and West. When they returned from Japan after meeting with Toyotomi, they gave divided opinions. Thus the Korean government was unable to form a firm policy toward Japan. However, the emissaries carried an arrogant letter which indicated that Toyotomi planned to attack Ming China, which meant that his forces needed to pass through Korea. Korea could not accept this demand. This meant the occupation of Korea by Japanese forces. The Korean government was still undecided about a possible attack by the Japanese. After two hundred years of peace, Korean forces were untrained in warfare and were scattered all over the country in small local garrison troops. Koreans were totally unprepared on land.

The only preparation at that time in Korea was made by Admiral Li Sun-sin (1545–1598), the commander of naval forces guarding the southwestern coastline. He secretly strengthened his fleet with the newly invented iron-clad battleships, which looked like turtles. The ship was covered with iron plates to protect sailors with sharp knives, pointed upward from the iron-plated roof to prevent enemies landing on its top. There were rows of portholes for guns and more oars than conventional ships for speed and maneuverability. It was a new invention, a true iron-clad battleship, the first of its kind in the world by several centuries. The admiral had a fleet of these iron-clad battleships built and trained his forces with them.[5,6] He was ready for the Japanese invaders who had to come across the sea.

KOREA–JAPAN WAR, 1592–1598

The Initial Stage of the War

Toyotomi Hideyoshi ordered his troops to assemble on the island of Tsushima between the Korean Peninsula and the main island of Japan on March 12, 1592. They waited for good weather and launched a surprise attack on April 13, 1592, on Pusan, before dawn. The commander-in-chief of the attacking Japanese forces was Konishi Yukinaga, who was supported by Kato Kiyomasa. The walled city of Pusan was totally unprepared. The magistrate of Pusan City, who was responsible also for the troops, was away on a hunting trip to a nearby island. The Japanese forces moved into the city, almost without resistance. The war diary of the chief Japanese commander described the first day of the war as follows:

> When we blasted the city wall with gunfire, no enemy stuck his head up. We climbed over the wall, we found people were running all over the place trying to hide. Those

> who could not hide started to wail loudly. They kneeled down on the ground, and put hands together in the front repeating same word "manora . . . manora." We presumed it to be begging for mercy. Regardless, our troops rushed on to them, and cut them up, kick them down. Men and women, and even cats and dogs were all beheaded. The head count came to thirty thousand. This was the sacrifice to the war god . . . our warriors' morale was ever high.[7]

It was a total massacre of the entire city. Practically all those killed were unarmed civilian residents. When the Pusan garrison chief Chōng Pal returned from his hunting trip with a handful of men, this mass slaughter was in progress. He plunged into the battle and was killed. This Japanese violence was only the beginning of the war.

The Korean commander of the naval forces of the area where the Japanese forces landed was an ineffective man named Wōn Kūn. He put up a brief fight, then withdrew. Admiral Li Sun-sin was given the responsibility of defending the entire seacoast. He had the position of commander-in-chief of all the naval forces. This was after the Japanese landing. Eventually the admiral was to save the nation.

The Japanese forces moved on to Kyōngju in the next few days and burned the historic capital of old Silla, destroying all the national treasures, including one-thousand-year-old temples. They moved on to the capital city of Seoul within twenty days and occupied it. The Korean King Sōn-jo escaped to P'yōngyang, then to the northern border city of Ūiju. When the Japanese forces attacked Seoul with nearly twenty thousand spearhead units, the Korean forces had less than one thousand men. When the Japanese reached P'yōngyang, the Koreans had only forty-four men. The Korean forces were practically gone. The king of Korea sent his messengers throughout the country to raise a volunteer militia, but such an effort took time. Korea was paying the price of neglecting its national defense. The Japanese forces were divided into two directions. Konishi's forces advanced to P'yōngyang, while Kato advanced on the east coast toward the Tuman River. At the border area Kato captured two Korean princes. The situation was turning from bad to worse. Korean citizens were being massacred by the Japanese everywhere. Countless numbers of people were beheaded, until the Japanese no longer could handle all the human heads. The Japanese general ordered the troops to cut off an ear instead. The number of ears taken was so great that when the troops retreated to Japan, they built a giant tomb called *Mimi-zuka* (tomb of ears). These mass murders were taking place without cause. Korea had done no harm to Japan. In fact, Korea had introduced the first (Yayoi culture), second (first central state of Yamato), and third (Golden Age of the Heian period) civilizations to Japan. Now these violent Japanese headhunters had turned into head-and-ear hunters. This cruelty had no match in the history of mankind.

The Second Stage of the War

Korean Naval Victories: The World's First Iron-Clad Battleship and the Total Destruction of the Japanese Fleet

The Japanese overall strategy was to invade Korea's southeast and central regions with a landforce and occupy that area, and its navy was to attack and occupy the rice-producing areas of Chōlla and Chung-chōng region and to supply food for the Japanese landforces. This plan did not work for the Japanese; Admiral Li Sun-sin with his newly invented iron-clad battleships began to attack the Japanese navy. There were a series of naval battles. First at Okp'o, and then at Sach'ōn, Tangp'o, and Tanghangp'o, Admiral Li gained decisive victories. The battle at Hansando was a significant victory for Koreans.

The Korean navy, led by Admiral Li, employed two major naval developments that were firsts in naval history. The first was the iron-clad battleship, and the second was a T formation. Koreans called the T formation the crane formation because the arrangement of naval ships was similar to the shape of a crane in flight. The wings were spread, embracing the enemy, but the main body of the attack force was aimed at the center of the enemy fleet, enabling the Korean naval forces to punch through the enemy line and scatter the enemy. Once the enemy lost formation and became disorganized, the Li forces could easily destroy ships one by one.

At the battle of Hansando Li's navy sank sixty-three large Japanese naval ships.[8] History records that both English Admiral Nelson who destroyed Napoleon's French fleet and Admiral Togo who destroyed the Russian Baltic Fleet at Tsushima Strait studied Admiral Li's naval tactics before gaining their decisive victories.[9] The remaining Japanese fleet escaped into Pusan harbor, its number of ships now 470. Admiral Li's navy launched a continuous attack and assaulted nine times. All of the Japanese ships were sunk or burned.[10] It was September 1, 1592, and Admiral Li seized complete control of the sea, dividing the Japanese forces in Korea from their homeland. No more reinforcements or supplies could be shipped from Japan, and the Japanese forces were stranded in a foreign country.

On land also events were not going well for the Japanese forces. The cruel manner in which the Japanese treated Koreans enraged Korean civilians, who began to volunteer for the militia forces by the thousands. One such large force occupied Haengju Castle south of Seoul, threatening the Japanese forces occupying Seoul from the rear. A force of ten thousand, including women, prepared for the Japanese assault. Korean women occupied a unique position in Korean society compared to women of other nations. They had more voice and participated to a greater degree in the affairs of society. The incident of the Haengju battle was such an example. The Korean women split their skirts in half, made them into large aprons, and used them to carry large rocks from the hillside, which they stockpiled on top of the castle walls. Ingenious Korean inventors invented rock throwing machines as well as a cannon which could discharge one hundred arrows or iron pellets with one gunpowder blast on enemy concentration. Then they waited.

Land Victory of Haengju

The Japanese, who were threatened from the rear by the Korean militia forces at Haengju Castle and concerned that their forces in Seoul might be cut off from their southern units, decided to attack the Haengju stronghold. On February 12, 1593, they sent forty thousand of their best forces, a force four times that of the Koreans. They launched an attack in good formation up the steep hill toward the castle. The Koreans waited until the last minute, then pelted them with big rocks, countless arrows, iron pellets, burning oil, and molten iron. At the day's end the Japanese forces were broken to pieces. More than half were dead and wounded, and they had to retreat. The Korean general was Kwōn Yul. The king, hearing of this smashing victory by the Koreans, appointed Kwōn Yul field marshal and commander-in-chief of all the Korean land forces. The top Japanese generals, Ukida Hideie, Ishida Mitsunari, and Yoshida Hiroie, who were Toyotomi's right-hand men, were all wounded in this battle.[11] The Japanese forces never tried to attack that castle again.

Korean Militia's Fire Attack on Japanese

The Japanese forces, which expanded like exploding bamboo, had become overextended by the winter. Their food supplies were not arriving. The Korean militia forces became more organized and more aggressive and launched fire attacks on the Japanese forces. With cries of "Burn, burn, any building or house Japanese devils are staying. Drive them out into the cold. Let them freeze to death. Let them starve to death!," the Korean militia set fire to all the buildings in which the Japanese soldiers were staying, including the king's palaces and government buildings. Kyōng Bok Palace, Chang Dōk Palace, and the government building were all burned down to the ground. With Admiral Li's blockade of the southern sea effective and the Japanese navy annihilated, nothing could go through this line to help the Japanese in Korea. Now the Japanese forces had suffered grave losses in land battles. The war finally turned in favor of the Korean forces.

Ming China's Participation in the War

About a month before the Haengju Battle, the Ming government decided to send an army to aid Korea in January 1593. After all, Toyotomi's ultimate goal in this war was to occupy and rule China. For China, it was better to fight a war in Korea than in China proper. In July 1592, a few thousand Chinese troops attacked the Japanese forces in P'yōngyang, without much success. The commanding general of Ming forces in the Manchurian region, Li Yō-song (Li Ju-sung in Chinese), was away commanding Ming forces in the western region of China to subdue a rebellion there. However, he was back at his post in

Manchuria by December 1592 and took up the command of two hundred thousand Chinese troops. Li Yō-song was a third-generation Korean whose grandfather became a naturalized citizen of Ming China. His name was Li Yong, and he became governor of Liaotung region. Yō-song's father was a Ming general who fought Nuchens and Khitans and was given the title of the Count of Lyong-won. Li Yō-song was the highest-ranking general of Ming at that time. Korea was his fatherland. Li Yō-song immediately organized his forces, personally led fifty thousand troops, crossed the Amnok River, and moved down to P'yōngyang.

On January 6, 1593, Li Yō-song's Chinese troops, joined by Korean forces, began to attack the Japanese forces in P'yōngyang. After four days of fierce battle Konishi Yukinaga's Japanese troops were defeated. With heavy losses, the Japanese hastily retreated to Seoul. The victorious allied forces of China and Korea pursued the retreating troops, but other Japanese forces, which were stationed in Seoul, joined in a battle at Pyōk-je-kwan north of Seoul. They set up an ambush force composed of a rifle brigade, and when the Chinese and Korean forces passed through a wooded area, they blasted them with rifle fire. Heavy fighting ensued, producing great casualties on both sides. The Japanese succeeded in stopping the allied forces temporarily. The Chinese and Koreans withdrew to Kae-sōng. Through these continuous battles, the Japanese suffered increasing losses without reinforcement from Japan, because of Admiral Li's blockade of the Japan Sea. The Japanese forces were dwindling, while the Korean militia forces were increasing. The war bogged down between the Chinese and the Japanese; however, the Korean militia continued its fire attacks and harassment.

The Koreans also won an important victory at Haengju Castle in February, inflicting heavy losses on the Japanese forces. The shortage of food and increasing casualties and cold weather put the Japanese forces in a desperate situation; the soldiers and even the generals wanted to withdraw and return home. One general remarked, "If I am to die anyway, I would like to die in my castle peacefully, rather than die here because of hunger and cold." If generals, who were the lords, were that hungry, one could imagine the condition of common soldiers. In this desperate situation, the Japanese forces were forced to retreat from Seoul in April 1593 and consolidate their forces on the eastern seacoast along the Japan Sea. They took up positions in the Ulsan, Masan, Sach'ōn, Sunch'ōn, and Ch'angwōn regions. The Korean stronghold of Chinju was located in the hub of all of these Japanese-held locations, blocking their coordination. The Japanese forces had to take Chinju Castle.

Fight to the Death at Chinju Castle

The Japanese mobilized all of their forces from the occupied nearby towns on the east coast. There were at least eighty thousand Japanese troops against three thousand Korean militia and about sixty thousand civilians. The civilians were unarmed, and most were women and children.[12,13] It was a mystery why the

Korean and Chinese forces did not send in more reinforcements, but perhaps it was too dangerous because it took place in the center of all the Japanese forces. It was also where in October 1592 the Korean militia soundly defeated a major Japanese force commanded by Hosokawa. The Japanese wanted to avenge the defeat. The second assault came a year later in October 1593, with seventy-nine thousand Japanese troops led by a hard-liner, the vicious Kato Kiyomasa, against a tiny militia force. Some Japanese liked Kato for being so ruthless, rough, and warlike, but others despised him because of that, including his superior, the commander-in-chief of the Japanese invading forces, Konishi Yukinaga. Once Kato arrogantly ridiculed Konishi, and the angry Konishi drew his sword, ready to slash Kato.

Most of the Korean castles were actually city walls, similar to Roman walls, which were designed to protect a city and its citizens. They were markedly different from some medieval European and Japanese castles designed to mainly protect warriors. Chinju Castle was no exception. The Japanese attack started on October 22 and continued until October 29. The Korean general Li Jong-in and his men fought well day and night. Each time the wall was breached and the Japanese soldiers poured into the castle, the Korean militiamen repulsed them. The tiny force of 3,000 fighting men could do only so much against 79,700 attackers. The Koreans fought to the last man. The Japanese soldiers poured into the castle on October 29, 1593, and butchered civilians: men, women, children, and even dogs, cats, and chickens. All sixty thousand civilian residents were slaughtered. This was recorded in the Korean history books *Ch'ung-yōl-lok* and *Ham-sōng-ki*. A similar slaughter of civilians at Pusan Castle was recorded by the Japanese commander himself, Konishi, in his war diary, as mentioned. Konishi described it as "actions of devils." Needless to say, all of these civilians were beheaded and ears were taken for credit.[14] These types of atrocities by the Japanese were commonplace during the war of 1592–1598. However, the Japanese repeated them in Korea in the twentieth century, and in the "Rape of Nangking" during World War II, when the Japanese army slaughtered two hundred thousand Chinese civilians in a few days in 1937 just to show their might.

Defections of Japanese Troops

The victory by the Japanese forces at Chinju Castle turned out to be an empty one. The heavy battle against diehard Korean defenders produced huge casualties for the Japanese forces, which were already reduced to less than half the original invading force. This additional large loss was unacceptable to the Japanese generals and soldiers alike. Reckless attacks ordered by Kato without considering the casualties produced huge losses by newly invented Korean weapons: rockthrowers, and cannons which spewed steel pellets and one hundred arrows with each blast. On top of these heavy casualties, when the battle was over, they found the town was in desolate ruin. There was nothing they could use: no food was left for the Japanese, all the houses had been burned. Hunger started to bite them. Soon after the Chinju battle, a strange occurrence began: The Japanese soldiers started to defect to the Korean side. Defection became so widespread that the Japanese units posted special guards to stop them, to no avail. Soon thousands had defected. Many volunteered to fight against their own former units.[15]

The Koreans formed Japanese units called *Hang-wae-dae* (units of surrendered Japanese soldiers). The number of these units increased over the months, to many thousands. The Koreans welcomed these soldiers, some of whom became high-ranking military officers and government officials when they accomplished meritorious services. One of them reached as high as the third grade, equivalent to a deputy cabinet minister in the Korean government. These former Japanese soldiers were now actively engaged in battle against their former forces. Changing sides like this was common in Japan during the prolonged warring period; to them it was not unusual. This situation not only drained the Japanese forces, but strengthened the Koreans. The Japanese forces could not sustain this situation for long; the top generals, Konishi Yukinaga and Ishida Mitsunari, began negotiations for a truce with the Ming forces because the Koreans would not even talk about truce as long as the Japanese stayed on Korean soil. The Ming forces wanted a truce as they desired to return home.

Truce Negotiations

What the Japanese generals were concerned about was the situation that existed in Japan. Hideyoshi, who came from a poor peasant family, lacked the centuries-long established clan foundation which many daimyos had. Although he inherited military and financial power from Ota Nobunaga, those very powers were wasted away in Korea in a war they had no hope of winning. In fact, their survival was in question. If Hideyoshi lost too much of his resources, there was no assurance that these powerful daimyos would not in the end destroy him and his supporters. They might lose Japan and their lives. Indeed, history has proved that their concern was warranted. Konishi wanted a truce at any price. For this he even deceived Hideyoshi. When Konishi contacted the Ming forces, Ch'im Yu-kyōng (Ch'en Wei-ching in Chinese) had the title of general but no post. An individual of dubious character who talked well but lacked trustworthiness, he volunteered to mediate. Much talk was going on without any agreement. Hideyoshi himself became involved in setting conditions. Emissaries were exchanged between Japan and China. While negotiations were going on, Japan withdrew almost all its forces from Korea, except a small unit in Pusan. Admiral Li and his iron-clad battleships let them pass the blockade, because preventing the withdrawal would prolong the Japanese stay. The Ming pulled most of its troops out from Korea also. However, the demands of each side were far apart.

Toyotomi Hideyoshi demanded that Korea cede to Japan four southern provinces, Ming send a daughter of the Ming emperor to Japan as a consort of the Japanese royalty (he intended to keep her as a hostage), commercial trade between Japan and China be opened, and two princes and several ministers of Korea be sent to Japan as hostages.

China refused all of the Japanese demands. Instead the Chinese emperor ordered Hideyoshi to give the Tsushima Islands of Japan to Korea as reparations for damages done by the Japanese forces. The emperor of Ming appointed Hideyoshi the king of Japan and said there would be no trade whatsoever between China and Japan. Upon receiving the letter, Hideyoshi screamed, "I am the king now. How dare he appoint me. Where is Konishi? I will behead him for making this kind of negotiation." Luckily, Konishi was still in Pusan with the small Japanese unit stationed there. Hideyoshi ordered a second invasion of Korea. A great force of 140,000 sailed again to Korea in 1597.

The Third Stage of the Korea–Japan War 1597–1598

The Japanese general Konishi Yukinaga, who was already in Korea, received the message about the new Hideyoshi invasion plan. He was the main advocate of a truce and the early end of the war. He was a devoted Christian, one of a quarter million Japanese Christians in the sixteenth century. From the beginning of the war he despised the cruel manner in which Japanese soldiers conducted the war, especially Kato Kiyomasa, the chief advocate for continuing the war and his archrival. He was informed that, as usual, eager Kato would spearhead the second invasion. He was also informed of his arrival date and place. Konishi blamed Kato for playing the main role in breaking the peace negotiations for which he had worked so hard. The angry Konishi informed the Korean general Kim Ūngsu of the impending invasion and told him that if Admiral Li's navy attacked Kato's incoming ships, Li would be able to destroy Kato's forces. This bespeaks how Konishi hated Kato, and it was unbelievable in normal circumstances. However, such betrayal was common among daimyos of the Japanese society during the warring period. The Korean general Kim reported it to Seoul, and the King ordered Li to attack the Japanese ships. Some historians thought it was actually a trick to ambush Li by Konishi, and Li thought so also. He could not believe one Japanese general was trying to destroy his colleague in front of the enemy. Li did not move, saying that it was a trick to ambush him. He did not understand the Japanese society of that time. Kato and his forces arrived on the indicated date at the indicated place. The angry king and his ministers removed Li from the admiral's post, demoted him all the way down to a buck private, and ordered him to join in the land battle—a foolish move. This opened the gate to the Japanese main units to land on the Korean coast. Wōn Kūn, who succeeded Li, did not do well. A cowardly man, he abandoned his ship when the sea battle was not going well and tried to escape to land. He was caught by the Japanese soldiers and was killed.

Sea Battles

King Sōn-jo and his ministers had no choice but to restore Admiral Li as commander-in-chief of the Korean naval forces. When he took up his forces, he was joined by the Ming naval forces of five thousand men. Li's Korean navy fought the Japanese naval forces at Orong (Ch'ingto), achieved a smashing victory in August, recaptured control of the sea, and blockaded Konishi's forces at Sunch'ōn.

Land Battles

The second invasion of the Japanese forces was ineffective. The Korean and Ming forces were much stronger and the Japanese forces did not enjoy the element of surprise. Korea mobilized its forces, and there were many battle-experienced soldiers this time. Ming, as soon as they heard the news, sent in 140,000 troops immediately. The Japanese, considering the reason for the failure of the first invasion, which was the shortage of food, moved into the rice-producing areas of Nam-won in the Chōlla Province and took it. However, at Chik-san the main Japanese forces were defeated by the Ming forces. Not only could they not take Seoul this time, they had to make a full retreat back to the east coast.

Konishi entered Sun-Ch'on, Kato entered Ulsan, and Shimazu took up position in Sa-ch'on, all on the seacoast. By December, all of these forces were completely encircled by Korean and Chinese forces, and at sea they were blockaded by Li's navy. Especially at Ulsan, Kato's forces were fiercely attacked by the Korean and Chinese forces. The Japanese suffered huge casualties and were in a desperate situation. Even the former Japanese troops who had changed sides launched a severe attack on their former friends. They constantly shouted in Japanese, telling them to surrender. Numerous battles were fought. And, each time, Kato's Japanese troops suffered heavy casualties. The Korean and Ming troops attacked them at midnight and throughout the night without pause. Kato, who had attacked the Koreans so severely during the first invasion, faced extinction this time. After several days of fighting, he had only thirty-five hundred troops left, a fraction of his original forces.[16] The food supply was completely exhausted. Kato's troops had to eat tree roots and leaves. The water flows into Ulsan were diverted to another direction; not a trickle was available.[17] Konishi in Sunch'ōn was not in any better situation; he was surrounded by the Ming forces on the land and blockaded by Li's navy. He sent a lavish gift to the Ming general in order to bribe him not to attack; this tactic delayed the battle somewhat.[18] However, the initiative of battle was shifted to the Korean–Chinese side, and all the Japanese forces could do was to maintain a defensive position.

Death of Toyotomi Hideyoshi and Full Disorganized Retreat of the Japanese Forces

With the Japanese forces holed up in several small castles and fighting desperate battles for survival, in August 1598, Toyotomi Hideyoshi suddenly died. His constant worry about the adverse circumstances of the Japanese forces proved to be fatal. His last request was to have the Japanese forces in Korea withdrawn. The news came as a shock; the problem was how to withdraw through Li's blockade. In November, the Japanese forces began retreating during the dark of night. All the units left behind the major portion of their troops. Because of the secrecy of the operation, coordination problems, and the disorganized retreat, each soldier was left to see his own survival: There were not enough ships to carry all, and so on. Tens of thousands of troops were abandoned.[19] Countless men who got on the boats were then sunk by Admiral Li Sun-sin's iron-clad battleships.[20] Thus the Korea–Japan War of 1592–1598 came to a conclusion, with the Japanese totally defeated and in full-scale retreat. The Korean victory did not come easily. Koreans paid an unacceptable price. Admiral Li, while attacking the retreating Japanese ships, was hit by a Japanese bullet and killed. Those Japanese troops who were left behind were accepted into Korean society. There was no historical record that they were beheaded as the Japanese had Koreans during the war. Most of them were rather well treated.

Aftereffects of the Korea–Japan War, 1592–1598

For the Japanese side, the war produced both positive and negative effects. On the positive side, although the context was hostile, the Japanese came into contact with the higher civilization of Korea, which Japanese society had not yet attained. The transmission of civilization in this case was done mostly through Japanese plunder and looting at gunpoint. Nevertheless, Japan undeniably benefited from it. National treasures, which had over several centuries accumulated, were taken away to Japan; this topic is discussed later in relation to the war's effect on Korea. The tens of thousands of Japanese soldiers who were left behind either voluntarily or involuntarily were treated with compassion by the Koreans and accepted into their society. They settled down in the area of Pusan, Masan, and Ulsan; married Korean women; and formed families. There are many families who are the descendants of such Japanese soldiers living in these areas even today. The author of *Yakimono-to Tsurugi* (Pottery and Sword), Noguchi Kakuchu, had an ancestor who was one of those soldiers.[21]

The Japanese soldiers who escaped the tiger's jaw of Admiral Li Sun-sin's fleet of iron-clad battleships and returned alive did not fare so well as those left behind in Korea. Tokugawa Ieyasu was the strongest warlord of Edo in the Kanto region. He and his ally daimyos decided that the crushing defeat of Toyotomi's forces in Korea left them tattered and weak; therefore, their opportunity to seize control of Japan had arrived. Tokugawa gathered forces and Toyotomi's forces had to meet them. The daimyos who fought in Korea, Ishida Mitsunari, Konishi, Kobayakawa, Mori, Ukita, and Shimazu, gathered the remnants of troops left from the Korean invasion and met Tokugawa's men at Sekigahara in 1600, less than two years after the Korean defeat. Some daimyos who were to support Toyotomi's forces turned their troops around and attacked his forces from behind. They would side with anybody who was stronger for self-preservation; that was the morality of the Japanese during the warring period. Toyotomi's forces were defeated. The Toyotomi troops were beheaded, and the head count reached fifty thousand. Most of them were the soldiers who had escaped from Korea. The generals who led the Korean invasions, Ishida Mitsunari and Konishi Yukinaga, were also beheaded.[22]

The last of the Toyotomi clan, Toyotomi Hideyoshi's wife, Yodo Gimi, and his only son, Toyotomi Hideyori, both committed suicide when the last of Toyotomi Hideyoshi's strongholds, Osaka Castle, fell in 1615.[23] The unnecessary war, which had created so much destruction to Korea, also caused the total demise of the Toyotomi clan. This historical happening was the repeat of Sei Yang-ti's Chinese invasion of Korea, which had cost his empire and his life a thousand years earlier. This was equivalent to a story of robbers who invaded someone else's house to take everything, but ended up losing their own lives as well as everything they possessed. Some old-line Japanese historians, especially those who were hired by the Japanese government Mombusho (Ministry of Education), glorified Hideyoshi's invasion of Korea, calling it *Chosen Seibatsu* (Conquest of Korea), and characterizing Hideyoshi as the greatest hero in Japanese history. But a miserably failed invasion was not a conquest, and furthermore, Hideyoshi's reckless venture led to the demise of his family and supporters. He could not possibly be considered a wise man, let alone a hero. The twentieth-century Japanese military expansionists and imperialists idolized him without conscience or introspection. Hideyoshi was indeed one of the greatest fools in the history of Japan, not a national hero. The new Tokugawa Shogunate realized Japan's mistake and sought friendly relations with Korea. It exchanged delegates with Korea, and when Korea's ambassador arrived in Japan, Tokugawa dispatched a welcoming group and treated him with courtesy equal to that of the highest-ranking daimyo. This continued until the second half of the nineteenth century, when the new regime of Meiji, which was far more imperialistic, came to power.

For the Korean side, the war of 1592–1598 left a great scar which could not be healed. The damage done by the Japanese was immeasurable, especially in Kyōngsang Province, where five-sixths of the farmland had turned into wasteland because of the war.[24] In addition to the massacre of civilians which took place everywhere, and the destruction of historical buildings, the following irreplaceable materials were rooted out of Korea and taken to Japan: (1) royal and governmental treasures; (2) art objects, paintings, and Koryō porcelains;

(3) tens of thousands of printed books;[25] and (4) hand-made cast movable metal type in hundreds of thousands, made over two centuries.[26]

Professor Kajimura Hideki has written that the Japanese troops burned and destroyed so many books during the war, that it is difficult to find source materials in Korea, even today. Rare books of Korea were taken to Japan by daimyos during the war, were stored, and had little use.[27] The Japanese could not even read them. These were the irreplaceable materials. The Japanese also abducted living national treasures of Korea, namely scholars and porcelain makers, by many thousands.[28] The famous Japanese pottery of Satsuma, Karatsu, Hagi, and Raku, were all made by the Korean potters who were kidnapped and taken to Japan.[29] Many of these products of civilization were in fact rooted out of Korea and replanted on Japanese soil. Japanese civilization, which had been far behind that of Korea, now gained some ground at the expense of Korea. The Japanese, who were never very inventive, took them from Koreans at sword point. From that time on, deprived of its national treasures, Korea went into a decline. However, the Li Dynasty managed to survive for another 312 years.

CHIN (NUCHEN) INVASIONS OF 1627 AND 1636

This book has discussed the origins of the Chin (Jin) nations. The Chins were the subtribe of the overall Korean nation of Tungus. They have the same ancestry of early Tangun Chosōn, Kija Chosōn, Puyō, Koguryō, and Palhae Kingdoms as the Koreans who live on the Korean Peninsula. After the Khitans (Liao) destroyed Palhae in 926, the Chins either moved into Koryō and received the protection of their kin in the south or remained in the Manchurian region, loosely organized as semi-independent states, especially in the southeast. The Chins, who were called Nuchens (Jurchens) by the Chinese, or Yōjin by their kin in the south on the Korean Peninsula, were horseriders, hunters, and fierce warriors. Unlike their kin to the south who settled in the fertile coastal lands of the peninsula and became settled farmers in mild climates, the Chins were still spending most of their lives on horseback, hunting and raising livestock. Once they had also had a high level of civilization shared with their kin in the south. However, after the Koguryō and Palhae Kingdoms, they fell behind after they lost nationhood.

The Chins came under the domination of the Khitans from 926 to 1115, nearly two hundred years. However, they rose again and created a mighty empire of Chin and ruled all of Manchuria, Mongolia, and northern China. The Chin Empire lasted until 1234, a little over one hundred years. It respected the kinship to Koreans on the peninsula and never invaded Koryō. They were fully satisfied with a signed diplomatic agreement that Koryō was their brother nation. The Mongols destroyed the Chin Empire in 1234 and Sung China in 1279. They occupied the Manchurian region until 1368; then Ming China replaced the Mongol rule of Manchuria into the early 1590s. For about 356 years eastern Chins lived without a central government, because Ming's power did not quite reach into their territory. The Chins looked upon their kin to the south and their civilization with awe and called them father and elder brothers. They always emphasized their kinship and common ancestry.

The Chins, who were always hard-pressed by both China and Korea, gained an unexpected opportunity to organize themselves when Korea and China pulled their military resources out of Chin territory to fight the Japanese during the Korea–Japan War of 1592–1598. In addition, they produced a great leader, Nurhachi (1559–1626). By 1592, the beginning of the war, Nurhachi had a considerable force under his command. He offered military assistance to Korea, stating that he was willing to assist a brother state in distress. Korea refused the offer, fearing the consequences.

Nurhachi was an outstanding organizer of military as well as political institutions. He was an expert in psychological warfare. He organized his army under eight banners of different colors. Under each banner he formed a military unit of ten thousand troops, mostly cavalry. He also used religious and psychological elements. Nurhachi spread the belief among the Chins that he was the reincarnation of the Buddhist god Man-chu, who was the spiritual ruler of the east. That idea worked: People started to call him and his domain *Manchu*.[30] The Chins, including rival tribes, were convinced that Nurhachi was invincible because he was a reincarnated god and gathered under his banners. These warlike nationals, once they united into a single fighting unit, became a formidable force that even the Chinese army could not stop. Nurhachi formally raised the standard of revolt against Ming in 1616 and named his new nation Later Chin. He declared war against Ming, announcing the "Seven Grievances" against Ming in 1618. Ming sent two hundred thousand troops to put down the revolt and asked Korea for assistance. Korea sent a token force of thirteen thousand men, but the Korean general surrendered without a fight.[31] Ming forces were soundly defeated by the Chins and most of Manchuria fell under Chin control.

The Chins released all of the Korean troops except the generals and requested "brother" state relationship with Korea. However, bickering Korean political leaders could not decide on Korea's policy toward the Later Chin Empire. Finally the hard-liners won out, and the Chins' request was denied. A few years later, in 1626, Nurhachi died of battle wounds. His son, Abahai, who succeeded him, was not as gentle toward Korea as his father had been. He invaded Korea in 1627.

The First Chin Invasion of Korea, 1627

Korea, after suffering major destruction by the Japanese invasion, was still under repair and had not yet fully recovered from the human losses. In fact, Korea was still in an exhausted state. Abahai's Chins, who now called themselves Manchus, crossed the Amnok River with thirty thousand troops and moved south. They passed Anju and P'yōngyang to reach the P'yōng-san area. The Manchus, while advancing, busily sent delegates to the Korean king and his officials, demanding a negotiated settlement. The Korean side also desired a peaceful settlement, and so they reached an agreement. The Koreans on the peninsula, who always called the Manchus *oranke* (barbarians), considered any agreement with the Manchus demeaning. However, a weakened Korea had no choice but to accept terms which established equal status with the Manchus as "brothers," a policy of nonaggression, and open trade. This trade agreement was especially important to the Manchus, because they needed food to support the war with Ming.

After the withdrawal of the Manchu troops, the Korean government's power structure changed. The ruling factions changed, and the new king and new nobles took over. King In-jo and his ministers did not like the previous agreement with the Manchus, and when the Manchu emperor sent an emissary with the emperor's personal letter, they did not even receive him, nor accept the letter. They displayed open contempt without the military power to support it. Korea was so exhausted that the country had no resources left to engage in another war. In 1636, the Manchus changed their official title to *Ch'ing* from Later Chin and began to invade Korea, personally led by the angry Emperor Abahai himself, with one hundred thousand troops. Abahai knew Korea maintained close relations with Ming China, and he could not afford to face two enemies from the west and south. The southern front had to be secured before he could invade Ming China.

The Second Invasion of Korea by the Chins (Ch'ing), 1636–1637

Abahai's troops were mostly cavalry soldiers who moved swiftly. They reached Seoul in a few days. The Korean King In-jo hurriedly escaped down to Namhansan-sōng Castle with barely thirteen thousand soldiers. Such retreats were the price Korea paid repeatedly for its lack of proper preparation for national defense and downgrading of the military. The Manchus encircled the castle and began to bombard the castle walls with Portuguese cannons captured from the Ming forces. The siege lasted for three months. The Korean forces ran out of food, and King In-jo had to surrender. A king of Korea had never surrendered to Liao, Chin, Mongols, Ming, or Japanese in this fashion, but this time, in 1637, he had to acknowledge the suzerainty of Ch'ing.

The Ch'ing emperor was gentle in his treatment of Korea. The Ch'ing forces did not destroy or kill people as the Japanese had. Ch'ing received sworn statements from the Korean king that Ch'ing would be the "elder brother." And King In-jo agreed that his sons would accompany the Ch'ing Emperor to Manchuria until such time when the emperor would decide to return them. Ch'ing of Manchus held them until Ming was conquered in 1644. One of these Korean princes, who later became the Korean King Hyo-jong, wanted to avenge his captivity and raised an army to attack the Ch'ing; however, nothing came of it. The Ch'ing never interfered with Korean internal affairs and respected the country's independence until the end of the dynasty.

After the rear front to Korea was secured, the Manchus could devote their full strength to Ming China. By 1634 the Manchus completed the conquest of Inner Mongolia and organized Mongolian forces into eight additional banners. What helped the Manchus most was the continuous rebellions which beset Ming China for two decades. The Ming generals surrendered to the Manchus without a fight with troops lured by the promise of higher positions and better pay by the Manchus. One such general was Hung Ch'eng-ch'ou, who surrendered with 130,000 troops.

By 1644, the Manchus had 170,000 forces ready to invade China proper.[32] These troops were led by the able regent Dorgon, uncle of the six-year-old child Emperor Shun-chih (1644–1661), as Abahai had died the year before. That year, in 1644, the capital city Peking (Beijing) was under occupation by the rebel leader Li Tzu-ch'eng. Li developed an intimate relationship with a famous beauty and entertainer who was the former lover of the Ming general Wu San-kuei, the commander of Shanhaikwan. *Shanhaikwan* literally means "the fortress between the mountains and the ocean." It was the last fortress guarding China proper from Manchuria. Upon hearing that the rebel Li had stolen his woman, Wu could not wait any longer. However, he did not have enough forces to attack Li. General Wu opened the gate of Shanhaikwan and invited the Manchus into China, asking them to help crush the Li forces in Peking.[33] The Manchus moved into China and occupied Peking without a battle in 1644. Prince Yung-ming and others tried to salvage south China; however, they were all crushed by the Ch'ing. Finally Yung-ming escaped into Burma, pursued by the Manchu forces, and was captured there in 1659. He was hanged and the Ming Dynasty ended.

Thus, a branch of Tungus, or the larger Korean nation, who shared the same ancestors of Koguryō and Puyō with the people on the Korean Peninsula, the Manchus (or Chins), set themselves up as the rulers of China and reigned until 1911. The Manchus conquered Inner and Outer Mongolia; Tibet; Turkestan; Dsugaria, reaching near the Caspian Sea; and Nepal, Burma, Vietnam, and Cambodia. Eventually they constructed one of the largest empires ever formed in the world. However, there was a negative side to such an expansion. The Manchu population was only two percent of the total Chinese population. When Manchuria was opened up to Chinese immigration by Manchu rulers, an avalanche of Chinese immigrants overwhelmed the Manchu population, and the Manchus as a separate nation disappeared. This was exactly what Wenyen Akuta had warned his people of Chin in 1115 to guard against. Korea, on the other hand, as a smaller nation, suffered greatly at the hands of its neighbors; nevertheless, it maintained its unique national identity. The Chins in Chosōn territory of the Korean Peninsula in the northeastern region became mixed with the southern Korean population who immigrated into that area from Kyōngsang Province of the old Silla region. The Chosōn government encouraged such immigration of southern Koreans to the north into Hamgyōng Province near the Manchurian border.

Notes to Part III

CHAPTER 9

1. Dun J. Li, *The Ageless Chinese* (New York: Charles Scribner's Sons, 1971), 223.
2. Gerald Leinwand, *The Pageant of World History* (Boston: Allyn and Bacon Inc., 1971), 241.
3. Ibid.
4. Li Pyōng-do, *Kuksa Taekwan* (History of Korea) (Seoul: Po MunGak Co., 1985), 335.
5. Ibid., 334.
6. Kajimura Hideki, *Chosen-shi* (History of Korea) (Tokyo: Kodansha Kendai Shinsho, 1989), 72.
7. Li Hui Song, Paek Ch'ol, et al., *Hanguk Inmyong Daesajon* (Encyclopedia of Korea's Historical Names) (Seoul: Sin-gu Publishing Co., 1970), 466.
8. Ibid., 38.

CHAPTER 10

1. Li Pyōng-do, *Kuksa Taekwan*, 431.
2. Sakamoto Taro et al, *Nihonshi Sho-jiten* (Encyclopedia of Japanese History) Origin of the Japanese Race (Tokyo: Yamagawa Publishing Co., 1970), 541.
3. Tanaami Hiroshi, *Shin-Nihonshi-no Kenkyu* (Research on New Japanese History) (Tokyo: Obunsha, 1967), 189.
4. Kajimura Hideki, *Chosen-shi*, 74–76.
5. Ibid., 77–78.
6. Noguchi Kakuchu, *Yakimono-to Tsurugi* (Pottery and Sword) (Tokyo: Kodansha, 1981), 119–120.
7. Ibid., 59–60.
8. Ibid., 131.

9. Li Pyōng-do, *Kuksa Taekwan,* 410–413.
10. Noguchi Kakuchu, *Yakimono-to Tsurugi,* 134–135.
11. Li Pyōng-do, *Kuksa Taekwan*, 414.
12. Noguchi Kakuchu, *Yakimono-to Tsurugi,* 158–171.
13. Li Pyōng-do, *Kuksa Taekwan*, 416–418.
14. Ibid., 418–419.
15. Noguchi Kakuchu, *Yakimono-to Tsurugi*, 171–172.
16. Ibid., 186–187.
17. Ibid., 188.
18. Li Pyōng-do, *Kuksa Taekwan*, 424.
19. Noguchi Kakuchu, *Yakimono-to Tsurugi*, 190.
20. Li Pyōng-do, *Kuksa Taekwan*, 424–425.
21. Noguchi Kakuchu, *Yakimono-to Tsurugi*, 192.
22. Sakamoto Taro et al., *Nihonshi Sho-jiten*, 383.
23. Ibid., 507.
24. Kajimura Hideki, *Chosenshi*, 78-79.
25. Ibid., 79.
26. Tanaami Hiroshi, *Shin-Nihonshi-no Kenkyu*, 195.
27. Kajimura Hideki, *Chosenshi*, 79.
28. Ibid.
29. Noguchi Kakuchu, *Yakimono-to Tsurugi*, 193–228.
30. Tamura Jitsuzo, *Sekai-no Rekishi* (World History) (Tokyo: Chuko Bunko, 1981), 197–198.
31. Li Pyōng-do, *Kuksa Taekwan*, 433.
32. Dun J. Li, *The Ageless Chinese*, 310.
33. Tamura Jitsuzo, *Sekai-no Rekishi*, 188.

Part IV

The Second Half of the Chosōn Kingdom—Li Dynasty, 1650–1910

11

The Gradual Decline of the Li Dynasty

The foreign invasions by the Japanese and Manchus caused massive destruction to human and material resources from which Korea could not recover fully. These were the beginnings of Korea's decline during the second half of the Li Dynasty. However, other factors contributed to the gradual decline: These were severe factional fights among high-ranking government officials which wasted away the national talents and continued indecision at the highest levels; increasing corruption; rebellions in local areas; increasing intervention by foreign nations and the ensuing rigid closed-door policy; and the longevity of the Li Dynasty, which continued too long without the reform and renewal needed to meet changing domestic and world situations.

FACTIONAL FIGHTS BETWEEN POLITICAL GROUPS

Koreans had been historically diligent, creative, inventive, and gifted in the arts, qualities demonstrated through the Golden Ages of the Three Kingdom period, Unified Silla, Koryō, and the first half of the Li Dynasty. During each of these golden ages, there were benevolent but strong leaders, such as King Kwang-kae-t'o of Koguryō, Kim Ch'un-ch'u of Silla, King Ko-jo (Wang-gōn) of Koryō, and King Se-jo of Li Chosōn. During these periods, Korea not only attained the pinnacle of civilized culture, but also was militarily strong. With the leadership of such people, Korea achieved great accomplishments.

The Korean people had many good qualities. However, Koreans also had a great shortcoming: It was their great fault to fight continuously, unable to agree on anything, putting petty differences above national interests even in dire crises. There was a saying that when three Koreans got together, they formed five organizations, and each of them wanted to be the chief of all five of the organizations. It is still true today. North and South Koreans are unable to agree on anything and continue to fight.

When Japan's Hideyoshi openly threatened to invade Korea, the Sō-in (West Faction) and Tong-in (East Faction) of Korea's high-ranking officials bickered with each other, unable to reach a decision on the defensive plan, and thus left Korea wide open to attack. Later, when Admiral Li annihilated the invading Japanese navy, because he had a few friends among the West Faction, although he did not belong to any group himself, the East Faction successfully plotted to downgrade him to a private in a land army unit. Thus Korea was again vulnerable to Japanese invasion. The East and West Factions bickered on during the Manchu invasion; the result was the Korean surrender to the Manchus.

After two wars, the struggle for power had even intensified. Each change in power through bloody purges took many lives. Each time a faction took power, the group splintered into many small groups. Between 1567 and 1834 political power was divided in roughly the following fashion:[1]

Political Factions

1. *Tong-in* (East Faction): 1567–1623
   a. *Nam-in* (South Faction)
      1. One *Nam-in* (South Faction) 1608–1623; lost power 1623
   b. *Puk-in* (North Faction) 1608–1674
      1. Two North Factions then divided into five North Factions; lost power 1674
2. *Sō-in* (West Faction): lost power in 1608; revived 1623–1834
   a. West faction then divided into four West Factions
   b. These factions then divided into senior and junior factions

This outline indicates how each faction was terminated or splintered into smaller factions. While each power struggle was going on, officials had no time to pay attention to national matters or the people, because they had to be engaged in a literal life-and-death struggle. Losing power usually meant loss of life or exile to a remote island.

This Korean tradition of bickering is still going on at the end of the twentieth century. The combined strengths of North and South Korea are about two million regular military personnel, and these standing armies are not maintained to guard against foreign intruders, but to destroy each other.

Dethroned Kwang-hae, while he still had power, helped Tong-in (East Faction) in the struggle against Sō-in (West Faction). However, he himself lost power in 1623 and was exiled to Kwang-hwa Island the same year. Sō-in (West Faction) regained power and eventually dominated the political scene.

Two kings, Yōng-jo (1724–1776) and Chōng-jo (1776–1800), tried their best to remedy the adverse situation caused by the nobles' factional fights, but without much success. A very wise King Yōng-jo during his long reign reformed the tax system and increased government revenue, revived printing and publication of books using movable metal type, and published numerous well-known books. He also improved military preparedness by manufacturing rifles and set up rifle brigades. He and his successor Chōng-jo slowed the rapid decline of the Li Dynasty.

INCREASING REBELLIONS

As high officials in the Li Dynasty government were too busy fighting among themselves and paid scarcely any attention to the welfare of the people, the conditions in the country deteriorated. It became common practice for local government officials to pocket a large portion of the tax collected for the national government, thus very little revenue would reach the central government in Seoul. Because of dwindling of income needed for running the central government as well as the king's household, the Seoul government was forced to sell some of the prized government positions. At the beginning of the Li Dynasty, all government positions were filled through the civil service examinations. The new situation by 1800 was that the civil service system existed in name only. The people were taxed at higher rates, but the government revenue increasingly dwindled. The peoples' living standard also declined. Only the middle men, the local officials, enriched themselves. Such corruption eventually led to rebellion.

The first major uprising came in the northwestern region of P'yōng-an Province north of P'yōngyang. The rebel leader was Hong Kyōng-nae, a member of the local gentry class. He was a man of clever organizational ability, who became greatly dissatisfied with the discrimination against northerners. He went to Seoul several times and took the civil service examinations and thought he did quite well. However, he was rejected as usual because of discrimination against northerners. He began to establish a secret network of political military establishments. Many wealthy landowners and well-educated scholars participated in it and provided support for the production of weapons and training of troops.

In 1811, Hong sent out a manifesto throughout the northern region of Korea against corruption in the central government and the centuries'-old discrimination against northerners. Tens of thousands of young people volunteered to participate in the revolt, and in December 1811 they struck and occupied eight counties in a matter of a few days around Kasan, Sōnch'ōn region. Hong proclaimed himself field marshal and Kim Sayōng deputy marshal. It seemed as if nothing could stop them. Then Hong was wounded by a turncoat who wanted to receive a reward from the government. While Hong was ill, momentum was lost. The rebel forces took up positions in Chōng-ju Castle and fought fierce battles. The battles lasted for four months, until April 1812, when the government troops dug a trench under the castle and blew down the walls with a large gunpowder blast. Hong and his supporters were killed and the largest rebellion during the Li Dynasty came to an end. The rebellion was not a spontaneous uprising of peasants, but a carefully planned revolt of upper-class elements of the northern region who harbored age-old resentments about discrimination against and exploitation of the northerners by southerners.

After this rebellion, there were several instances of unrest in the areas of Chōnju, Ch'ungji, as well. In addition to such rebellions, unprecedented natural calamities of severe famine and floods followed, thus hastening the decline of the Li Dynasty. One day rainfall reached 190 millimeters, a record. In 1818, cholera swept across the land and killed many hundreds of thousands.[2] It started in India, spread across China, and entered Korea, where it spread like wildfire. While the people were suffering, local government officials were engaged in systematic exploitation of the peasants.

In 1868, in Chin-ju, there was a peasant uprising. The peasants took up weapons and marked themselves with white caps. They killed government officials and burned down buildings. The central government dispatched troops, put down the rebellions, and punished corrupt officials. In order to check corruption of local officials, the central government established a spy system called *Am-haeng-ō-sa*, which literally means "king's personal secret emissary." The emissary was empowered to punish corrupt officials on the spot. Such extraordinary measures were not very effective. However, people liked the system and stories of the king's personal emissaries. Such stories were written into novels, such as *Ch'un-hyang-jōn*, and read by many.

EARLY WESTERN CONTACTS WITH KOREA

The earliest Westerners who traveled to Korea, in 1629, were a Dutch sailor named Weltevree and two others who were shipwrecked and landed in Korea. Eventually Weltevree went to Seoul and was given a position in the Korean army. He was skilled in production of cannons; took up a Korean name, Pak Yōn; and married a Korean woman and had children. A Dutch ship wrecked again in 1651, and Hendrick Hamel and thirty others landed in Cheju Island and were sent to Seoul. They were assigned to work under Weltevree and engaged in the production of cannons. In 1664, Dutchmen including Hamel escaped from Korea to Nagasaki. Later Hamel published a book describing their shipwreck in Korea, which included descriptions of Korean culture and customs.[3] In the seventeenth century, the Dutch established colonies in Indonesia, occupied a portion of Taiwan, and monopolized trade with Japan at Nagasaki, Hakada, and Hirado.

In 1658, Korea dispatched one hundred fifty troops to Manchuria at the request of the Ch'ing government and fought Russian troops at the Amur River basin. This was Korea's first contact with Russians.[4]

Korea's Closed-Door Policy: The Hermit Kingdom

By the first half of the nineteenth century, the nobles' power in the Korean court was such that they eliminated the potential threat to their power among the king's relatives through purges. Able, intelligent members of the royal family were purged and exiled. When King Ch'ōl-jong died in 1863, the king did not have an heir. The court had to reach down to the third cousin level. After political maneuvers, the second son of Duke Hūngsōn was selected as the new king, but he was only twelve years old. The dowager Cho was supposed to assist the young king, but in reality she relied on the king's father, Hūngsōn, in political affairs. His title was upgraded to Duke Taewōn, and he took up dictatorial power as the king's regent. Although he was a member of the royal family he was financially impoverished. He had spent his youth among undesirable elements in Seoul, drunk most of the time, and often slept in the streets drunk. This was one reason he was not purged by the ruling nobles.

He was a radical conservative man who had adhered to old Sinicized concepts. He was against new ways, especially anything to do with the West. For ten years, until 1873, when he lost power, he maintained the closed-door policy. It was a critical ten years, during which Korea's neighbor Japan rapidly became modernized after the United States Navy Commodore Perry demanded Japan adopt an open-door policy with seven warships at Tokyo Bay in January 1854. The U.S. Consul General Harris concluded a friendship treaty with Japan in June 1858. The Tokugawa Shogunate government lost power in 1868, and the new Meiji government took up full-scale Westernization of Japan. While this was going on, Korea remained isolated from the world because of its rigid closed-door policies.

Persecution of Christians

Taewōn-gun (Duke Taewōn), as soon as he attained power, began hiring officials from the North and South Factions who had been out of power for a long time, in order to counterbalance power with the West Faction's senior and junior sections. He instituted some reforms. He also undertook a major construction effort to rebuild Kyōng-bok Palace, which was in disrepair. In order to raise funds for the project, which began in 1865, he raised taxes and devalued the currency by one hundred to one, thus creating economic problems for the nation. While this was happening, he tightened the closed-door policies even more. To enforce these policies, in 1866 he ordered the persecution of Christians because they had close contact with the Western missionaries. In the second half of the nineteenth century Western imperial expansion was strongest, and practically all of Asia was colonized by the Western nations, except Japan and Korea. Even China was divided into several spheres of influence by the Western nations after the Opium War and the Treaty of Nanking of 1842. Korea, aware of these facts, became grossly afraid of the Western powers. Taewōn-gun considered the Western missionaries spearheads of Western aggression.

In 1866, nine French missionaries were killed together with Korean Christian leaders. Taewōn-gun issued an order to all eight provinces of Korea to persecute Christians, as a result, many were executed. Some French missionaries such as Ridel, Feron, and Calais escaped and reported the persecution to the French Admiral Rose, who was stationed in China. The French consul in China protested to China; however, China replied that it had no jurisdiction over Korea and never interfered with Korea's internal affairs. The French admiral decided to take action on his own and sent three warships in August 1866 to the Inchon coastal area to investigate. In September he dispatched seven warships to Kanghwa Island and occupied a portion of the island. The Korean government was greatly alarmed and quickly dispatched a rifle brigade of five hundred troops. The French forces were ambushed by these troops and had to withdraw quickly. This emboldened Taewōn-gun and he tightened his grip on the closed-door policy. By this time, Korea had become known as the Hermit Kingdom.

American Merchant Marine Ship *General Sherman* and the U.S. Navy's Brief Battle in Korea

After U.S. Admiral Perry encouraged Japan to open its doors and the United States established a foreign legation in Peking, American merchant ships frequented the waters of East Asia. In 1866, when an American merchant marine ship went to China, Korea was in the midst of its closed-door policy, and it was the same year that Korea was bombarded by the French fleet. The orders from Seoul to repulse any foreign forces were still in force throughout Korea. The American merchant ship *General Sherman* was loaded with merchandise and manned by soldiers of fortune who were seeking quick profits. It was risky to venture into Korean waters, but the adventurous merchants sailed toward the northwest of Korea, up the Tae-dong River toward P'yōngyang. They did not know that the river was flooded after heavy rain. Soon the river water receded, and the ship was stuck in sand. The American merchant sailors tried to get help from the Koreans, who would have nothing to do with them, because they had received strict orders from the central government not to make contact with foreigners. Their food and water ran out and the sailors were forced to raid nearby villages. An angry mob from the villages dashed out and set the ship afire. The unfortunate end of the *General Sherman* was largely due to mutual misunderstanding. Korea, which had suffered many centuries of Japanese and Chinese piracy, mistook it for a pirate ship, and it was so recorded even in the history books.[5]

Five years had passed since the *General Sherman* incident when the American government ordered the U.S. Naval Command stationed in China to investigate the matter. In 1871, five U.S. warships commanded by Admiral Rodgers sailed toward the Han River estuary near Kanghwa Island and met bombardment from the Korean fortress. The American warships returned fire and destroyed most of the fort. The Korean commander was killed in the battle. The Korean guns were not powerful enough to reach the American ships;

however American shells could hit the Korean fortress. When American marines landed on the island and tried to set up camp during the night, about five hundred Korean troops attacked them.[6] The casualties on the Korean side were heavy, with over two hundred wounded, while the Americans suffered less than half a dozen wounded. However, this determined defensive action by the Koreans caused the Americans to withdraw. Both sides claimed victory. This provided another impetus for Taewōn-gun to continue his closed-door policy.

POLITICAL CHANGES IN JAPAN, TAEWŌN-GUN'S LOSS OF POWER, AND THE SUBSEQUENT OPEN-DOOR POLICY

It was customary that during the Li Dynasty the king's in-laws enjoyed power in the court. Taewōn-gun, knowing that a threat might come from his son's in-laws, did everything to prevent the possibility. When his son was sixteen years old, he selected an orphaned girl among his wife's relatives, Min, as a new queen. He thought he would be safe with this woman, who had no family; however, he did not take into consideration the cleverness and intelligence of the woman herself. After Queen Min came into the court, she recruited all her relatives and appointed them to influential positions, using the king's command. She also allied with the political enemies of Taewōn-gun. By 1873, they had enough power to oust Taewōn-gun from power.

While Taewōn-gun was still in power, there was a radical change in the power structure in Japan. The Tokugawa Shogunate, which reigned for 265 years, was replaced by the new regime of Meiji in 1868. Unlike the Tokugawa regime, which maintained friendly relations with neighboring Korea, the new ruler took up an aggressive policy toward Korea; the new government demanded new commercial trade with Korea. The letters of demand were rude and undiplomatic, and the Korean government returned the letters to Japan. This act angered the Japanese politicians, especially Saigo Takamori, who in 1873 advocated an armed assault on Korea. He was opposed by other politicians, such as Okubo and Kido. Saigo resigned and returned home to Kyushu, but in 1877 he revolted against the Tokyo government and was killed in battle. This was the beginning of the aggressive nature of the new Japanese government toward its neighbor Korea.

While Saigo was still alive, in 1875, the Japanese government dispatched a warship to the Korean shore and engaged in spy activity. The Korean coastal battery responded with fierce bombardment, and the Japanese warship was forced to withdraw. Japan dispatched a special envoy, Kuroda and Inoue, and complained of Korea's attack on the Japanese ship, at the same time demanding trade. Many Korean politicians were still opposed to the open-door policy; however, Prime Minister Li Ch'eung prevailed and signed the Kanghwa Treaty with Japan in 1876.

12

The Last Forty Years of the Li Dynasty, 1870–1910

THE OPEN-DOOR POLICY OF KOREA

The 1876 Kanghwa Treaty with Japan formally ended the closed-door policy of Taewōn-gun. The treaty recognized Korea as a fully independent state; it also agreed to the exchange of foreign missions and the opening of three Korean ports for trade with Japan. China, witnessing the Japanese approach to Korea, became concerned about Japanese influence on the mainland of Asia and secretly suggested to Korea that Korea conclude a similar treaty with the United States in order to counterbalance the Japanese influence on the peninsula. Thus, in 1882, the United States signed the West's first trade treaty with Korea. After the United States–Korea treaty, European countries demanded similar treaties. In 1883, England and Germany signed trade treaties, and in 1884 Russia and Italy; in 1885 France joined the group. In a few years, Korea was wide open for trade with the Western nations. Taewōn-gun, who was out of power and opposed such treaties, wrote protests to the government, which was now controlled by Queen Min and her relatives. Such protests had no effect.

Taewōn-gun was to have one more chance, when Korean soldiers did not receive pay for thirteen months and hungry soldiers revolted against Min as they believed that she and her relatives were stealing their pay. Soldiers killed the Prime Minister and Min Kyōng-ho, who was responsible for controlling soldiers' pay. The queen had to escape from the palace in disguise. Taewōn-gun, using that opportunity, moved in and seized power, but not for long. In desperation, the Korean government asked China to intervene. It was a chance for Ch'ing (Qing) China to reclaim suzerainty over Korea. China sent forty-five hundred troops to Seoul and captured Taewōn-gun. The ringleaders of the revolt were captured and executed. While the revolt was in progress, the

Japanese consulate was attacked by the rebellious soldiers. Japan protested, and in July 1882 concluded the Chemulp'o Treaty with Korea. Korea made a formal apology, paid five hundred thousand yen, and sent a delegation to Japan which included Pak Yōng-ho and Kim Ok-kyun. They were to become progressive pro-Japanese leaders who wanted to bring about radical reforms in Korea.

THE STRUGGLE BETWEEN THE PROGRESSIVE AND CONSERVATIVE FACTIONS

Those who went to Japan as national delegates or private students noted Japan's rapid Westernization and progress and wanted to model Korea on Japan's new reforms. They formed *Tok-lip Tang* (pronounced *Tong-nip-tang*, meaning "Independence Party"). They were younger nobles. Opposing the Independence Party was the *Sadae Tang,* literally "Serving Big (China) Party," who wanted to maintain power with the help of China. China, in the Ch'ing Dynasty, had previously never interfered in Korea's internal affairs. Now it became actively involved, by invitation of Queen Min and her relatives.

The young members of the political faction of Tok-lip Tang who wanted rapid reform reasoned that the only way to do this was to remove the Min clan from the government by forcible means. They staged a coup d'etat. In 1884, when the high-ranking government officials held a celebration party for the opening of the national post office, the Independence Party sent in assassins and killed and wounded many Conservative Party members. The Independence Party members, Kim Ok-kyun, Pak Yōngho, and Sō Kwang-bōm, escorted King Ko-jong to the small Kyōng-yu Palace and placed him under the protection of the Japanese troops. They killed six Conservative Party members and formed a new government. However, the surviving Conservative members invited the several thousand Chinese troops who were already stationed in Seoul to intervene. The Chinese troops led by Yüan Shih-k'ai quickly attacked the Japanese troops and dispersed them, thus restoring power to the Conservative elements.[1] The new government formed by the progressive faction did not last more than a few days and was a total failure. All the leaders of the plot escaped to Japan. The following month, Japan dispatched an army of two battalions to Seoul, matching the Chinese troops in number. The armies of the two neighboring nations were glaring at each other in the capital city of Seoul, and the situation was critical for Korea.

In April 1885, the Japanese government dispatched Ito Hirobumi as an ambassador to T'ien-chin (Dian-jin), China, and concluded a treaty with Li Hung-chang. Both China and Japan agreed that they would each withdraw troops from Korea, and each party would notify the other party in advance when it intended to send troops to Korea.[2] China pulled its troops out of Korea, but its commander, Yüan Shih-k'ai, remained as the Chinese representative of commercial affairs and interfered with Korean politics. Even the Mins began to dislike this.[3]

THE NEW NEIGHBORS OF KOREA: AMERICA AND RUSSIA

Early American Influences in Korea

For millennia, Korea's neighbors were Chinese and Japanese, and occasionally Mongols and Manchus. However, during the second half of the nineteenth century, Korea acquired new neighbors: the Russians and Americans. King Ko-jong expressed his feeling that among all these nations the only one he could trust was the United States. This was the reason Korea signed its first trade treaty with a Western nation, with the United States. The treaties that followed with Germany, France, England, Russia, and Italy were signed reluctantly.

Korea gave concessions to American businessmen for some of the best mines in Korea and for the building of Korea's first railroad and streetcar lines. American Christian missionaries were welcomed and American churches became well established. Korea today is the only major Christian nation on the Asian continent; the churches were founded by the American missionaries who started to arrive toward the end of the nineteenth century.

Not only did American missionaries establish churches, they also founded colleges, which grew to be the most prestigious universities in Korea. This is discussed further in later chapters. The U.S. government did not arrive in Korea until 1945, but before that American civilians played a predominant and beneficial role in Korea. By comparison, the role of the Japanese was extremely destructive to the Korean people and culture. Before the American government arrived in 1945, American civilians, for over a half century, were winning the hearts of the Korean people. Soon after the Korean American Trade Treaty was signed in 1882, Americans began to arrive in Korea. By 1897, there were two hundred fifty Americans in Korea, of whom one hundred fifty were missionaries.[4] These were unusually select and high-quality missionaries. One of them was Horace N. Allen, who later became the U.S. Minister in Korea. He was a most responsible diplomat who served eight years during the most critical period for Korea, from 1897 to 1905. He sincerely cared about the situation in Korea and worked hard for Korea's independence. He was often reprimanded by the U.S. State Department, which took a policy of complete "neutrality" in the three-way power struggle among China, Japan, and Russia in Korea.

In 1897, Secretary of State John Sherman sent Allen a message marked "Confidential" which set U.S. policy toward Korea. It read:

(1). The U.S. representative in Korea is not to "take sides with or against any of the international powers."
(2). The U.S. is not "bound to Korea by any protective alliance" despite the "good offices" clause in Article 1 of the Treaty of 1882.

(3). The U.S. does not wish to take on the role of "counselor [*sic*] of Korea as to its internal destinies."[5]

This U.S. policy toward Korea continued until November 24, 1905, when U.S. Secretary of State Elihu Root telegraphed instructions to then U.S. Minister in Korea Edwin V. Morgan, who served for only five months, to "withdraw from Korea and return to the United States, leaving the premises, legation property and archives in the custody of the Consul General." Thus the United States became the first nation to recognize the Japanese Protectorate over Korea, twenty-three years after the Treaty of 1882.[6]

King Ko-jong desired more U.S. involvement, but the United States turned him down cold. As explained, because of Korea's vital geopolitical location, any power which controlled the Korean Peninsula eventually could control East Asia. By letting Japan control Korea, the United States risked Japanese control of East Asia, and, in fact, the emboldened Japan, using Korea as a military base on the Asian continent, eventually occupied Manchuria and the heartland of northern China proper. Later Japan attacked America itself.

Unlike the indifferent U.S. government in Washington, D.C., American civilians played a pivotal role in the progress of Korea in modern times. American missionaries had headquarters in Seoul and fanned out to areas of Taegu, Pusan, Taejon, Chōnju, and P'yōngyang, where they introduced Christianity. The number of Christians in Korea grew by leaps and bounds, literally increasing by the thousands every month. The American missionaries were genuinely concerned about the welfare of the Korean people. They not only built churches, but also established schools, colleges, hospitals, and orphanages.[7] The Protestant influence was particularly strong in northern Korea, where there were three hundred thousand converts by the mid-1940s. Today, in the 1990s, the estimated number of Christians in South Korea alone is close to ten million, the largest number outside the Western nations. During the Japanese occupation period, the Christians were in the front ranks of the struggle for Korean independence.[8]

American entrepreneurs and engineers played a very important role in Korea beginning in 1895. The American firm Hunt and Fasset was given a concession for a rich gold mine at Unsan in 1895,[9] which generated such huge profits that the grateful American firm built a magnificent Western-style palace for the king in the Tōk Su Palace in Seoul. Today, it is a part of the Korean national museum system. American economic influence continued to increase. In 1896, a financial firm represented by the American James R. Morse was given a contract to build Korea's first railroad, running from Seoul to Chemulp'o (Inch'ōn). And in 1898, a large contract was awarded to the firm of Collbran and Bostwick to build an electric railway and lighting plant.[10] This firm realized a huge profit for many years.

EARLY RUSSIAN CONTACTS WITH KOREA

When China was forced to cede the maritime region east of the Ussuri River in 1860 by the Peking Treaty, Russia's territory reached to the Tuman River, which forms the northernmost boundary of Korea. Thus, Russia became a new neighbor by virtue of its geographical location. Russians founded the city of Vladivostok, close to the Korean border, which became the largest Russian port as well as a naval base in East Asia. After the Korea–Russia Trade Treaty was signed in 1884, Russian minister Woeber was stationed in Seoul. He was an able diplomat. At that time China was interfering daily in Korean governmental affairs, something that had not occurred since the Mongol Yüan Dynasty of the fourteenth century. Korean governmental officials began to invite Woeber often into the king's court to offset the Chinese influence.[11]

While Russia began to enjoy the king's confidence, England, which had conflicts with Russia in Afghanistan, sent the British fleet to Korean waters and occupied Kōmundo Island. They called it Harbor Hamilton and constructed a fort in 1885. England withdrew from Korean soil only after an official assurance from Russia that Russia would not invade Korean territory.[12] The Russian influence in Korea steadily increased until 1905 at the end of the Russo–Japanese War. By the early 1890s, Korea had become a focal point for the three-way power struggle of the larger nations of China, Japan, and Russia. The Li Dynasty, which had lasted more than five hundred years since its founding in 1392, had outlived its usefulness and become corrupt and feeble. It tried to survive by playing one power against another, while it could not defend itself. It was like an injured and feeble deer unable to stand on its own feet and at the mercy of three wolves snapping at each other to get to the food.

THE SINO–JAPANESE WAR: 1894–1895

Tong-hak Rebellion of 1894–1895

By the 1890s, Korean government officials were so corrupt that the tax collected for the central government was sidetracked by local officials. Hardly any money flowed into the government in Seoul. This caused continuous increases in taxes which did not yield any positive effects. This situation impoverished peasants at the lowest level. The nation was ripe for a peasant rebellion.

About the same period a new semireligious group called Tong-hak became popular among peasants and some intellectuals. *Tong-hak*, meaning "Eastern learning," was founded by Ch'oe Che-u in 1860. Ch'oe believed that Korea's traditional four religions and philosophies, Confucianism, Buddhism, Taoism, and Catholicism, were not really suitable for Koreans and that each contained significant shortcomings. He selected the "best" of each of them and devised the new philosophy, Tong-hak. In addition, he intermixed these with native shamanistic practices. Tong-hak followers were promised a prosperous and egalitarian new world along with the magic power of healing.[13] This belief made the followers fearless and daring. Ch'oe was accused of teaching heresy and was arrested and executed. However, his teaching survived and picked up a large following in the southern part of the Korean Peninsula in the farming areas. The group became so large that it had become a political force by the early 1890s. The Tong-hak group took an antiforeigner, especially anti-Japanese, stance. They began demonstrations, which developed into open revolt involving many thousands. In 1894 the Korean government dispatched an army unit to suppress this armed revolt, but the army was defeated by the mobs. The unruly mob occupied Chōlla and Ch'ung-Chōng provinces and began to march north toward Seoul. The desperate Seoul government asked the Chinese government for help.

Sino–Japanese War Fought on the Korean Peninsula

In 1885, China and Japan had signed the Treaty of T'ien-Chin (Dian-jin) stipulating that both nations must not station their troops in Korea, and in the event that this agreement were broken, the other nation would be informed of it beforehand. China, at the call for help from Korea, quickly dispatched a sizable army of three thousand. Japan responded to China's move by quickly sending its own army. Then the Japanese government declared war on China on August 1, 1894. Essentially this war was to control Korea. Japan sent seven warships and seven thousand troops to Korea, occupied Seoul and Inch'on and the central region, and together with the Korean army eventually put down the Tong-hak rebellion. The leader of the rebels was captured and executed. While the Japanese forces were in the central areas of Korea, the Chinese forces landed at Asan, occupied P'yōngyang, and tried to attack the Japanese forces from the north and south. However, both Chinese armies were defeated. The most disastrous was the destruction of the China's prized Peiyang fleet.

The Japanese won victories on land and sea and penetrated into southern Manchuria, threatening Shanhaikuan and Peking itself. Japan occupied the Liaotung (Liaodong) Peninsula. The world, until that time, had considered Japan a small, backward nation. Japan's quick defeat of China startled them. Japan proved itself to be an emerging power and China came to be considered as a sick old giant. As the capital city of Peking (Beijing) itself was threatened, China quickly sued for peace. The Treaty of Shimonoseki was signed on April 17, 1895. The treaty called upon China (1) to recognize the full and complete independence of Korea; (2) to cede the southern part of the province of Fengtien (Fengtian), which was the Liaotung Peninsula; (3) to cede Taiwan and the Pescador Islands; (4) to pay a war indemnity of two hundred million Kuping taels; (5) to open ports for trade and grant Japan most-favored-nation treatment.[14]

After the Sino–Japanese War the position of Japan in Korea was greatly enhanced, because the main obstruction was removed. Russia, on the other hand, felt its interests in East Asia threatened and began to reinforce its troops in East Asia. At the same time, Russia persuaded Germany and France to join in forcing Japan to relinquish its claim over the Liaotung Peninsula. In the face of joint pressure from three Western nations, Japan capitulated. Russia did this because it planned to occupy the Liaotung Peninsula itself. Three years later, in 1898, Russia leased the Liaotung Peninsula from China, as well as the right to construct the southern Manchurian railroad. Russia also moved into Korean politics, actively influencing the Korean government. These events enabled Russia to replace Japan's dominance in Manchuria and the Korean Peninsula, angering Japan.[15] In June 1895, the pro-Japanese politician Pak Yōng-ho lost power, and his government was replaced by the pro-Russian faction of Queen Min and her relatives.[16] Thus most of the Japanese gains of the Sino–Japanese War were nullified by Russian efforts in Korea.

THE MURDER OF KOREA'S QUEEN MIN BY THE JAPANESE

Korea's King Ko-jong was a gentle, kind man but indecisive, and easily swayed by the opinions of others. In this critical period, Korea needed a ruler who could provide strong leadership in order to survive the rampant imperialism of the late nineteenth century. As King Ko-jong himself could not provide such leadership, his wife, Queen Min, ruled the best way she knew how. She gathered her relatives and gave them key posts that held real political power. She also put political allies in key posts. Thus, Queen Min had become the power behind the throne of Korea.

First she drove her father-in-law from power. Then she allied Korea with China to counterbalance the increasing Japanese influence in Korea. When China was defeated by the Japanese in the Sino–Japanese War of 1894–1895 and Japan was about to monopolize influence in Korea, Queen Min engineered the ouster of the pro-Japanese cabinet of Pak Yōng-ho in June 1895. The Japanese, who had already lost the Liaotung Peninsula, were in danger of losing Korea altogether. About the time the pro-Japanese government was ousted and Pak Yōng-ho was exiled to Japan, the Japanese government in Tokyo appointed a new Minister of Japan to Seoul, Miura Goro. As soon as he arrived in Seoul, he secretly organized a group of Japanese unemployed gangster-like people called *Ronin.* On August 20, 1895, merely three months after Japanese influence had shrunk to almost nothing, Miura personally led a group of Japanese Ronins and launched a surprise attack on Kyōng-bok Palace, where Queen Min lived. The palace gates were open as usual and there were only a few soldiers guarding them, because such an attack was totally unexpected. The guards were killed, and, as planned, the attackers dashed into the queen's chamber. The Japanese attackers caught the queen before she could even realize what was happening. They stabbed her numerous times, and when she was dead, they dragged her body out to the courtyard, sprayed kerosene over it and set it afire.[17] They burned it until it could not be recognized. Miura, the official representative of Japan, could not have done this without an order from the highest level of the Tokyo government. Such a barbaric, cruel act was deplored even by the new generation of Japanese historians.

When Queen Min of Korea was murdered by the Japanese Minister Miura and his gang, Japan had extraterritorial rights in Korea. Therefore, Miura was tried in the Japanese courts by Japanese judges. The mock trial found Miura "not guilty" because of "insufficient evidence," even though there were numerous eyewitnesses. Not only was Miura freed, but soon after, he was appointed by the Japanese government to one of the most prestigious positions in Japan as the headmaster of Gakushu-in, the school which educated children of the Japanese royalty and nobles.[18] This type of award proved that the Japanese government was involved in the plot to murder the queen of Korea. Unlike the European imperial powers, who treated the resident royal families gently, these crude Japanese activities angered the Korean people to the extreme; they also angered other powers such as Russia. Russia sent more troops to East Asia, consolidated Manchurian bases, and became involved even more deeply in Korean affairs. Korea now faced two foreign enemies, Japan and Russia.

The angry Korean people mobilized several *Ūibyŏng* (volunteer) units and began killing soldiers of the pro-Japanese cabinet headed by Kim Hong-jip. Pro-Russian elements in Korea made contacts with the Russian Woeber, invited Russian sailors into Seoul from Inchon, and moved King Ko-jong and the crown prince to the Russian legation. The pro-Russian faction dispatched police units to the government buildings at the king's command and killed the pro-Japanese Prime Minister Kim Hong-jip and many other cabinet ministers. Those who escaped the killing had to flee to Japan. There was no trace of the pro-Japanese element left by February 1896. Subsequently a pro-Russian cabinet was formed and controlled Korean political affairs. In August 1896, the king moved back from the Russian legation to Kyōng-bok Palace. He declared a new name for Korea, *Tae-Han Che-guk* (Great Han Empire), and assumed the title emperor. He initiated a new Western-style governmental organization, a military academy, and educational systems. Although outwardly the new Korea took on the appearance of an independent state, Russian influence was dominant. For Japan, the murder of Queen Min, staged to remove an obstacle to the Japanese domination of Korea, had backfired. Japan had lost control of Korea completely.

AMERICAN-EDUCATED KOREAN LEADERS FORM THE INDEPENDENCE PARTY AND THE INDEPENDENCE PRESS

Sō Chae-p'il (Philip Jaisohn), who participated in the coup d'etat of 1884 with Kim Ok-kyun and others and failed, exiled himself to Japan and then to the United States. There, he earned a medical degree from Washington University and married an American woman, Armstrong. He became an

American citizen. Although he was practicing medicine, he never ceased to participate in political activities in Washington, D.C., and continuously advocated Korea's full independence from the aggression of Japan and Russia. He returned home in 1896 and quickly organized a political party with the American-educated leaders Li Sang-je, Yun Ch'i-ho, and Li Sūng-man (Syngman Rhee). This political party was called *Tong-nip Hyōp-hoe* (Independence Association). The same group published the newspaper *Tong-nip Shin-mum* (Independence). Sō was appointed as a consultant to the Privy Council of the Korean government and associated with high-ranking officials of the government. He received a donation of five thousand wōn, which was a considerable sum at that time, from the Interior Ministry.[19] The crown prince donated one thousand wōn also. The newspaper was printed in both Hangūl (Korean alphabet script) and English. It was designed to awaken the people of Korea on civil rights, autonomy of the nation through rejection of Japanese and Russian influences, modern science and technology, and, most important of all, the ideal of democracy learned from America.

The founders of this association and press were all American-educated or had resided in the United States. Li Sang-je became first secretary to the first Korean ambassador to the United States in 1887. As the first Korean diplomat, he worked, attended school, and lived in Washington, D.C.,[20] and was profoundly influenced by the American system of democracy.

Yun Ch'i-ho went to America when he was seventeen to study journalism. When the first Korean–American Friendship Treaty was to be signed in 1883, he returned to Korea with the American minister Foote as his interpreter and translator. After that he returned to America and attended Emory University in Atlanta, Georgia. He returned to Korea in 1895 and formed the Independence Party with Sō.[21]

The youngest of the leaders, Li Sūng-man (Syngman Rhee), had not yet gone to the United States by 1896. However, he graduated from Pae-jae Middle School, founded by American missionaries, and his English was so proficient that he was appointed an English teacher at the school.[22] He participated in the founding of the Independence Party and Press. Later he was to become the first president of the Korean Provisional Government in Shanghai. He received a Ph.D. degree from Princeton. In August 1948 he became the first president of the Republic of Korea (South Korea).

These were the young American-educated leaders who wanted to free Korea of the encroachment of Japan and Russia. The newspaper *Independence* was well received, and its circulation had increased tenfold in a matter of a few months. At this time, Korea was undergoing a critical period. In August 1895, Queen Min was murdered by the Japanese, and King Ko-jong took up residence in the Russian consulate building for safety. Although Japanese influence was temporarily curtailed, Russian influence was increasing phenomenally. The king, who was grateful to the Russians for their protection, delegated all kinds of power to the Russians. They were given power in finance and the military.

The Korea–Russia Bank was formed. A lease of Chōryōgdo Island (off Pusan on Korea's southeastern coast) to Russia was considered. Although *Independence* was designed to be a nonpolitical newspaper, it began to criticize the overdependence of the Korean government and king on the Russians. After all, Russia at the end of the nineteenth century was one of the most aggressive imperialist powers in the world. Whatever Russians did in Korea was not for the benefit of Korea but for the Russians. Such criticism offended the king. He ordered publication of *Independence* suspended.[23] Sō Chae-p'il returned to America; however, the Independence Party and newspaper reopened and were continued by other members.

THE RUSSO–JAPANESE WAR, 1904–1905

Two-Way Alliances in East Asia

After the Sino–Japanese War, the southern part of Manchuria, especially the Liaotung Peninsula with its two excellent ports, came under Japanese influence. This was somewhat alleviated by Russian, French, and German intervention. However, the Japanese encroachment in Manchuria had become a great concern to China. Li Hung-chang, who was personally humiliated by signing the Treaty of Shimonoseki, wanted to stop Japanese aggression by using Russian power. When he visited St. Petersburg in 1896 to attend the coronation of Tsar Nicholas II, he signed a secret treaty with Russia. Under the treaty, Russia and China would provide mutual assistance. Russia was to use Chinese ports in case of war, and China would agree to Russia's construction of the Chinese Eastern Railroad, which would link the Liaotung Peninsula to Harbin and then to Vladivostok. For the exchange of these concessions, Russia would guarantee that Manchuria would remain a territory of China.[24] This was in essence a Sino–Russian alliance to stop the Japanese. After this treaty Russia sent in 180,000 troops and occupied not only the Liaotung Peninsula but major Manchurian cities.

On the other hand, Japan, which had lost the Liaotung Peninsula and influence in Korea, wanted to have the backing of a European power. England, which feared increasing Russian influence in East Asia, agreed to sign a mutual defense treaty with Japan. The first Anglo–Japanese alliance was signed on January 30, 1902. This treaty recognized the independence of China and Korea and safeguarded British interests in China and Japanese interests in Korea. In the event that either party became involved in a war with more than one country, then the other party would join the war to assist its ally. A second Anglo–Japanese Treaty was signed on August 12, 1905, recognizing Japan's "guidance, management, and protection" over Korea.[25] Two years earlier, in 1903, Japan had proposed to Russia that the two nations exchange spheres of influence, namely, that Japan would recognize Russian influence in Manchuria in exchange for Russian recognition of Japanese influence in Korea. This proposal was met with a cold Russian refusal. Japan began to prepare for a war against Russia.

The Russo–Japanese War and Its Effect

Russia not only refused the Japanese proposal, but also increased its involvement on the Korean Peninsula. Finally Japan broke off diplomatic relations with Russia on February 2, 1904; initiated an attack on Russian warships in the Yellow Sea; and sank a Russian warship. Thus the war began. The primary reason for this war was, like that of the Sino–Japanese War of ten years earlier, control of the Korean Peninsula. The government of Korea declared strict neutrality; however, Japan ignored this and sent in troops as if Korea were Japan's territory without permission from the Korean government.

Japan was victorious in the land war on the Liaotung Peninsula and in Mukden. The Japanese navy destroyed the Russian Baltic Fleet at the Korean Strait. England helped Japan by blocking the passage of the Russian Fleet at the Suez Canal, which forced the Baltic Fleet to circle the African continent, sapping their fighting power. In the eighteen months of the war, Japan was victorious but paid an enormous price. The war produced over two hundred thousand casualties and cost one hundred fifty million yen, exhausting Japan's human and financial resources.[26] Japan no longer could continue the war. Russia also had domestic unrest problems. Japan requested that President Theodore Roosevelt mediate. The Treaty of Portsmouth was signed on September 15, 1905, concluding the war.

With the prodding of Roosevelt, Russia agreed to (1) Japan's superior rights in Korea on political and military affairs and, if necessary, Japan's right to exercise "guidance, protection and management" of Korea; (2) the lease of Port Arthur and Dalien (Darien) and their adjacent territories, and lease of Changchun and Port Arthur Railroad (South Manchurian Railroad) with all its branches; (3) the secession of the southern part of the islands of Sakhalin and all the islands adjacent thereto.[27] Needless to say, the greatest gain for Japan was the domination of the Korean Peninsula, and Roosevelt was involved in handing Korea over to Japan. With the Russian opposition gone and Great Britain and the United States tacitly recognizing Japanese occupation and control of Korea, Korea was left at the mercy of Japan.

Two months after the Portsmouth treaty, Japan dispatched Ito Hirobumi as ambassador to Korea and presented a draft of the Korea–Japan Treaty which prescribed conditions to make Korea a protectorate of Japan. According to these Japanese conditions, Japan would appoint a *Tokan* (commissioner or resident general) who would oversee Korea's governmental affairs and control Korea's foreign affairs and treaties. Ito used threats and intimidation toward the Korean cabinet ministers in conference, demanding the treaty be signed. Most of the Korean ministers strongly opposed such a treaty; however, the Minister of Education, Li Wan-yong, came out in support of Ito after several days of discussion. He persuaded several others to join him. Encouraged by Li's attitude, Ito pressed harder. On November 17, 1905, Korea signed the treaty with Japan and abandoned its status as an independent state. The name *Li Wan-yong* lives on in history as the greatest traitor in Korea. The Li Dynasty was to continue for a few more years, until 1910, when Japan finally annexed Korea. Ito Hirobumi was immediately appointed the first Tokan in Korea. He took all of Korea's political affairs into his own hands in November 1905.

The once-proud Korean army, which had crushed the mighty invasion forces of Yang-ti of Sei China, Taitsung of T'ang, Khitan, and even the Japanese of the sixteenth century, was nonexistent by the beginning of the twentieth century. The nation was helpless against the encroachment of Japan, the result of many centuries of neglect of national defense. Ito Hirobumi, the chief mastermind of Japanese imperialism in Korea, twice Japan's prime minister and top official in Japanese political society, was shot and killed on October 26, 1909, by An Chung-gūn at the Harbin railroad station in Manchuria while he was inspecting the Russian troops. Li Wan-yong was also shot but survived to sign the Korea–Japan Annexation Treaty of August 22, 1910, thus formally ending the Li Dynasty Chosōn Kingdom. The official name of Korea was *Tae-han Che-guk* (Great Han Empire) when it was annexed by Japan. This was the first complete loss of independence by Korea in a history of more than five thousand years. However, the Korean people's spirit did not succumbed to Japanese imperialism, and the struggle continued.

INTERNATIONAL EFFORTS FOR KOREA'S INDEPENDENCE

The beginning years of the twentieth century was a time when world powers were still busy trying to open up new colonies for themselves, and, therefore, the desperate cries of Koreans for help were largely ignored. Nevertheless, Koreans did their best to alert the world to the victimization of Korea by the Japanese. After the 1905 treaty that was forced upon Korea by Japan, the Korean emperor Ko-jong secretly sent Syngman Rhee to the United States to appeal to President Theodore Roosevelt to intervene on Korea's behalf. Since Roosevelt was committed to the Treaty of Portsmouth which he himself had sponsored, the appeal was ignored.[28] Rhee arrived in the United States too late, after the signing of the Taft–Katsura agreement, which gave Japan tacit recognition to occupy Korea in exchange for Japanese consent to the U.S. takeover of the Philippine Islands.

As a last-ditch effort, in 1907 Emperor Ko-jong, trying to save his country's independence, sent secret envoys to the Second World Peace Conference, held at the Hague, Netherlands. He wanted to plead to the world body that Korea regain independence because the 1905 treaty was forced upon Korea by Japan. The Envoys Li Chun and Li Sang-sōl, joined by Li Wi-jong at St. Petersburg, Russia, carried Emperor Ko-jong's signed and sealed letter to the conference in the Hague. Upon their arrival, the Japanese delegates began fierce lobbying to obstruct the Korean envoys' attendance. The conference did not formally accept the Korean delegates; however, the three envoys visited the representatives of each country and the press club, asking their help for the Korean cause. None of the nations was willing to intervene. Li Chun died there of heartbreak, and the mission was a failure. Lacking a foundation of economic or military strength, the international effort was ineffective.

JAPANESE ANNEXATION OF KOREA: 1910

By 1905, Japan had successfully eliminated the competing powers of China and Russia from the Korean Peninsula by two wars and had gained tacit recognition of its occupation of Korea from the Untied States and England. There was nothing left to stop Japanese aggression in Korea. As usual *ūibyōngs* (civilian volunteer army units), in the national crisis, were organized and tried to salvage the situation. However, poorly equipped and poorly trained civilian troops were no match for the huge Japanese forces. The Korean ūibyōngs were massacred by many thousands. The Japanese executed those Korean civilian volunteers who escaped killing in battles by stringing them up on crosses, as they had executed Christians in Japan in earlier times. In a similar manner, the Japanese executed thousands of Korean farmers who protested the Japanese confiscation of their ancestral farmlands.

The Korean independence movement moved overseas to the United States and China. Armed partisan units were organized in Antung (Andong) Province in Manchuria in the deep forest of the rugged Paektu Mountains and continued resistance. Some Japanese and pro-Japanese Korean masterminds were personally attacked and killed or wounded. However, these efforts were not strong enough to dislodge the Japanese forces from Korea.

The Japanese resident general in Korea appointed the pro-Japanese traitor Li Wan-yong the prime minister of the puppet government. As Li Wan-yong was not appointed prime minister of Korea by Korean King Ko-jong, but by the Japanese, his position was illegal from Korea's standpoint. During the summer of 1910, the Japanese Resident General Terauchi Masatake had a series of secret consultations with Li Wan-yong and formulated the so-called Korean–Japanese Annexation Draft. This draft was signed by Terauchi and was forced on Li Wan-yong in a ceremony guarded by thousands of Japanese troops. According to this treaty, the Korean king would be a subject of Japan; the national name would revert to *Chosōn* from *Tae-han Che-guk*; all treaties between Korea and other nations were to become null and void; and the Japanese Governor-General's Office was to be established to rule Korea. Thus, more than five thousand years of Korean independence and self-rule came officially and finally to an end. Outrageous and unchecked exploitation of Korea by Japan began.

Terauchi Masatake was appointed the Japanese governor-general in Korea. Li Wan-yong was given the Japanese title of marquis for selling his country. He was the Korean Benedict Arnold and worse, because his treason had a worse effect on Korea than Arnold's had on America. Li Wan-yong succeeded whereas Arnold failed. Li Wan-yong was motivated by personal greed, putting his own interest above the interest of his country, the king, and the Korean people. Although Li Wan-yong was rewarded by the Japanese government, he and his family were completely ostracized by Korean society and his name appears in every history book in Korea as one of the worst traitors in history. However, the most blame must be placed on the Korean government and its ruling class for failing to safeguard the national security with strong Korean armed forces.

The Japanese annexation of 1910 firmly secured Korea as the military base and springboard of Japan onto the East Asian continent. Using Korea as a base, Japan completely occupied Manchuria in 1932 and in 1937 launched an attack on China proper, which produced an estimated loss of thirty million Chinese lives. The British, who were so eager to help Japan occupy Korea; had to meet the Japanese forces directly, were driven out of Hong Kong, Malay, and Singapore; and had to battle for Burma, at great sacrifice. America also had to deal with Japan in the Philippines during the war. Yet the combined efforts of Britain and America could have checked the Japanese advance onto the Korean Peninsula, limiting Japanese military expansion before 1910. Hilary Conroy, in *The Japanese Seizure of Korea: 1868–1910*, concludes,

> A little more sense of involvement by the American State Department would have lessened the Japanese sense of urgency that Korea had to be made secure . . . Even after America and Japan became Pacific rivals after the turn of the century, since there was a certain ideological kinship . . . in the Philippines and Korea, they might have exchanged inspection teams . . ., instead of delimiting spheres of influence. When the Korean secret mission appeared at the Hague, the United States might have volunteered to allow the Hague court to investigate American management of the Philippines if the Japanese would allow the same for Korea.[29]

Notes to Part IV

CHAPTER 11

1. Li Pyōng-do, *Kuksa Taekwan* (History of Korea) (Seoul: Po MunGak Co., 1985), 398–400.

2. Ibid., 489.

3. Ibid., 447.

4. Ibid., 48.

5. Kajimura Hideki, *Chosen-shi* (History of Korea) (Tokyo: Kodansha Kendaishinsho, 1989), 99.

6. Li Pyōng-do, *Kuksa Taekwan*, 501.

CHAPTER 12

1. Dun J. Li, *The Ageless Chinese* (New York: Charles Scribner's Sons, 1971), 419.

2. Ibid., 513.

3. Li Pyōng-do, *Kuksa Taekwan*, 513.

4. Scott S. Burnett, *Korean-American Relations* (Honolulu: University of Hawaii Press, 1989), 11.

5. Ibid., 10.

6. Ibid., 12.

7. Louis R. Mortimer (ed.), *South Korea* (Washington, D.C.: Federal Research Division, Library of Congress, 1992), 124.

8. Ibid.

9. Scott S. Burnett, *Korean-American Relations*, 11.

10. Ibid.

11. Li Pyōng-do. *Kuksa Taekwan*, 513–515.

12. Ibid.

13. Lawrence Ziring and C. I. Eugene Kim, *The Asian Political Dictionary* (Santa Barbara, CA, and Oxford, England: ABC-Clio Inc., 1985), 412.

14. Dun J. Li, *The Ageless Chinese*, 420.

15. Tanaami Hiroshi, *Shin-Nihonshi-no Kenkyu* (New Research on Japanese History) (Tokyo: Obunsha, 1985), 362.

16. Li Pyōng-do, *Kuksa Taekwan*, 544.

17. Kajimura Hideki, *Chosen-shi* (History of Korea) (Tokyo: Kodansha Kendaishinsho, 1989), 128-129.

18. Ibid.

19. *Handbook of Korea* (Seoul: Korean Information Service, 1990).

20. Li Hui-Sung, et al., *Han-Kuk Inmyong Tae-sa-jon* (Encyclopedia of Historic Names of Korea) (Seoul: Shin-ku Mun-hwa-sa, 1982), 645.

21. Ibid., 573.

22. Ibid., 667.

23. *Handbook of Korea*, 93.

24. Dun J. Li, *The Ageless Chinese*, 421.

25. Tanaami Hiroshi, *Shin-Nihonshi-no Kenkyu*, 369.

26. Ibid, 370.

27. Lawrence Ziring and C. I. Eugene Kim, *The Asian Political Dictionary*, 401.

28. *Handbook of Korea*, 147

29. Hilary Conroy, *The Japanese Seizure of Korea: 1868–1910* (Philadelphia: University of Pennsylvania Press, 1960), 507.

Part V

Japanese Occupation and Rule of Korea: 1910–1945

13

Establishment of the Colonial Government

Korea, which had enjoyed continuous independence and self-rule for over five thousand years, for the first time in its history completely lost its independence in 1910. To maintain such long independence was not easy for a smaller nation among larger countries. There were many crises. The first was the Han Chinese invasion in the second century B.C., when the Chinese established four provinces around P'yōngyang in the northwestern region of the peninsula. However, Koreans maintained independence in the southern part of the Korean Peninsula and central Manchuria.

The Chinese influence had beneficial effects on the Koreans also, because the higher level of civilization of China of that time flowed onto the Korean Peninsula. China tried to recreate the Han's accomplishment when Sui Yang-ti and T'ang Ta'i-tsung led invasion armies onto the Korean Peninsula and were defeated by the Korean forces in the eighth century A.D. T'ang Kao-tsung, with the help of the Silla Kingdom, managed to defeat Koguryō; however, Silla survived, and in fact unified the peninsula. The Khitans in the eleventh century and Japan in the sixteenth century invaded with large forces, but Korea was victorious in both wars. The Mongols in the thirteenth century and the Chins (Ch'ing), another branch of the Korean nations in the seventeenth century, defeated Korea militarily, but Korea was able to maintain full independence through diplomacy. It all came to an end when Japan annexed Korea and took its independence away completely in 1910.

Koreans gave Japan its first civilization of the Iron Age, the unified government of the Yamato state, and the first golden ages of Nara and the Heian cultures, which all had a beneficial impact on the Japanese culture. However, once the Korean influence declined after ten centuries of dominance in Japanese society, the Japanese reverted to the violent society they had been before the Koreans arrived. The Japanese entered Korea with a vengeance with piracy, which started in the beginning of the thirteenth century. The harassment of the Japanese pirates continued for many centuries until it was capped by the Japanese invasion of Hideyoshi's army of 1592–1598, which looted Korea to a skeleton. However, the Japanese army was defeated by the allied forces of Korea and China. That humiliating defeat was always in the minds of the Japanese.

The Tokugawa *Bakufu* (Shogunate) took up a policy of peaceful relations with Korea because they had witnessed the quick downfall of the Toyotomi clan after the Korean debacle. The venture in Korea did not pay the invaders, as it brought the demise of Toyotomi, as well as their supporters. After two hundred sixty-five years of peace between the two nations, the new Japanese government of the Meiji regime adopted an aggressive attitude toward Korea. It started with Saigo Takamori's desire to attack Korea and his rebellion in Kyushu when his idea was rejected. Japan opened its doors to the West about thirty years earlier than Korea and thus had the advantage of Westernized armaments. Japan utilized this advantage to the fullest extent. After the Sino–Japanese and Russo–Japanese Wars, Japan set out to occupy Korea. However, unlike the Chinese, Mongolians, and Manchus, who respected Korean civilization and independence, the Japanese paid no respect to history and set out to rule Korea as a colony.

When the Japanese resident-general was appointed governor-general in Korea, in effect the Japanese military dictator of Korea, he sang loudly at the annexation celebration party, saying that Koreans had one of two choices to make: obey the Japanese or die. He boasted that what Toyotomi could not accomplish in the sixteenth century, he would accomplish in the twentieth century.[1] His open statement was an understatement of the harsh Japanese rule to come.

Thirty-five years of Japanese rule of Korea was thoroughly destructive and harmful, producing no benefit for the Korean people. It was unique in its notoriety and viciousness, unmatched anywhere or anytime in the history of mankind, except perhaps in Nazi Germany. After Japan annexed Korea, Japan forcibly took independence and political, diplomatic, and military power away from the Korean people. Step by step, Japan systematically set out to destroy anything Koreans possessed as a sign of nationhood. The following are a few examples of what Japan did in Korea to destroy all identity as a nation.

CONFISCATION OF KOREAN LANDS BY THE JAPANESE

For many centuries beginning in 1223 A.D., the Japanese robbed Koreans of personal and national treasures through piracy and invasion. One thing they could not take away was the land. However, after 1910, Japanese began to steal even land from Koreans.

Before 1910, during the Li Dynasty, there were three types of public lands in Korea: *yukto*, which were assigned to postal stations; *tunto*, which were assigned to support military forces; and *kunto*, palace-land, lands for the royal family and the government. These farmlands were exceedingly large. The Japanese governor-general's government confiscated land without compensation and put it under Japanese ownership. The land was registered as 252,000 acres.[2]

The Japanese occupation government was not satisfied with the confiscation of the public lands and began to confiscate the land owned by private citizens. To do this, the Japanese occupation colonial government used two methods: land registration documents and a new land survey. The governor-general's office allocated twenty million yen[3] (two yen per one U.S. dollar in 1910 currency) for the farmland survey of Korea, especially in the best farm regions of the southwest seacoast areas of the peninsula. This great sum of money, exceeding U.S. $100 million in 1990 dollars, was used to measure all the lands of farmers, not for the purpose of helping the farmers, but to find fault with recorded measurements of their farmlands. If their centuries-old measurements of their ancestral lands proved inaccurate by the Japanese survey, the lands were confiscated. The Korean farmers who worked on many-centuries-old ancestral farms were evicted from their lands naked without compensation.[4]

Those who did not register their lands properly at the Japanese colonial government offices by the set date also lost them. Thousands of Korean farmers who protested the Japanese confiscation were executed without trial. By 1918, when the Japanese land survey was completed, the Japanese governor-general's office had added 130,000 acres, boosting the total acreage of farmland owned by the Japanese government to a total of 382,000 acres.[5]

Korea was basically an agrarian nation, and rice production was the center of the agricultural industry. Concentrated farming in the rich coastal soil produced bumper crops that kept the Korean living standard one of the highest in Asia. This large-scale confiscation of the best lands drove Koreans into widespread poverty overnight. The Japanese colonial government in Korea was not satisfied by these initial land seizures. In order to increase their landholdings, they created a company called *Toyo Takushoku Kaisha* (Oriental Development Company) with a land grant of 24,500 acres from the governor-general of Chosen.[6] The shares of the company were largely held by Japanese royalty and nobles. The company was the Japanese semiofficial colonization organization in Korea; with assistance and a subsidy from the Japanese colonial government, it started to bring in Japanese settlers and created large Japanese landowners.

Dr. Hoon Koo Lee, who has conducted the most thorough research on the Japanese activities in Korea from 1910 to 1930, sponsored by the Institute of Pacific Relations and the American National Geographic Society, found that the Japanese large landowners and their private holdings increased by leaps and bounds. The Japanese landowners and their holdings in Korea increased from almost nothing in 1910 to 538 persons holding more than seventy acres per person in 1929, with an aggregate total acreage of 585,542.[7] This does not include those Japanese farmers who held less than seventy acres. The average Korean farmer owned about two acres, and anyone who owned fifty acres could dominate an entire village and town. The Japanese Oriental Development Company brought in an average of eighteen thousand Japanese settlers per year, granting an average of six acres of land per settler from 1921 to 1930 and replacing Korean farmers.[8] In the fertile coastal plains of the southwest Korean Peninsula, Japanese towns and villages sprang up like mushrooms, driving Korean farmers off their ancestral lands.

While the Japanese settlers were busy grabbing Korean land, as if they were never satisfied, the governor-general's government, acting as a great landlord who owned 380,000 acres, raised the rent payment of Korean tenant farmers by forty percent in 1914. In 1919, the rent was increased again, by another twenty-four percent, which left the Korean farmers almost nothing to eat.[9] By these aggressive and merciless actions of the Japanese colonial government in Korea, in 1930, Japanese private landowners, whose number did not exceed 7.8 percent of the total farm population of Korea, owned more than fifty-nine percent of the total Korean farmland.[10] And this did not include the direct landholdings of the Japanese governor-general's government. The Japanese holdings were the best, most fertile lands of Korea. Koreans were left with only the poor hillside terraced lands. Thus Koreans lost their major economic resources and livelihood and drifted away.[11] Those Korean farmers who protested the Japanese land seizures were executed.

THE JAPANESE MONOPOLY OF RAILROADS, INDUSTRY, UTILITIES, FINANCIAL INSTITUTIONS, AND COMMERCE

Transportation

The Japanese and some Westerners who accept Japanese contentions at face value often cite Japanese railroad building as a Japanese benefit to Korea. However, they ignore the fact that the railroads were primarily built for the movement of the Japanese armed forces and the transportation of Japanese industrial products and foodstuffs. They also forget to take into consideration that the Japanese monopolized the railroad system one-hundred percent and took all the profit from it. These people who allege beneficial effects of the Japanese in Korea try to point out that Koreans were incapable of building railroads in their own country; therefore, the Japanese built railroads for the Koreans. That is one of the worst fallacies any historian could establish. Railroad building was a relatively simple technological matter; many railroads were built the world over in the middle of the nineteenth century. Compare this to the building of superhighways, involving a high level of technology and engineering. The Japanese never gave Koreans an opportunity to build a railroad system in their own country during the Japanese colonial period. Once the Koreans had the opportunity after 1950, they built superhighways crisscrossing South Korea, which were of world-class quality.

South Koreans also built long-distance four-lane superhighways for Saudi Arabia, Indonesia, and other countries. Such high-quality superhighways are practically nonexistent in communist China, and even in Japan they are not as extensive as in South Korea in the 1990s, measured in relation to the size of the countries. These engineering achievements prove Koreans could have built railroads, which were relatively simple to build, if they had been allowed to do so before 1945. Japan used this same excuse time and time again, telling the world, "Koreans are not capable; therefore, we rule Korea."

The first railroad was built by an American company in 1900, four years after a contract was awarded to the American James R. Moore, between Seoul and Chemulp'o. A Japanese company constructed a line between Seoul and Pusan in 1904. As Japanese–Russian war became imminent, Japan rushed the construction of the Seoul–Sinūiju Line, which was completed in 1905, in order to carry troops and supplies to Manchuria.[12] The Pusan to Sinūiju Line became the main artery of Japanese troop movements for aggression into the Asian continent by the Japanese imperialists. Upon the annexation of Korea in 1910, all railway control was transferred to the Railway Bureau of the Japanese governor-general's government in Korea. It became predominantly a Japanese government monopoly. The rail lines gradually increased from 674 miles in 1911 to 1,777 miles in 1930.[13] Some minor privately owned railroad construction was allowed only to the seven Japanese companies, a total of 676 miles by 1931. Secondary railroad lines were built to link the northeastern seacoast Japanese factories in Wōnsan, Hamhūng, Hūngnam, and Najin. Other lines were constructed in the southwestern Korean Peninsula in the region of large Japanese-owned farms.

Japanese-Owned Financial Institutions, Industry, Utilities, and Commerce

While the southern part of the Korean Peninsula had rich farmlands which could feed hungry Japanese who had large-scale rice riots in 1918 in Japan, the northern part of the Korean Peninsula had large deposits of mineral reserves of more than seventy different kinds of minerals, including iron, gold, copper, coal, silver, tungsten, and zinc. Geologists call the region of the T'ae-baek Mountains a miracle of the earth. To take advantage of these abundant mineral resources, the Japanese built complex factories along the northeastern seacoast cities, which had large supplies of cheap labor. By 1940, this area had become a region of heavy industry and was linked with a railroad line. In order to supply power for this industrial complex, the Japanese built the huge Supung Dam with a hydroelectric power station on the Amnok River. Needless to say, all of these were solely owned by Japanese. Koreans, or any other foreigners, were not allowed to participate in these industries. This region played a major role in the World War II effort. As much as a quarter of the total Japanese industrial production came from this northern Korean region.[14]

To finance the construction of these Japanese mines and industries in the northern part of Korea and the newly developing Japanese factories in Manchuria, the Japanese government-owned central bank in Seoul, *Chosen Ginko* (Bank of Korea), was reinforced. It had become a center of finance for Japanese enterprises in Korea and Manchuria. It was exclusively for the Japanese, and Koreans were not allowed to use its resources. There were several Japanese-owned commercial banks; however, their services were largely limited to the Japanese residents in Korea, whose numbers increased to about two million in the 1940s. Deprived of financial resources, Koreans began to rely on traditional *Ke*, a credit union type of organization whose members mutually assisted each other in financial matters. However, this type of organization had limited scope and was only useful for the capitalization of small businesses. The Japanese government of the governor-general in Korea also had a monopoly on utilities, such as gas and electricity, and production and marketing of tobacco and ginseng, of which Korea was a major producer in Asia.

EXPLOITATION OF FARM PRODUCTS BY THE JAPANESE

The major commerce between Korea and Japan was the export of processed rice and cheap labor from Korea to Japan for the benefit of the Japanese. By 1930, only twenty years after the annexation of Korea by Japan, Japanese farms of great size owned fifty-nine percent of the total farmlands in Korea, concentrated in the best fertile plains. This did not include the 380,000 acres of land directly held by the Japanese colonial government in Korea. This meant that as much as eighty percent of the annual crops produced in Korea were in Japanese hands. As explained earlier, the Japanese seized these Korean lands by force. Most of the rice harvest was taken to Japan for its war effort. Table 13.1 indicates the amount of rice production in Korea from 1915 to 1936:

Table 13.1
Total Rice Production and Annual Per Capita Consumption in Korea (in U.S. Bushels)

Average	Total Production In U.S. Bushels	Export to Japan	Korean Consumption	Japanese Consumption
1915–1919	71,577,600	9,881,600	3.64	5.73
1920–1924	73,830,400	16,896,000	3.28	5.79
1925–1929	75,878,400	29,952,000	2.61	5.73
1930–1936	86,220,800	41,779,200	2.20	5.53

Source: Chosenshi Kenkyukai (Chosen-no-Rekishi: Research Association on the History of Korea). (Tokyo: Sansho-to) Kajimura Hideki, *Chosen-shi* (Tokyo: Kodansha, 1989), 161.

This table shows that total production of rice in Korea steadily increased from 71,577,600 U.S. bushels to 86,220,800, an increase of about fourteen percent; however, rice taken to Japan increased by 315 percent in the twenty years from 1915 to 1936. During the same period, Korean consumption of rice decreased from 3.64 U.S. bushels a year to 2.20 bushels, about forty percent of the Japanese consumption of 5.53 bushels.[15] This table does not really give the entire picture, because the figure ends in 1936, the year before the Second Sino–Japanese War in 1937–1945. During these years, the Japanese exploitation of Korean farmers increased radically for the Japanese war effort. The Japanese employed a method called *Kyoshutsu* (*Kongch'ul* in Korean), "allocated offering from the harvest." Usually this allocated offering, designated by the Japanese, was in excess of the actual total crop of the year. Those farmers who could not meet the allocated offering without any compensation were sent to jail. Koreans lost most of their lands, and when they had land, they could not keep what they had produced.

The Japanese, who took all the Korean rice harvest in the period 1940–1945, in order to stave off mass starvation in Korea, imported bean residue from Manchuria, left after extracting oil from the beans. Bean residue was normally used as fertilizer in Manchuria; however, the Japanese colonial government distributed it to Koreans as food after taking away all the Korean rice harvest. These types of atrocities were common in Korea under Japanese rule. The Korean fishery and forestry industries suffered the same fate and were also taken over by the Japanese.

SUPPRESSION OF EDUCATION IN KOREA DURING THE JAPANESE COLONIAL PERIOD

Historically, Koreans were highly motivated to obtain an education. As explained earlier, Koreans during the Silla and Koryŏ periods as early as the fourth century built universities, some of which were the earliest in the world. They built not only the central universities in their capitals, but also many hundreds of local schools. The highly sophisticated and difficult civil service examinations ensured that only highly educated people could reach the higher positions. This emphasis on education encouraged the Korean society to develop the world's first printing with movable metal type and widespread publication, which in turn helped to create the three later golden ages in Korea.

The traditional Korean enthusiasm for education gained additional special meaning when Korea came under Japanese occupation in the first half of the twentieth century. Developing and maintaining the intellectual resources of the nation were ways to fight the Japanese and keep alive hope for eventual independence and self-rule. As schools were the only place in which Koreans were allowed to gather in groups, the number of private schools increased rapidly, reaching three thousand by 1908. They became the centers of resistance to the Japanese and created a movement and tradition for freedom.

These private schools, which were established throughout Korea, taught Western science, history, geography, political science, law, arithmetic, and algebra.[16] In these private schools, the students were taught not only the Western sciences, but Korean nationalism. These students later became fighters for freedom and independence such as Syngman Rhee.[17] The Japanese, who were quick to recognize the danger of educating Koreans, did everything possible to destroy the eager Korean educational movement by closing down more than half of the Korean private schools and denying licensing of schools.[18] By 1910, the number of schools was reduced to 820.[19]

Unlike the Japanese, who obstructed Korean education, American missionaries played a pivotal role in development of education in Korea. The American educators founded some of the earliest modern Western types of schools. The schools founded by the American Christian missionaries included Paejae Boys' School, Ewha Girls' School, Paewha and Chungshin Girls' schools, and Kyungshin Boys' School, all in Seoul. Sungsil Boys' School and Sungeui Girls' School were established in P'yōngyang, and Hosudon in Kaesōng.[20] All of these schools were founded between 1886 and 1905. These schools were the great learning centers of Korea and still flourish today. Many of these century-old schools produced countless numbers of Korean leaders in every field and built the foundations of modern Korean society. The gratitude and admiration of Koreans toward America are not just for the liberation of Korea in 1945 and the subsequent political and military protection of South Korea, but go back to the nineteenth century. This is one reason Korea has become the dominant Christian country in Asia.

The Japanese feared world public opinion and were hesitant to crack down on these American-founded Christian schools in general; therefore, most of them survived. However, there were exceptions, such as the Union Christian College (Sungsil College) in P'yōngyang, which was forcibly closed by the Japanese. American Christian missionaries founded most of the colleges for Koreans, also in the early twentieth century. They were Chosōn Christian (Yōnhūi) Men's College, Ewha Women's College, and Severance Medical College in Seoul and Union Christian College in P'yōngyang. In 1937, the Japanese began to force the worship of the Japanese Shinto ghosts at all the schools by requiring faculty and students alike to attend and worship Shinto shrines at least once a month. Dr. George S. McCune, president, and Dr. Hoon Koo Lee, vice president, of the Union Christian College in P'yōngyang, refused to obey the Japanese demands, and the Japanese governor-general's government forcibly closed the college. In 1945, it was revived as the Kim Il-sung University in P'yōngyang. The faculty and students of this college, who moved to Seoul, created another university, Sungsil University, in Seoul after 1945. All of these American-founded universities in Korea are now among the greatest in the world, with student enrollment of from ten to thirty thousand.

Following these American models, Korean leaders also created schools of great tradition, such as Posōng, Hūimun, Yangjōng, and Osan Boys' schools, and Sukmyōng and Chinmyōng Girls' schools. Posōng Men's College and Sukmyōng Women's College, founded by Koreans, have become great universities (Korea University) today. However, they all went through a very difficult time during the Japanese occupation period.

The Japanese, on the other hand, did not build a single college for the Koreans, whose population exceeded thirty million. However, for themselves, the Japanese built one university, one business college, one engineering college, one agricultural college, two medical colleges, and one marine college. These schools were built exclusively for the two million Japanese settlers, and Koreans were seldom admitted. The educational opportunities for Koreans were limited to the extent that only about one in twenty applicants was admitted to the beginning grades at middle schools. This was all due to the Japanese education policy of destroying Korea's intellectual resources.

THE DESTRUCTION OF ALL FREEDOMS IN KOREA BY THE JAPANESE

There was no freedom in Korea between 1910 and 1945. Koreans had to suffer the indignity of attending Japanese shrines built in Korea and were forced at gunpoint to pretend to worship Shinto spirits of dead Japanese ancestors alien to Korea, or else have their businesses and schools closed, as at Union Christian College. The Japanese stole Korean land, food, and bodies and even attempted to seize Korean minds and gods. Nothing the Japanese did was acceptable, as all their acts were malicious after 1905, when Korea became Japan's protectorate. However, matters became worse after a Japanese army general named Minami Jiro was appointed the Japanese governor-general in Korea. Minami Jiro, who was to be sentenced to life imprisonment by the judgment of the War Criminal Tribunal in Tokyo in the post–World War II period, initiated the notorious so-called assimilation policy in 1937. He forced Koreans to worship Japanese Shinto ghosts and closed schools and newspapers. These were some of his many "ideas."

Freedoms of speech and publication for Koreans were not any better than freedom of religion. The Newspaper Law (Shinbunshi hō, 1907) and the Publication Law (Shutpan hō, 1909), which were promulgated during the protectorate period by the Japanese, had become the legal foundation to control publications in Korea. From 1910 to 1919, under Terauchi Masatake's governorship, the Japanese did not permit any Korean newspaper managed by Koreans. This was what historians call the "dark period" (*amhŭkki*).[21] Such severe repression eventually exploded into Korea's nationwide independence movement of March 1, 1919 (*Sam-il Tok-nip Undong*). This brought a temporary relaxation of control of newspaper publications in Korea by the Japanese, although censorship continued. The daily circulation of the three Korean newspapers grew gradually to 163,134 in 1939.[22] In 1940, Minami Jiro, however, decided to close down two of the largest Korean newspapers (*Tonga*

Ilbo with 55,977 and *Chosŏn Ilbo* with 95,939 daily circulation),[23] leaving only the minor pro-Japanese *Maeil Sinbo*. This was the reinstatement of the earlier "dark period." From 1940 to 1945, there was no trace of freedom of speech or press left in Korea, because the two Korean language magazines were also closed down by the Japanese.

THE PROHIBITION OF THE KOREAN LANGUAGE AND KOREAN NAMES BY THE JAPANESE

In 1937, soon after he was appointed Japanese governor-general of the colonial government in Korea, Minami Jiro sent out an order to extinguish Korean culture altogether by strictly prohibiting use of the Korean language in all Korean schools, offices, and businesses. All teaching materials written in Korean were forcibly destroyed. Teachers or students who spoke Korean in the schools were expelled from them. All government offices or business firms had to write documents in Japanese. Koreans were forced to use the Japanese language and anyone who used the Korean language in Korea was persecuted. The scholars who organized a Korean linguistic association, *Ŏhakhoe*, for Korean language research were all sent to prison, and the association was disbanded in 1942.

The Japanese passed a law in 1939 requiring Koreans to use Japanese names. The foundation of the Korean society and its strength were built on the family and clan systems. This was especially strong among intellectuals, most of whom came from the old gentry class of Yangban. They took pride in their clan and were jointly responsible for all activities. The cohesiveness of the clan members formed by many thousand families sharing the same clan origin, called *Pon-kwan*, was, in fact, the strength of the Korean society. The history of some of these clans, as recorded in the family registries, goes as far back as the Silla period, for over fifteen hundred years. The Japanese set out to destroy this millennia-old system by forcing Koreans to adopt Japanese names. Under this new system, even brothers would have different family names, destroying the clan system. Those who refused to take Japanese names were discriminated against in every part of the society dominated by the Japanese.

THE DISPLACEMENT OF KOREANS FROM KOREA BY THE JAPANESE

The Japanese used many different methods to dislodge Koreans forcibly from Korea. As the war continued, the Japanese had to produce more military hardware while the labor supply was becoming critically short. The Japanese forcibly drafted Koreans, often from the streets and farm fields, and took them to forced labor camps for mines, factories, and military construction. By the end of World War II, there were 2,616,900 such persons in the forced labor camps within Korea.[24] Many more were forced to move outside Korea. Many were drafted into the Japanese army and millions were forcibly sent to Japanese factories in Japan (see Table 13.2). Some Koreans who lost land went to Manchuria (Table 13.3).

Table 13.2
Koreans Who Moved to Japan

1935	625,678
1940	1,190,444
1945	2,100,000

Source: Kajimura Hideki, *Chosenshi* (History of Korea) (Tokyo: Kodansho, 1989), 163.

After the war, most Koreans returned home. In 1946, 647,006 Koreans remained in Japan.

Table 13.3
Koreans Who Moved to Manchuria

1935	807,506
1939	1,163,000
1943	1,540,583

Source: Kajimura Hideki, *Chosenshi* (History of Korea) (Tokyo: Kodansho, 1989), 173.

In addition to those in Japan and Manchuria, there were over one million Korean immigrants to Russian Siberia, China proper, and the United States, comprising about 4,600,000 overseas Koreans. Most immigrated to other countries to escape the Japanese rule in Korea, except those who went to Japan as forced laborers. With these dislocated overseas Koreans and 2,600,000 dislocated Koreans within Korea, the total dislocated population was about seven million people, of about thirty million in 1945.

"Comfort" Women (*Imong-fu*)

Among these dislocated people were about two hundred thousand young Korean women, mostly teenagers, who were taken from their homes by the Japanese through force and fraud to the front lines of China and Manchuria as "comfort women" for the Japanese soldiers. The favorite trick of the Japanese recruiters was the promise of a good job with good pay in the factories or business firms in the cities. Once the young innocent girls boarded the train, they were kept prisoner until they arrived at the front lines, where they were raped many times each night for years by Japanese soldiers. Fifty years later, in 1994, the Japanese Prime Minister Tomiichi Murayama publicly apologized for this "mistake." However, these women's ruined lives could not be recovered. The orders for these atrocities came from the highest level of the Japanese government. The recruiters were the Japanese police and the local government officials. The Japanese government as a unit was deeply involved in this crime. The Japanese government, supposedly a legitimate legal government, planned and managed this criminal operation for many years on a massive scale never before seen.

OTHER JAPANESE ATROCITIES NOTED BY HISTORIANS

The continuous Japanese atrocities were not limited to the Korean Peninsula proper. Large-scale massacres of Koreans by the Japanese took place in Japan and Manchuria, as well.

In 1923, when there was a great earthquake in the Tokyo region, the Japanese government and police, in order to divert the minds of the shocked and disoriented people, started baseless false rumors which said that the Koreans were rioting and putting poison into the wells. The angry Japanese mobs started to murder Koreans on sight. The Japanese officials not only failed to stop this massacre, but secretly encouraged these slaughters for many days until the number of murdered Koreans reached sixty-six hundred.[25] A major portion of the Korean residents of Tokyo at that time were massacred. The helpless Koreans fell victim to the endless Japanese atrocities time after time, in and out of Korea. It is difficult to understand why the Japanese people have been so violent and cruel throughout the ages. The Korean residents in Tokyo were victims of the earthquake, like the Japanese, yet they met this additional punishment by the Japanese without cause. No Japanese was ever punished for this mass homicide.

THE NECESSITY FOR GOODWILL AND FRIENDSHIP BETWEEN KOREA AND JAPAN

The relationship between Korea and Japan was not always bad. Historically, these two closest neighbors were quite good friends most of the time. At the beginning of known Japanese history, it was Koreans who traveled to Japan and introduced new civilizations many times over, including the Iron Age, a unified Japanese government, and a golden age of the Heian period. The Japanese people should remember that what they call the "Yamato nation" was created by Korean settlers, who gradually assimilated the indigenous natives and established a centralized government in the Nara and Kyoto areas. Japan's capital city of Nara, 710–784, was named from the Korean word *nara*, which means "nation," "the king," and "the king's seat; the capital city." There was no such word in the Japanese language.

For more than one thousand years, Japanese society responded to these Korean contributions with warmth and respect, until the thirteenth century, when the central government lost control over local regions and Japan turned into a vicious society controlled by local feudal lords. Korea suffered also from this harsh situation in Japan, through Japanese piracy capped by the invasion of the Japanese warlord Toyotomi Hideyoshi's troops. When Japan was secured and these hostile warlords were put under the control of the new Shogun Tokugawa Ieyasu, his government took up a policy of friendship toward Korea.

Close, friendly relations were maintained by both the Korean and Japanese governments for 265 years, from 1603 to 1868.

The modern era Japanese government has been unfriendly to her neighbors, Korea and China, and for that matter, to the world. This aggressive imperialistic tendency caused unbearable suffering among Japan's neighbors until 1945. Although Japan had been defeated physically by the power of the United States, the Japanese leaders' aggressive attitudes have not changed greatly, as the world is still witnessing through their predatory commercial dealings toward other nations. Japan still maintains harsh discrimination against the Korean residents in Japan, in every possible way, spearheaded by the Japanese government and business firms. They should realize that Japan cannot survive alone in the community of neighbors while being selfish and looking after only its own interests. They need to reflect and to recognize what they have done to other people without self-centered denial of past wrongdoings.

Korean people want to forget past atrocities by the Japanese military and look forward to having genuine friendship with Japan. Japan must also show a true eagerness for such friendship, through deeds, not just lip service. The Japanese people also want such friendship with Korea and its people. Why else would they visit South Korea as tourists on an average of one million visitors per year, spending so much money? The Japanese people as a whole must consider that Korea is a beautiful land and its people are friendly, to find it worthy of visits. They would not travel in such huge numbers to an ugly land with hostile people and waste their money. This is proof that the Japanese people desire genuine good relations with Korea. Japanese government and business leaders should give heed to this public trend and resolve the existing unfriendly attitude toward Japan's neighbors.

14

Korea's Fight for Independence and Wartime International Conferences

The Japanese colonial government, in order to rule Korea with an iron hand, instituted *Kenpei Seiji* (rule by military police) after the annexation of 1910. The traditional ŭibyŏng (voluntary units) were crushed and their members were executed. All firearms and any tools that could be used as weapons were confiscated. An attempt to assassinate the Japanese governor-general in 1911 failed. A resistance organization, Sinmin-Hoe, and the Independence Volunteer Headquarters were forcibly dissolved. During the "Dark Period" of the Terauchi regime of 1910–1919, all assemblies and publications were disbanded. However, after the First World War, a ray of hope was illuminated for the Korean people.

In 1918, the American president Woodrow Wilson proposed at the Versailles Peace Conference that treaties of peace be founded upon his Fourteen Points. One of the points was the principle of self-determination; that the existence of a nation and the form of governance be freely determined by its people, and that no people were to be dominated by others against their will. This was a god-sent opportunity for the Koreans. A Korean group which was active in the Korean independence movement in Shanghai quickly sent a delegate, Kim Kyu-sik, to Paris. This also activated the Korean underground movement in Korea and An Ch'ang-hō and Syngman Rhee's groups in the United States to prepare for a concerted independence movement. The movement started to surface openly. About six hundred Korean students gathered on February 8, 1919, at the YMCA in Tokyo and sent out a manifesto demanding Korean independence from Japan.

SAM-IL UNDONG (MARCH 1, 1919, MOVEMENT), THE KOREAN PROVISIONAL GOVERNMENT, AND KOREAN ARMIES

In Korea, major religious leaders, especially Christians, secretly gathered and drafted the Declaration of Independence, signed by thirty-three Korean leaders, and proclaimed Korean independence to the world. The proclamation was made first at a conference center called T'aehwa-kwan.

Simultaneously massive demonstrations started throughout Korea. Many thousands of people demonstrated at Pagoda Park in Seoul. The objective of this demonstration was to inform the world that the Japanese had seized Korea against its people's will so that world opinion would force Japan to free Korea and its people. The independence movement vibrated into all parts of Korea like a tidal wave, lasting several months. Over two million people participated in fifteen hundred demonstrations. However, unlike those who initiated the American Revolution for independence, Koreans lacked the military power ultimately needed to support such a movement.

The surprised Japanese initially were disorganized. Later they retrenched and cracked down on the movement. The leaders of the Korean independence movement were arrested, and the Japanese government sent out an order "to shoot to kill" the unarmed civilians who were participating in the peaceful demonstrations. The Korean leaders had decided against violence, and, furthermore, people did not possess any weapons because all had been confiscated. The Japanese fired into the unarmed crowd indiscriminately, and about seven thousand were killed and fifteen thousand wounded.[1] About forty-six thousand were arrested. Again, Japanese cruelty came to the fore in many instances. When people were meeting inside church buildings, the Japanese locked the doors from the outside and set the buildings afire, burning people alive.[2] After all the sacrifices, the March First Movement did not attain its stated goal of independence.

The Japanese were determined to stay in Korea, and the Western nations, including the United States, were colonial powers in Asia and would not do anything to encourage the liberation of a colony, which might put them in a difficult position. Regardless, this March First Movement inspired the spirit of independence and freedom, which led to the establishment of the Korean Provisional Government in Shanghai, China, which received the official recognition of the Chinese Nationalist Government. The Korean political leaders, including Syngman Rhee, Kim Koo, Kim Kyu-sik, Cho Pong-am, and Yō Un-yōng, participated in forming the cabinet, and all of them played an important role in modern Korean history. The form of this government was a republic, modeled after the democratic government of the United States. It guaranteed people freedoms of speech, assembly, press, and religion; an elected government with a president and legislature; and separation of state and religion. The fight against Japan now had a headquarters and democratic ideals.

Under the Korean Provisional Government, a Korean volunteer army, *Kwang-bok-kun* (Korean Liberation Army), was formed in China. This army was trained and received supplies of uniforms and weapons supported by donations from Korean sources, as well as the Chinese Nationalist Government. During the Second Sino–Japanese War of 1937–1945, many young Korean men were drafted into the Japanese army forcibly and were sent to the Chinese theater. Many of them escaped from their Japanese captors and went over to the Chinese side and joined the Korean Liberation Army, which was fighting alongside the Chinese army against the Japanese invaders. The number of Kwang-bok-kun troops grew to such an extent that two regular Korean divisions were formed with about forty thousand troops. These troops were commanded by General Li Ch'ōng-ch'ōn.

The Korean Provisional Government, which was formally recognized by the Chinese Nationalist Government as the legal government of Korea, officially declared war against Japan in February 1945, although its army Kwang-bok-kun had long been fighting the Japanese army in actual battles. As there were over 1.5 million Koreans who resided in China and Manchuria, some of them joined the Chinese Communist force's operation out of Yenan (or Yan'an) China. Their hatred of the Japanese was especially strong, because these were the people who had lost their ancestral lands to the Japanese land grabs through forced confiscation. The Korean Communist volunteer army that fought against the Japanese formed two separate Korean divisions, about forty thousand troops. After World War II, these Korean Communist troops campaigned against the Chinese Nationalist army in Manchuria and played a significant role in attaining victory for the Chinese Communists in 1948–1949. They returned to North Korea in 1949 and formed the battle-experienced core of the North Korean army. The Korean armies of both Nationalists and Communists numbered a total of about eighty thousand in the 1940s. These were the significant forces. Koreans did not sit idly, but actively fought against Japan.

KOREAN PARTISAN FORCES IN THE KOREAN–MANCHURIAN BORDER REGIONS

Traditionally most of the fighting powers of Korea, especially during the Li Dynasty, came from ūibyōng. The ūibyōng did most of the fighting during the invasion led by the Japanese warlord Toyotomi Hideyoshi in 1592–1598. They were victorious over the Japanese in that war. Toward the end of the Li Dynasty, the ūibyōng forces were again organized; however ill-equipped, outnumbered ūibyōngs without much government support were no match for the modern Japanese army. Eventually, about thirty thousand Korean ūibyōngs moved into the mountainous Korean–Manchurian border areas to become partisan forces. Battles between the Korean partisans and the Japanese troops continued from the 1910s to the 1940s. It was a true Korean people's army, because ordinary Korean citizens took up arms in the national crisis. They were strong because they were motivated by patriotism.

This ūibyōng was very active, even after the Korean annexation by the Japanese. According to Japanese military police records, the Japanese battled the Korean ūibyōng on 1,060 occasions and the total number of Korean ūibyōng involved in the battles were 38,305 from 1910 to August 1913.[3] As it became increasingly difficult to engage the Japanese forces in Korea, ūibyōng forces moved into the mountainous regions of eastern Chien-tao (*Kan-do* in Korean) Province in Manchuria, where the Japanese forces could not reach them easily and formed partisan forces. Li Tong-hi even established a military academy there in the 1920s and trained young men. The ūibyōng in this region became the Korean military stronghold and a bastion for the Korean independence movement.[4]

As the number of Korean immigrants gradually increased to 1.5 million in Chien-tao Province, the financial and manpower base also increased during the 1930s. Accordingly, the power of the partisan forces also increased in the same period. In the late 1930s and early 1940s, these partisan forces in Chien-tao Province in Manchuria established joint operations with the Korean residents, more than five hundred thousand people who had immigrated into Siberian Russia across the Tuman River near the Korean border in order to escape the Japanese repression. These Koreans in both areas formed more than two million supporters for the Korean freedom fighters. Those Koreans who moved to Manchuria developed fertile farmlands with new irrigation systems in the vast Manchurian grasslands. The word *Korean* became synonymous with the word *wealthy* in the southeastern Manchurian region. These Korean farmers were the people who had lost lands through the Japanese land policy in Korea and had escaped into Manchuria; therefore, their anti-Japanese sentiment was very strong. With this financial and population base, the Korean partisan forces grew rapidly.

By 1933, this force established seven liberated districts in the mountainous areas of Manchuria near the Korean border.[5] Weapons were imported from nearby Soviet Russia, and the forces were so entrenched in the rugged mountains that the crack Japanese Kanto Army was unable to dislodge them. To support this Korean partisan force, a secret organization, *Kwang-bok Hoe* (Liberation Party), was established with two hundred thousand members in Manchuria and Korea.[6]

The Japanese historian, Noritake Mizuo, in *Oryoku-ko* (Yalu River), with material sources obtained from the Japanese Kanto Army, described the Japanese military losses due to the Korean partisan forces during the period 1931–June 1936 as follows: Number of battles: 23,928; Japanese dead and wounded: 4,321; Japanese captured: 18,114; captured weapons to the Korean partisans: 3,179 items. This shows that the Korean partisans were a formidable force already by the early 1930s.[7] The strength of the Korean partisan forces grew to such an extent that they could carry their battles into Korea proper. The

Japanese army based in Po-ch'ōn-po (June 1937) and Musan (May 1939) was attacked and destroyed. This struggle continued into the 1940s, intensifying in ferocity.

The North Korean sources credited this struggle to Kim Il Sung,[8] who was born Kim Sōng-ju in 1912. However, the authenticity of his origin was uncertain, because he died in 1994 at the age of eighty-two, which meant that he was the leader of the already well-established Korean partisan forces in 1931, at the age of nineteen. It is reasonable to think that perhaps he assumed the name of the legendary Korean hero and used it effectively to gain support when he entered Korea in 1945, as this theory was believed by most South Koreans. Most people believe that the legendary name of the Korean hero Kim Il-sōng goes much further back than the 1930s. The total number of this partisan force was over ten thousand toward the end of the 1930s.

Kim Il Sung was a midlevel guerrilla unit commander, whose largest command was approximately three hundred men. He had many superiors, both Korean and Chinese. O Sōng-yun (or Chon Kwang), Yang Jingyu, and Wei Zhengmin were Kim Il Sung's superiors. Therefore, it was erroneous to credit all Korean partisan activities to Kim Il Sung alone, although he played a part in them. There were many other partisan members who fought for the freedom of their country, if not more significantly. Kim's propaganda in the latter years in North Korea built up his credit far more than his actual contribution to the partisan activities.

The Japanese forces in Manchuria felt uneasy about the existence of the Korean partisan forces and began to crack down on them after 1940. Many partisan members paid the ultimate price for their activities. Whenever the Japanese caught partisan members alive, they guillotined them without a legal trial. The Japanese collected their heads and put them on public display. The shamelessly cruel Japanese occupiers also took photographs of many of the collected human heads of the Korean independence fighters and published the photographs. Actual photographs of the Japanese atrocities remain in many Korean history books in perpetuity. One such book was by Dae-sook Suh, published by Columbia University Press in New York.[9] The ancient Japanese custom of headhunting was still alive and well in the twentieth century (see Chapter 10; the section on Korea–Japan War, 1592–1598).

In 1941, most of the partisan forces escaped into the maritime provinces of the Soviet Union. There, the Soviet Union created an international army of ten thousand strong, composed of both Korean and Chinese. At Khabarovsk, some partisan officers were given Soviet army officer ranks. Zhou Boazhong, commander of the Second Route Army, and Chang Shoujian were appointed colonels; Kim Ch'aek and Feng Zhongyun were appointed lieutenant colonels; Pak Kil-Sōng was appointed major. At Voroshilov Camp and Okeanskaya Field School, Kim Il Sung was appointed major in the 88th Division of the international unit of the Far Eastern Command of the Soviet army. When Kim returned to P'yŏngyang in 1945, he was wearing a Soviet army uniform of the rank of major.[10]

What appeared to be a defeat by the Japanese for Kim Il Sung turned out to be a boon for him. It gave him a chance to learn the Russian language while he stayed in Russia for five years, and thus he was able to communicate with the Russian occupational commanders of North Korea after 1945. While in Russia, Kim Il Sung married a fellow partisan, Kim Chŏng-suk, who bore him a son on February 16, 1942. He was named Kim Chŏng-il (Kim Jung Il), and he was often called Yura.[11]

WARTIME CONFERENCE OF THE ALLIED POWERS ON KOREA

There were six major Allied powers' wartime conferences during World War II. They were the Quebec Conference of the summer of 1943 in Quebec, Canada; the Moscow Conference of October 1943; the Cairo and Tehran Conferences of November–December 1943; the Yalta Conference of February 4, 1945, in the Russian Crimea; and the Potsdam Conference of July 17–August 1, 1945.

Quebec Conference

The Quebec Conference was attended by the leaders of the Allied powers, including President Franklin D. Roosevelt and Prime Minister Winston S. Churchill. The conference determined that more aid should be provided to China, and that the South Asian Command would be created under Lord Mountbatten. The conference also questioned Soviet participation in the Pacific war against Japan. This conference was organized primarily for the purpose of weakening Japanese military power in Asia, and therefore, was indirectly related to Korea, although it did not discuss Korean matters specifically.

Moscow Conference

The Moscow Conference, held by the foreign ministers of the United States, Great Britain, and the Soviet Union, with China's later approval, issued a declaration which pledged creation of an international organization for the maintenance of world peace and security. This principle created the United Nations, which in 1950 dispatched the United Nations Forces to defend the Republic of Korea from the North Korean invasion.

Cairo Conference

The third international meeting, the Cairo Conference, attended by President Roosevelt, Prime Minister Churchill, and Generalissimo Chiang, dealt with future military actions against Japan in Asia. Generalissimo Chiang, mindful of the fact that the Korean army of Kwang-bok-kun with tens of thousands of troops was fighting alongside the Chinese troops against the Japanese army, and mindful also of the existence of the Korean Provisional Government in China, recognized as Korea's legal government, promoted the idea of Korean independence. The joint communiqué issued on December 1, 1943, contained a statement on Korea that "Japan will . . . be expelled from all . . . territories which she has taken by violence and greed . . . The aforesaid three great powers, mindful of the enslavement of the people of Korea, are determined that in due course Korea shall become free and independent."[12]

Tehran Conference

The Tehran Conference, held immediately after the Cairo Conference, from November 28 to December 1, 1943, attended by President Roosevelt, Prime Minister Churchill, and Premier Josef Stalin of the Soviet Union, dealt with strategy against Japan after the end of the European war and possible Russian participation in the Pacific war. Stalin was also informed of the decisions made at the Cairo Conference.

Yalta Conference

The three leaders met again at the Yalta Conference of February 1945. At this conference, the Soviet Union endorsed the Cairo Agreement, which promised Korean independence. Russia also agreed to join the war against Japan within three months after the European war. This conference was known to the West, which conceded too much to Russia on Eastern Europe. It was long thought that the United States secretly agreed with Russia regarding the divisional occupation of Korea at the 38th parallel line into North and South Korea. That belief turned out to be erroneous.

Potsdam Conference

The last of the series of major wartime summit conferences was held at Potsdam from July 17 to August 1, 1945, attended by President Harry Truman, Prime Minister Churchill and then Clement Atlee of Great Britain, and Marshal Stalin of the Soviet Union. It was decided that: terms for the Japanese surrender were to be unconditional; Japanese sovereignty was to be limited to the islands of Honshu, Hokkaido, Kyushu, and Shikoku; Japan would be occupied by the Allied Powers until the establishment of a new order devoid of Japan's warmaking power; and full implementation of the Cairo Declaration.[13] This meant that Korea would be outside Japanese sovereignty with full implementation of Korean independence.

THE END OF WORLD WAR II AND KOREA'S LIBERATION

After an atom bomb was dropped on Hiroshima on August 6, 1945, it became clear that World War II would not last much longer. The Soviet Union, which had made a commitment to join the war at the Yalta Conference, decided not to miss the opportunity to leap at the spoils of war. Only two days later, the Soviet Union declared war against Japan and it sent a large army into Korea and Manchuria on August 8, 1945. A week later, on August 15, 1945, Japanese Emperor Hirohito announced over the radio in a halting, quivering voice that Japan surrendered to the Allied Powers unconditionally. By this time, the army of the Soviet Union was deep into the Korean Peninsula. Its forces quickly overran Manchuria, because the Japanese Kanto Army had largely withdrawn to fight a battle at Okinawa. At Yalta, the leaders of the Allied Powers had agreed to disarm the Japanese troops in Korea, yet they had not specified how to do it.

A hasty decision had to be made in Washington to draw a demarcation line dividing Korea into two occupation zones, before the Russian forces could overrun all of Korea. The "temporary" line separating the two zones was agreed to be the 38th parallel. The Cairo Conference of October 1943 promised that Korea was to be free and independent, but nobody ever expected that Korea would be divided into two parts. Koreans were overjoyed when they were liberated from the Japanese; however, this joy was short-lived when they learned that their country was to be divided into two parts. This division later became permanent and tragedy struck Korea once again.

In the meantime, more than two million Japanese residents in Korea were ordered by the Allied Forces to evacuate back to Japan within a few months. The Japanese, who took almost everything away from the Koreans by force, lost everything and left Korea bare. Despite all the atrocities committed against Koreans for so long, when the Koreans had their chance for revenge, they were strangely compassionate. For months, until all the Japanese had withdrawn, no violence was reported. Instead many Japanese families in distress were helped by Koreans. This situation was a contrast to that in Manchuria and China, where many thousands of Japanese were shot and killed in the streets. This Korean postwar generosity was similar to what happened after the 1592–1598 Korea–Japan War ended in Korean victory, with much sacrifice and destruction. However, Koreans treated tens of thousands of stragglers of the Japanese army who could not return to Japan with compassion.

Notes to Part V

CHAPTER 13

1. Kin Tatsu-shu, *Chosen* (Tokyo: Iwanami Shin-sho, 1990), 118.

2. Hoon K. Lee, *Land Utilization and Rural Economy in Korea* (New York: Greenwood Publishing Group, 1969), 203 (originally published by Chicago: Chicago University Press, 1936).

3. Kin Tatsu-shu, *Chosen*, 119.

4. Ibid.

5. Hoon K. Lee, *Land Utilization and Rural Economy in Korea*, 203.

6. Ibid.

7. Ibid., 288.

8. Ibid., 285.

9. Ibid., 203.

10. Ibid., 148.

11. Kin Tatsu-shu, *Chosen*, 120.

12. Hoon K. Lee, *Land Utilization and Rural Economy in Korea*, 203.

13. Ibid.

14. Ramon H.Myers,Mark R. Peattie (eds.), *The Japanese Colonial Empire* (Princeton, NJ: Princeton University Press, 1984), 487.

15. Kajimura Hideki, *Chosen-shi*, 161.

16. *The Handbook of Korea* (Seoul, Ministry of Culture and Information, 1979), 148, 641.

17. Ibid.

18. Ibid.

19. Ramon H.Myers,Mark R. Peattie (eds.), *The Japanese Colonial Empire* (Princeton, NJ: Princeton University Press, 1984), 296.

20. *Handbook of Korea*, 148.

21. Ramon H. Myers, Mark R. Peattie (eds.), *The Japanese Colonial Empire* (Princeton, NJ: Princeton University Press, 1984), 323.
22. Ibid., 326.
23. Ibid.
24. *Handbook of Korea*, 156.
25. Ibid., 162–163.

CHAPTER 14

1. *Handbook of Korea*, 153.
2. Kajimura Hideki, *Chosenshi*, 152.
3. Kin Tatsu-shu, *Chosen*, 125.
4. Ibid., 126.
5. Kajimura Hideki, *Chosenshi*, 174–178.
6. Kin Tatsu-shu, *Chosen*, 138.
7. Ibid., 139.
8. Baik Bong, *Kim Il Sung, Biography II* (Tokyo: Mirasha, 1970).
9. Dae-Sook Suh, *Kim Il Sung: The North Korean Leader* (New York: Columbia University Press, 1988), 43.
10. Ibid., 50.
11. Ibid., 51.
12. Eugene Kim and Lawrence Ziring, *The Asian Political Dictionary* (Santa Barbara, CA, and Oxford, England: ABC Clio Inc., 1985), 370–371.
13. Ibid., 371.

Part VI

South and North Korea: A Divided Nation

15

Period of Occupational Governments of the United States and the Soviet Union

SOUTH KOREA: SEPTEMBER 1945–AUGUST 1948

During the Second World War, most of the fighting in Asia against the Japanese forces was conducted by the United States, with great sacrifice of human lives and materials. On the other hand, the Soviet Union, which had a nonaggression pact with Japan, was a bystander until the last days of the war. Once Russia realized that the Japanese surrender was imminent, Russian forces quickly moved into the northern part of the Korean Peninsula. By August 15, 1945, the day of the Japanese surrender, Russian forces occupied most of northern Korea. The American forces did not even arrive in any part of Korea until a month later, in mid-September.

To prevent Russian occupation of all of Korea, a hasty decision was made in Washington to draw a line of demarcation dividing the Korean Peninsula into respective zones of occupation by Russian and American forces. In the beginning, this line was never intended to be a political division into two spheres. It was intended only for the military purpose of disarming the Japanese forces.

When the Japanese had withdrawn and American and Russian forces moved in, Korea was thrown into confusion. Koreans did not expect two occupation zones. And because Koreans were forbidden by the Japanese to form any political organizations for thirty-five years, Korea lacked any major political entity. Many political parties sprang up overnight, each vying for political influence. The overseas Koreans arrived quickly to confuse the situation further.

Five major political groups appeared in South Korea. Three were formed by the people who were underground in Korea; two arrived from overseas, one from the United States, and one from Nationalist China. The Korean Democratic Party, under Kim Sōng-su, Song Jin-u, and Chang Dōk-su, representing the landowners and moneyed people; the Korean Labor Party, under the Communist Pak Hōn-yōng; and the moderate socialist group, under Yō Un-yōng, were the three major groups led by people who had lived in Korea during the Japanese occupation. Those who had maintained the Korean Provisional Government in China, Kim Ku and Kim Kyu-sik, arrived in Seoul, as did Syngman Rhee from the United States. Among these five groups, the Communist (Labor) Party, which was formed in Seoul in October 1945, was coordinated closely with North Korea and received orders from it.

Lieutenant General John R. Hodge, commander of the United States occupation forces in Korea, was under a severe handicap to maintain peace and order while Korea was undergoing political and economic turmoil. Before the U.S. forces moved in, the Japanese printed paper money to such an extent that inflation skyrocketed to over one thousand percent in a few months. They did this to create economic trouble for the Americans and Koreans alike in Korea. The political scene was also dangerous. The political leaders of Korea, Song Jin-u, Yō Un-yōng, Chang Dōk-su, and later Kim Ku, were assassinated one after another, demonstrating the unsettled situation.

The Koreans, when they were liberated from the Japanese, proclaimed two "governments" in Korea. One was the *Korean People's Republic*, formed by the Socialist Yō Un-yōng. The other was the *Korean Provisional Government*, headed by Kim Koo, who returned from China with his group. Syngman Rhee, who was the first president of the Korean Provisional Government in China in 1919, had become a rival of that group.

The United States did not recognize either of these two "governments."[1] They were incensed by the order to disband given by the U.S. Military Government in Korea, which imposed direct rule. However, the U.S. Army personnel, who lacked language skills and knowledge of Korea, were assigned at various levels and faced numerous difficulties. American-educated Koreans who had stayed underground during the Japanese occupation came to assist. The leaders included Dr. Lee Hoon Koo Minister of Agriculture and Forestry, who chaired the National Economic Board (composed of five Korean cabinet ministers). The National Economic Board was able to check runaway inflationary economic pressures and instituted fair land reform and redistribution of the vast lands previously owned by the Japanese to the Korean tenant farmers. Another leader was Dr. Cho Pyōng-ok, who headed the Ministry of Police and Justice and was able to maintain law and order in the unruly postwar society. Those leaders who assisted the U.S. Military Government in South Korea also contributed to the founding of the new Republic of Korea, after the independence of South Korea in August 1948. For example, Dr. Lee Hoon Koo, who became the chairman of a political party, was among the twenty congressional members who wrote the first constitution of the Republic of Korea. Dr. Cho Pyōng-ok, became the leader of the opposition party, the *Korean Democratic Party* (*Han Min Tang*), during the Rhee regime.

Another special mention should be given to the return of Dr. Philip Jaisohn (Sō Chae-p'il), a Korean revolutionary of the 1890s who became an American citizen. Dr. Jaisohn was invited to Korea as the special political adviser to Lieutenant General Hodge of the U.S. Military Government in Korea. That was his last contribution to the country in which he was born. The U.S. Military Government was able to settle down as an effective governing body with the support of the American-educated Koreans. A governmental system was formed that was readily transferable into a new democratic elected government in 1948. A well-functioning body was established. There were, however, many problems which the U.S. Military Government had to tackle in the meantime.

The Political Developments

The foremost political problem facing South Korea was not in Korea, but in Washington, D.C. There were people in the U.S. government who considered Korea unimportant, too far away, too costly, or too dangerous to maintain. They were scarcely aware of Korea's geopolitical location, in the hub of East Asia. The people in Washington, D.C., especially in the U.S. State Department, had not learned the historical fact that control of Korea had resulted in eventual domination of all of East Asia by any power throughout the millennia. They had forgotten that when the United States and Great Britain let Japan occupy Korea, the Japanese had created unrest and turmoil in East Asia in the twentieth century. They had forgotten that a free, independent, and unified Korea was essential to peace in East Asia.

When the power of the Chinese Nationalists faltered, U.S. strategists began to question the defense of South Korea. Soon, it became apparent that South Korea was the only tiny area under Western influence in the vast Asian continent. According to one highly placed official, this was an "exposed, unsound military position, one that was doing no good."[2] This same attitude caused the United States to abandon Korea to Japan in 1905, an action which eventually invited the Second Sino–Japanese War and World War II. This same pessimism caused the United States to pull forces out of South Korea in 1949 and invited the Korean War. To them, any positive support to the U.S. Military Government in Korea was a waste. The Washington authorities refused to provide the necessary financial support for the security of South Korea, including military training and equipment. The Republic of Korea (ROK) was left unprepared and vulnerable to an attack from the North. Insufficient support to strengthen South Korea's economy or military came from Washington, D.C. When the Soviet Army trained two hundred thousand North Korean troops and turned over military equipment, including six hundred T34 tanks, four hundred YAK fighter planes, and many thousands of artillery pieces, the South Korean force of eighty thousand troops was training with wooden rifles because insufficient modern rifles were available. South Koreans had not a single tank or plane.

The second major problem faced by the U.S. Military Government in Korea was the political and civil unrest caused by the failures of international conferences on Korea. The first such unworkable decision by the international conferences was made in Moscow in December 1945. The three powers, the United States, Great Britain, and the Soviet Union, agreed, without consultation with Koreans, to move toward eventual independence of Korea under a four-power, five-year trusteeship which included Nationalist China.[3] World history indicated that trusteeship was synonymous with colonization. This Moscow agreement infuriated South Koreans. Only the Communists supported the idea. They reasoned that such an arrangement would give them fertile ground for a takeover of all of Korea. Without Korean support, this decision could not be implemented. It created only needless unrest for the U.S. Military Government. This Moscow agreement also provided for the formation of a joint American–Soviet commission which was supposed to help organize the provisional Korean democratic government.

The joint commission was held in Seoul from March 1946 to October 1947. The Soviet side insisted that only those parties and organizations which upheld the trusteeship be allowed to participate in the formation of an all-Korea government. This effectively left out every Korean organization, except the Communists. This would leave all of Korea under Communist control and was totally unacceptable to the United States and the Korean Nationalists. The joint commission was dissolved in October 1947 without reaching agreement.

Establishment of the Republic of Korea (ROK)

The United States submitted the Korean problem to the United Nations in September 1947 for a new resolution on Korea.[4] In November 1947, the United Nations adopted a resolution which stipulated that the formation of a Korean government be left to the elected representatives of the Korean people, and the U.N. Temporary Commission on Korea be formed to observe the election process. The Soviet Union objected to this UN resolution, and in January 1948 it refused to admit the commission into the northern half. A free democratic election was held only in the southern part of Korea on May 10, 1948. One hundred congressional seats were reserved for the North Korean delegates. However, these seats were never filled. On the basis of population (one for every one hundred thousand), the government created three hundred seats in the Korean National Assembly. Only the two hundred delegates from South Korea filled the seats. The assembly selected twenty members, who wrote the constitution while electing Syngman Rhee as its president. The constitution adopted by the assembly set forth a presidential form of government modeled after that of the United States and specified a four-year term for the presidency. With this constitution ratified by the National Assembly on August 15, 1948, the *Republic of Korea* (*Tae-han Min-guk*) was proclaimed. Syngman Rhee took office as the first president.

The Economic and Social Problems

Other than unresolved political disputes, there were many social and economic problems faced by the U.S. Military Government in Korea during the short period of only three years. However short its administration, it had left a giant legacy which continued a half century later toward the turn of the twenty-first century in South Korea.

The first order of business was the evacuation of the Japanese. There were roughly two million Japanese on the Korean Peninsula; of this number, about seven hundred thousand were in South Korea. About the same number of Japanese had moved down from the north to avoid the Soviet troops. There were about four hundred thousand Japanese troops in Korea who were disarmed by the American and Russian forces. Many of the Japanese who remained in the Russian occupation zone were sent to forced labor camps in Siberia. All the Japanese in the American zone were evacuated to Japan without exception. The American forces were fair to the Japanese, and all were evacuated in an orderly manner.

Soon after this, the overseas Koreans started to pour in. There were over two million Koreans in Japan, and about 1.5 million were repatriated, except about 600,000 who chose to remain in Japan. At the end of the Second World War, there were 1.4 million Koreans in Manchuria, 600,000 in Siberia, and 130,000 in China. Of these, about 500,000 returned to Korea, making the total repatriated from overseas over two million.[5] Most of them chose to go to South Korea. In addition to these, more than 500,000 people, many of them Christians, went over the 38th parallel to South Korea from the north in the period 1945–1946. This produced a sudden increase in the population of more than 2.5 million, which created a huge problem for the U.S. Military Government.

Agricultural South Korea in the period 1945–1948 was severed from the north, which was more industrialized at that time, and the number of unemployed among the working population was above fifty percent. The main source of electricity was the Supung Electric Plant in the north. North Korea did not hesitate to cut off the electric supply to South Korea. This forced a rationing of three to four hours per day for the use of electric power for the average South Korean family. In addition to these economic difficulties, South Korea experienced severe runaway inflation caused by the reckless printing of money by the Japanese in 1945 and the Communist counterfeiting of money in 1946. The economic policy formulated by the National Economic Board under the U.S. Military Government effectively checked this inflation by the end of 1947.

THE MAJOR ACCOMPLISHMENTS OF THE U.S. MILITARY GOVERNMENT IN KOREA: SEPTEMBER 1945–AUGUST 1948

The revolutionary reforms carried out by the U.S. forces in Korea in the short period of only three years accomplished solid results. Some of these reforms, such as land reform, had immediate effects. However, other, such as education reform, had more gradual effects. Many of these reforms took place for the first time in the Korean history of more than four thousand years. All are still in effect after half a century and have become solidly rooted in Korean society. These reforms were modeled after reforms enforced by the Supreme Command for the Allied Powers (SCAP) in Japan for Japanese society. However, the situation in Korea was different from that in Japan; therefore, the changes took different forms. The major aims of SCAP were to ensure that Japan would never again menace the United States and the world; to try war criminals; and to dissolve the *zaibatsus*. These simply did not apply in the Korean situation. However, reforms for the establishment of democracy in Korea, land reform, social and educational changes to promote equal opportunity, and enfranchisement of women and protection of their full equality were very much needed for Korea.

Land Reforms

Many years of systematic confiscation of Korea's best lands by the Japanese colonial government had deprived Koreans of their ancestral lands. By 1945, as much as an estimated seventy to eighty percent of Korea's best lands were in the hands of the Japanese government, land companies, or individuals. The Japanese civilians took ownership of fifty-nine percent of the Korean lands by as early as 1930. This situation became worse in the late 1930s and 1940s. The United States government, realizing that the Japanese had confiscated the lands by illegal means, redistributed all of the land to the Korean farmers in a fair and equitable manner. These land reforms involved a major portion of the Korean land and were the largest in scale in the history of Korea. After this American-instituted land reform of 1946–1948, the Rhee government, in 1949–1950, followed suit and instituted land reform for acreage owned by large Korean landowners. They were obliged to divest of most of their lands. However, this land reform was relatively small-scale because there were few Korean large landholders left by 1949. These reforms gave lands to land tillers, a process which had not occurred for many centuries.

Educational Reforms

Koreans were extremely motivated toward education. The history of Korean effort for better education goes back to the seventh century of Silla's time. The oldest universities in Korea predate the oldest universities in Europe by several centuries. Before the Japanese occupation of Korea, there were three thousand private schools which taught Western learning, including mathematics, history, geography, and science. The Japanese, in order to deprive Koreans of intellectual resources, closed most of the Korean schools (see Chapter 13). The Japanese built a university and many colleges for Japanese residents and barred Koreans from attending them. American missionaries built several colleges for the Koreans; however, the Japanese closed down one such major college, the Union Christian College in P'yōngyang. The Japanese had not built a single college for thirty million Koreans. Because of this Japanese colonial educational policy, Korean educational opportunities had become extremely limited.

As soon as the U.S. Military Government was established in Korea, the first order of business of Americans was to open up educational opportunities to everybody. The new education system of Korea was modeled after the U.S. school system, with six years of primary school, six years of secondary school, four years of higher education, and additional years for graduate studies. Attendance up to the ninth grade was made compulsory. Permits were freely given to build high schools and colleges. American-educated people in the United States and Korea played dominant roles in the radical expansion of postwar educational opportunities. The floodgates were open. People rushed into schools to get an education. Seoul University, Korea University, Yōnsei University, Ewha Womans University, Suk-myōng Womans University, Tong-Kuk, and Sōng Kyung Kwan Universities all increased their student enrollment to over ten thousand each from a mere five hundred to six hundred for each. The new universities of Tan Kuk, Sung Sil, Pusan, and many others were open. All of these universities boasted enrollments of ten thousand to forty thousand students by the 1980s.

The U.S. Military Government initiated the policy of mass education, and the educated manpower resources that were created by this educational revolution were primarily responsible for Korea's astonishing economic and industrial progress. South Korea has been a nation of poor natural resources. However, it has acquired rich manpower resources through education. With it, South Koreans have been able to build an industrial nation which ranked as one of the ten greatest economic powers in the world by the mid-1990s. It all started from the educational reforms of the U.S. Military Government in Korea in 1945–1948.

In the mid-1980s, approximately 4.8 million students in the eligible age-group were attending primary school. The proportion of students going on to middle school the same year was more than ninety-nine percent.[6] About thirty-four percent, one of the world's highest rates of secondary-school graduates, attended institutions of higher education in 1987. This rate was higher than Japan's roughly thirty percent, and much exceeded Britain's twenty percent.

South Korea's literacy rate was ninety-seven percent in 1990, and the proficiency scores of the Korean high school students on all subjects consistently ranked first or second among world students, based on objective measurements of more than one hundred countries. Historians tend to minimize the American accomplishments in Korea; however, due recognition must be given to them. The Americans set the stage for South Korea's astonishing progress of the 1980s and 1990s, through the radical reforms of the period 1945–1948.

Reforms of Social Class Structures

Social reforms introduced by the U.S. Military Government were no less revolutionary than land and educational reforms. Traditionally, Korea had rigid social class structures. The people who ruled the nation were nobility and gentry classes, *Yangban*, who constituted about eight percent of the population. The rest of the population was called *Sangin* or *Sangsaram*, meaning "commoners." On some occasions they were called, usually by *Yangban*, *Sangnom*, which has a derogatory connotation. Within the *Sangin* class, there were several divisions. The class structure was so rigid that social mobility in any direction was not permitted.

When the Japanese went into Korea in 1910, they abolished the *Yangban* class; however, they imposed their own social class in Korea, including the Western-style nobility system of peerage. This Japanese class structure was no more democratic than the old Li Dynasty class system.

As soon as the U.S. Military Government was established, everybody in South Korea was made legally and socially equal. Thus, the very foundation for democracy was established. Gone was the old Li Dynasty or Japanese type of class system.

Reforms of Human Rights and Freedom

During the Japanese occupation, there were absolutely no human rights or freedoms. People were sent to prison without a trial. Thousands of people just disappeared without a trace. Newspapers and magazines were closed down. Koreans were not allowed to speak their own language in their own country. All of these conditions changed when the Americans moved in. Just as schools and colleges mushroomed overnight, publication enterprises exploded. Freedom of assembly, press, speech, and religious worship were all guaranteed by the U.S. Military Government. These rights were written into the new constitution of the Republic of Korea in 1948.

Reforms of Equality of Women

Traditionally, the social and family positions of Korean women were quite different from those in the neighboring countries of China and Japan. In the old society of Puyō horseriders, women controlled religious affairs, which had a close relationship with affairs of state. Quite often Korean women were reigning queens. This was true as late as the seventh and eighth centuries of Silla.

Customarily Korean men lived with the wife's family. Korean families tended to have matriarchal characteristics. Women's opinions were respected by husbands and sons. All this began to change from the beginning of the fifteenth century, when the Li Dynasty kings adopted the Chinese Confucian philosophy, which treated women as inferior beings. Nevertheless, Korean women kept their free spirit; they even participated in active battles in national emergencies. Toward the seventeenth and eighteenth centuries, Korean women's social position fell somewhat. However, it was still a far cry from the slave-like position of Japanese or Chinese women.

When the Japanese occupied Korea after 1910, they imposed their civil law and customs on Korean women also. Japanese civil law did not permit women to inherit money or property from a father or husband as long as a male heir was alive. These Japanese laws and customs which treated women unequally made Korean women's position even weaker. Education opportunities for them were severely limited, except at the schools founded by the American missionaries. All the discrimination against women officially came to an end and women became socially and legally equal to men when the U.S. Military Government was established. Korean women now had equal voting rights, equal right of inheritance, and equal opportunity for education. All the colleges and universities were made coeducational, except some women's universities, such as Ewha Womans University, which preferred to remain female institutions. Korean woman's position improved radically through the American-initiated social reforms.

Establishment of a Well-Functioning Transitional Government in South Korea

During the Japanese colonial government, Koreans were barred from important policy-making positions. Some Koreans worked in the Japanese government as low-ranking civil servants, who were mostly clerical staff. When the American forces took over governmental management, Americans were essentially unfamiliar with the Korean language or Korean affairs. Many Koreans, especially American-educated Koreans, were given advisory positions. This was mutually beneficial because Koreans could acquire valuable managerial experience heretofore denied them by the Japanese, while they were helping Americans.

About a year later, in 1946, the U.S. Military Government in Korea switched American-held personnel positions with Koreans. The Americans let the Koreans take over managerial positions, while they started to function only as advisers. By early 1947, all the ministries, departments, and bureaus were managed by Koreans. A Korean civil governor, An Chae-hong, equal in rank to the American military governor, was appointed in the latter part of 1947. Thus, a well-functioning government body, manned by Koreans, was firmly established by 1948. This proved that Americans did not have territorial ambitions in Korea. Because of this, when the government of the Republic of Korea was established, a smooth transfer of power from the U.S. Military Government to the government of the Republic of Korea took place.

NORTH KOREA: AUGUST 1945–SEPTEMBER 1948

After the troops of the Soviet Union moved onto the Korean Peninsula north of the 38th parallel, North Korea went through rapid political changes. It took several months for the Korean Communist elements to infiltrate the localities. At first, a non-Communist Nationalist leader, Cho Man-sik, who commanded a broad respect among northern Koreans, was set up as the chairman of the new executive establishment called the North Korean Five Province Bureau, which was organized on October 28, 1945. However, the bureau governed in name only, and the actual political power was wielded by the Soviet occupation forces, assisted by the Korean Communist elements. At that time, there were four major Communist groups: the Soviet Koreans; Kim Il Sung's followers; the group returned from Yenan in Communist China; and the domestic Korean Communist groups. The power struggle of these groups continued for at least a decade; however, Kim Il-Sung held the upper hand with the help of the Soviets.

Kim Sōng-ju, self-named Kim Il-Sung sometime in the 1930s, moved into the Soviet Far Eastern region in 1941 and received formal military training from the Russians. When he moved into North Korea in October 1945, Kim held the rank of Soviet major. He was an overseas Korean, lacking a political foundation in Korea proper. The Soviets, who did not trust Koreans who lived in Korea, heavily relied on Kim's group to maintain Soviet power. The movement to organize Communist cells was pushed throughout North Korea in 1945 and 1946. The first Soviet move to strengthen Soviet power was made at the expense of the domestic groups, resulting in the organization of the North Korean Communist Party in December 1945. Kim was designated to lead the party. Rapid infiltration by the Communists took place in every segment of the population. By January 1946, the Communists were confident enough to do away with the Nationalists and imprisoned Cho for opposing the trusteeship plan formulated by the three foreign ministers in Moscow in December 1945. The Communists took over direct control.

The following month, February 1946, the North Korean Provisional People's Committee was organized as the new governing body, and its cabinet initiated sweeping socialist reforms beginning March 1946. All lands were expropriated and redistributed to the peasants. A law was passed to nationalize all the basic industries, and transportation, financial, and communication facilities. By August 1946, as much as ninety percent of the total industries were nationalized.[7] A new law guaranteed equal rights for men and women.

The consolidation of power under Kim Il-Sung with the help of the Soviet Union could not be carried out without challenge. In mid-1946, the New People's Party, formed by returnees from Yenan, China, under Kim Tu-bong, demanded participation in the Communist movement. As a result, in August 1946, the two groups merged and established a new party, the *North Korean Workers Party*, under the nominal chairmanship of Kim Tu-bong. Kim Il-Sung held real power as the vice-chairman. In order to legitimize the reforms that had already taken place in early 1946, in November 1946 elections were held to select local delegates. In February 1947 there was a convention of the People's Committee, and this in turn elected the North Korean People's Assembly. The assembly approved the creation of the North Korean People's Committee, which became the highest executive governing organization under Kim Il-Sung. North Korea was under Soviet occupation, and therefore the Yenan group could not exercise real power in the government.

Establishment of the Democratic People's Republic of Korea (DPRK)

As the preparations to form a Communist government in North Korea approached completion, the North Korean People's Assembly appointed a committee to prepare a constitution, which was promulgated on July 10, 1948. By this time, South Korea had completed a general election (on May 10, 1948), and a new national assembly had appointed a constitutional committee, which began to write a constitution for South Korea. It should be noted that the constitutions of both countries claim all of the Korean Peninsula as one united territory and do not recognize the division of the country into north and south. The Supreme People's Assembly of North Korea ratified the constitution. On the basis of this constitution, the establishment of the *Democratic People's Republic of Korea* (*Chosŏn Minjujuui Inmin Konghwaguk*) was formally proclaimed on September 9, 1948,[8] about three weeks after the establishment of the *Republic of Korea* (*Tae-han Min-guk*), on August 15, 1948, in South Korea. Thus Korea, which had been united as one nation in one territory since 676 A.D. became divided into two nations.

16

Korea Before and During the Korean War: 1948–1953

SOUTH AND NORTH KOREA BEFORE THE WAR

The Republic of Korea (ROK) proclaimed its independence in South Korea on August 15, 1948, claiming legitimacy for the entire Korean Peninsula, including North Korea. North Korea (DPRK) similarly declared its sovereignty on September 9, 1948, claiming all of Korea. The Republic of Korea was immediately recognized by the United Sates and Nationalist China, followed by more than one hundred nations around the world, except the Communist nations. A resolution passed by the U.N. General Assembly on December 12, 1948, referred to the government of the ROK as the "only lawful government in Korea."[1] Despite this, in reality, Korea was divided into two parts, each possessing great potentiality and power and hostile to the other after more than twelve hundred years of united government and culture. Each claimed the title "Korea," not recognizing the other part.

While this was going on, the political and military situation in East Asia was turning unfavorable for the ROK. In 1949, Mao's Chinese Communist army was triumphant against Chiang's Nationalist army. This placed the ROK in a precarious situation. Under these circumstances, the United States government, particularly the State Department, was uncertain about its policy toward Korea. The United States canceled previously allocated aid (U.S. $500 million) to Korea and withheld all military and economic assistance to the ROK.[2] And U.S. military intelligence was not functioning well enough to know what was happening in North Korea. There was no economic or military aid to the ROK from the United States at a critical moment. Not only that, officials at the U.S. State Department considered Korea unimportant to U.S. interests and declared it too dangerous to become involved.

This notion was badly mistaken. The history of East Asia had proved over many centuries that Korea is located at the hub of the East Asian political–military powers of China, Russia, Japan, and lately the United States, as any power which lost influence in Korea eventually lost all of East Asia. The U.S. Secretary of State, Dean Acheson, who was primarily preoccupied with European affairs,[3] timidly decided to abandon Korea rather than take a firm stand. Acheson declared that the Korean Peninsula was outside the defense perimeter of the United States.[4] He drew a U.S. defense line on the East Asian map, leaving out South Korea and Taiwan, and announced it to the world. It was an open invitation to an attack by the Communists. The United States occupation forces had already been withdrawn by June 29, 1949, except a handful of military advisers. There were less than one hundred thousand ROK army troops, with no heavy military equipment, as the United States refused to turn equipment over to the ROK when the U.S. Army was withdrawn. The ill-trained, ill-equipped ROK army had suffered great damage through the October 1948 Communist-led army rebellion of Yōsu-Sunch'ōn, which consumed much of the ROK Army's resources. A massive purge within the army further weakened it.

While these events inside and outside Korea kept South Korea militarily unprepared, North Korea and the Soviet Union wasted no time. They built a formidable military and political structure in North Korea. Between 1946 and 1949, large numbers of North Korean youths, at least ten thousand, were taken to the Soviet Union for military training.[5] They formed the North Korean army cadres when they returned. A draft was instituted. The Soviet occupation forces, secure in the knowledge that the Communist regime and its military were firmly established, had withdrawn from North Korea by December 26, 1948.

To strengthen the North Korean Army in 1949, two divisions, about forty thousand troops of the former Korean Volunteer Army, who fought the Japanese Army and then the Chinese Nationalist Army in Manchuria, returned to North Korea.[6] They were trained and battle-experienced troops who had played a pivotal role in the Communist victory in Manchuria, which was the beginning of the Chinese Communists' final drive in the Chinese civil war.

To strengthen these military resources, the Soviet Union left behind all its equipment and arms, including T34 tanks, Yak fighter planes, and heavy artillery pieces. Dr. Claude A. Buss states in *The United States and the Republic of Korea* that the United States had scarcely noticed that the arms and equipment left behind by the Russians were far superior to the materials left by the Americans.[7] Premier Stalin of Russia was personally involved in the North Korean military buildup. After Dean Acheson's statement, which left South Korea outside the U.S. defense line, Stalin knew the United States would not go to the aid of South Korea if it was attacked. He summoned Kim Il Sung to Moscow and asked whether the DPRK were ready to attack South Korea. When Kim told him that he was not quite ready, Stalin became very angry and told him to speed it up. Knowing that the United States was the mightiest nation on earth, Stalin would do anything to avoid a direct confrontation with it. He wanted to unify Korea by force before the United States changed its mind about the defense perimeter which left out Korea. The North Koreans strengthened their arms might quickly to be confident of their ability to occupy South Korea in the shortest period of time, so that the Communist unification of all of Korea would be a fait accompli before the United States could even react.

THE BEGINNING OF THE KOREAN WAR

On June 25, 1950, North Korea launched an invasion across the 38th parallel. On a Sunday before dawn, when everyone was still asleep and more than half of the ROK troops were away on leave, nearly two hundred thousand North Korean troops attacked, spearheaded by T34 tanks. The ROK army, without a single tank or antitank gun, had no means to stop them. Seoul was occupied in three days. The Korean War was in full swing. In retrospect, this war could have been prevented easily. The Russians had gone through the Second World War and had twenty-seven million of its people killed only five years earlier, and men and materials were exhausted in the devastating war. It could not have risked another major war against the United States, the mightiest nation at that time, and the only nuclear power. Communist China had barely won the civil war and nothing was secure in 1949. North Korea could not have attacked the ROK without Russian backing and assurance from Dean Acheson that South Korea was outside the U.S. defense perimeter. Instead of issuing such a foolish and unnecessary announcement, which was nothing less than an invitation for an invasion, the United States could have maintained a naval fleet containing an aircraft carrier or two with war planes and marines in nearby Korean waters and issued a stern warning to the Communists not to tamper with South Korea. This could have effectively prevented the war. The blunder of the U.S. State Department announcement, which assured North Korea of U.S. noninvolvement in the East Asian continent, was one of the direct causes of the Korean War. Not only was it an unnecessary absurdity, but also it was utterly irresponsible because it totally ignored the fate of twenty million people in the friendly nation of South Korea. U.S. President Harry Truman later overruled Acheson's U.S. defense perimeter and withdrew it officially. However, his action came too late. The Korean War was on full scale.

THE KOREAN WAR AND ITS EFFECTS

One day after the North Korean forces crossed the 38th parallel, on June 26, 1950, a man of fortitude and one of the great presidents in American history, Harry S. Truman, lost no time and ordered the use of United States war planes and naval vessels against the North Korean forces. On the same day, the United Nations Security Council held an emergency session and ordered North Korea to cease hostilities immediately. However, it was ignored. The United States dispatched ground troops to Korea on June 30, the Twenty-Fourth Division of about twenty thousand troops. By this time, North Korean forces had already passed Seoul and Suwōn and were on their way down to Taejōn, where they met American troops. The vastly outnumbered American and South Korean allies fought valiantly; however, they were soon overrun by the Communist forces.

Only a few months earlier, the United States had drawn a defense line and was ready to abandon South Korea and Taiwan. Now it realized the mistake. Fearing that inaction in Korea would be interpreted as appeasement of Communist aggression throughout the world, the United States was now determined to defend South Korea. The United Nations was asked to intervene militarily. General Douglas MacArthur was appointed the commanding general of the United Nations forces in Korea. For three months, the North Korean forces pressed the United Nations troops hard into the triangular southeast corner of the Korean Peninsula, linking lines of Taegu-Masan and Taegu-P'ohang. The North Korean forces were stopped at the Naktong River, just north of Taegu City. The United Nations forces were still outnumbered by the Communist forces, and each time the Communist forces attacked, the UN forces had to move troops to plug the hole, exposing other defense lines. It was a risky move. For some reason, the North Koreans did not attack the whole front at the same time. Because of this, UN forces were able to hold the critical beachhead around Pusan.

On September 15, 1950, General MacArthur personally led troops that landed at Inchōn, cutting off enemy troops to the south.[8] The course of the war changed abruptly. About one hundred fifty thousand enemy troops who were encircling the UN forces in the south had disintegrated. They threw down their weapons, changed their uniforms for civilian clothes, and scattered. The Inchōn landing was a textbook case, a brilliant military strategy that would be recorded in history. After this, the North Korean forces became practically nonexistent. The UN forces easily occupied the city of P'yōngyang, the North Korean capital. By November 1950, they were approaching the Manchurian border. When the U.S. Marines reached the Manchurian border of the north-central Korean Peninsula, they realized that they were in the midst of a large Chinese Communist force.

As the history of East Asia had witnessed on so many occasions, no nation could afford to have the Korean Peninsula held by another great power next to their borders. Both China and Russia shared their borders with Korea, and if the United States took control of Korea, they would both face the United States directly across a river. China sent an army of one-half million men into Korea, while the Soviet Union mobilized its air force into Manchuria, manning the MIG fighters themselves. The American pilots of the war planes actually engaged in combat with Russians, not Chinese, as was commonly believed at that time.

By December 1950, three great powers of the world were directly involved in this war: the United States, the Soviet Union, and Communist China. To a lesser degree, fifteen other nations fought alongside the American forces. They were the United Kingdom, Australia, Canada, New Zealand, Turkey, Belgium, Colombia, France, Ethiopia, Greece, the Netherlands, the Philippines, Thailand, Luxembourg, and South Africa. Five other nations (Denmark, India, Italy, Norway, and Sweden) provided medical assistance.

In reality, the Korean War was the third world war, except it was not called such. The United Nations forces temporarily lost their balance in the sudden, unexpected attack by the Chinese. Actually, most of these Chinese forces were former Nationalist forces who had surrendered to the Communists and used military equipment supplied by the United States during the World War II. It was said that Mao wanted to get rid of them, hence used human wave tactics against the Americans and South Koreans.

Seoul once again fell into Communist hands on January 4, 1951. The U.N. forces took three months to regroup and mount a counterattack, retaking Seoul on March 12, 1951. Seoul had gone through four battles and was occupied by great forces on both sides. Seoul was utterly destroyed. It is difficult to imagine that this same city had risen again, as a shining city, like a phoenix, with countless high-rise modern skyscrapers, boasting twelve million citizens by the 1990s.

The Korean War continued. However, the battle line was settled close to the 38th Parallel, where the war had begun. This new battle line was more defensible for the U.N. forces. As the war dragged on, the Russians called for truce negotiations. These began in July 1951, at Kaesong. However, the war dragged on for another full two years, while representatives of both sides bickered endlessly. On July 27, 1953, the armistice was finally signed at P'anmunjōm. A war which could have been prevented, cost the world astronomical damage in terms of human lives and materials. The United States alone suffered fifty-four thousand killed and three hundred fifty thousand wounded. Over 1.3 million South Koreans, many of whom were civilians, lost their lives because of the Korean War.[9] More than one million Chinese and five hundred thousand North Koreans were killed. Other UN forces also suffered lesser casualties. The total war deaths of the Korean War were estimated to be more than three million.[10] The war was one of the largest in world history. Both North and South Korea were devastated by it. The Korean War was far greater than the Vietnam War in the extent of damage to life and property. During the war, more than six hundred fifty thousand North Koreans abandoned their homes and the Communist way of life to stream south for freedom.[11] The North Korean population was reduced by 1.15 million, about ten percent of the population. The fighting ended in 1953; however, South and North Korea were technically still at war nearly one half century later. It was a tragedy unseen in more than five thousand years of Korea's recorded history. All South Koreans have become staunch anti-Communists.

17

South Korea: 1948–1990s

During the Korean War, the South Korean political and military leaders were more or less united to oppose the North Koreans and Chinese. However, once the war was over, they broke off to form different groups, creating an unsettled political climate which lasted over four decades, into the 1990s. Power-hungry political and military leaders rose and fell, one after another, each changing the form of government and the national constitution radically to suit his personal greed for power. Each called such change a revolution, while putting his personal ambitions above the interests of the nation and people. The extremity and cruelty of their methods were reminiscent of the second half of the Li Dynasty period, when corrupt nobles jockeyed for power, purging opponents endlessly for many centuries, weakening the nation.

For over two hundred years, the United States has had one form of government and one constitution, although there have been some amendments. Compared to this, South Korea, in the short period of forty years, has had six radically different forms of government and constitution, each arising from a violent turnover. Since its independence on August 15, 1948, the Republic of Korea has had six different republics.

THE FIRST REPUBLIC: 1948–1960

Although Syngman Rhee lacked grass-roots support, he was handily elected president by the Korean National Assembly in 1948, by a vote of 180 of 196 votes cast, as a reward for his lifelong struggle against Japanese rule. As he faced his second term in 1952, he had increasing difficulties with the assembly, which no longer had the same sentiment. As he had no prospect of being reelected, he proposed a constitutional amendment, introduced in November

1951, for popular election of the president. This proposal was soundly defeated by the assembly, with a vote of 143 to 19. Rhee began to force the assemblymen into his Liberal Party. He declared martial law in May 1952 and imprisoned many members of the opposition. Finally, he succeeded in passage of an amendment for direct election by the people. As the Korean War was still going on and a radical change of government might adversely affect its outcome, the Korean people reelected Rhee in 1952.

Although Syngman Rhee organized the Liberal Party, he had not a single strong political ally, except three people around him who influenced him on all affairs. They were his wife, Francesca Rhee; her friend, Maria Pak; and Maria's husband, Li (or Yi) Ki-bung. The Austrian-born Francesca went to Korea with Rhee in 1945 and befriended Maria Pak. Because of this connection, Li Ki-bung was made Rhee's personal secretary. As Rhee had started his presidency at the age of seventy-three and was rapidly aging, the idea of Li Ki-bung's succeeding him became an obsession in this inner circle. In 1956, when Rhee's second term was to end, with the maximum of two terms prescribed by the constitution, Rhee again forcibly amended the constitution so that he could serve another term.

Rhee was elected to a third term. However, Li Ki-bung, who had run for the position of vice president on a separate ticket, was defeated by Chang Myōn, an opposition leader. Rhee won the 1956 election with only fifty-five percent of the vote, although his Democratic Party opponent, Sin Ik-hui, had died of a heart attack a few days before. The possibility of an opposition leader's succeeding the aging Rhee made Li and his group very uneasy. In 1956, Rhee was eighty-one years old and was, in fact, a captive of the trio, who held actual power behind the scenes.[1] In a society where the family connection was important, Li Ki-bung and his wife came up with the scheme of letting the Rhees adopt Li's son. There was nothing they would not do to bolster their political power.

After twelve years and three full terms as president, at age eighty-five, Rhee ran for a fourth term. Li Ki-bung also ran for vice president. Rhee won by default, as his opponent, Cho Pyōng-ok, died just before the election. Because of Rhee's age, the vice presidential contest was all-important. Li and the trio were determined to win and rigged the election. Li "won" 8.3 million votes against Chang Myōn's 1.8 million votes.[2] On April 19, 1960, student rebellions broke out. The young Korean students would have no part of such corruption. Rhee and the trio mobilized the police force to put down the revolt, and in the process 142 students were killed. The students launched a frontal attack on Rhee's presidential mansion and forced him to step down on April 26, 1960. Having lost all hope of Li's becoming president, the next day all four of Li Ki-bung's family members died in a suicide pact. The Rhees were exiled to Hawaii, where Rhee died in 1965 at the age of ninety. Rhee was a patriot who spent almost all of his life fighting for Korea's independence. Had he not become a captive of the power-hungry people who surrounded him and had he not been so self-serving, rejecting good and able people, he might have been revered as the founder of the Republic of Korea, as George Washington had been to America. Rhee failed in his last years.

Economy, Social, and Military Affairs During the Rhee Regime

Economic conditions during the Korean War were a matter of bare survival. Most of the large buildings and factories were destroyed. Most of the young men who could be a major labor force were called into the military. To make matters worse, there was an influx of more than one half million North Korean refugees, who needed assistance. Foreign aid, mainly from the United States, helped. The United States economic aid was U.S. $200 million in 1954, topped at $365 million in 1956, and fell to an average of $200 million in the mid-1960s. Much of the economic aid was used to support more than six hundred thousand ROK military forces, increased to that level by 1953 and maintained at the same level thereafter. The ROK military had become the largest and single most potent force in the ROK. The Rhee government maintained its power with the support of the military and police forces. The bulk of the United States economic aid was in the form of the United Nations Korean Reconstruction Agency (UNKRA). However, when UNKRA folded after 1957, the United States continued to supply economic aid in the form of direct assistance. Most of the war destruction was repaired by 1960, and the economy grew at an annual rate of 5.5 percent. However, the ROK had not reached the level of economic takeoff. Korea's most valuable asset, its educated work force, had not reached the point of fruition. However, Korea's educational expansion grew at the fastest rate during the period up to 1960, laying the foundation for the ROK's future industrial development.

The other major development of the Rhee period was the ideological setback for the Communists in South Korea. South Koreans were so enraged against the Communists for causing the war, destruction, and atrocities that the whole nation had become a solid anti-Communist camp. The Communists had no room to function in the ROK. Together with the strong anti-Communist trend, the Christian movement became very strong. By 1960 the number of Christians grew to an estimated six million of a population of thirty million, making South Korea the only major Christian nation on the continent of Asia. Of course, all these social happenings could not be attributed to the policies of the Rhee government. Rather, they were the spontaneous undertakings of the Korean people after they gained independence, although the new country was only half of the peninsula.

THE SECOND REPUBLIC: 1960–1961

When the twelve years of the Rhee government ended, there was no administration to fill its place. Hō Chōng, who was appointed foreign minister one day before Rhee resigned, was given the task of forming an interim government until a new election could be held. He was acceptable to the opposition groups. From April 26 to July 1960, a period of three months, he had to organize a new election, revise the constitution, and exile Rhee to Hawaii. The revised constitution established a parliamentary form of government with a bicameral legislature. The lower house was the National Assembly and the upper house was the Senate. It was similar in structure to the United States Congress, except that the Korean Congress was to elect the titular president and the prime minister, who held political power. In July, the Democratic Party won 175 of 233 seats in the lower house, and 31 of 58 seats in the Senate.

The Democratic Party was a coalition of parties that had previously opposed Rhee. Once they seized power, they began to struggle against each other. Yun Po-sōn, the titular president, wanted real power and threatened to break up the coalition. Chang Myōn, who as prime minister held real power, reshuffled the cabinet three times in five months to satisfy Yun. In November, Yun formed a new party, *Sin-min Tang*, or New Democratic Party. As they had for centuries, Korean political leaders put their own political ambitions ahead of the interests of the nation.

In reality, the Second Republic was the only true democratic government in the period of more than forty years after the ROK was established. However, it was a politically unstable period. Emboldened student groups who had helped topple the Rhee government staged daily demonstrations against the new government. The army and the police needed to be purged of political appointees, as they had supported the dictatorship of the Rhee government. These agencies became demoralized and ineffective. In the meantime, North Korea was regaining its military strength. Young ROK army officers, deprived of a decent living under the corrupt senior officers who regularly sidetracked military rations, were eager to risk their lives. This situation provided fertile ground for a radical move, a military coup.

The constitution of the Second Republic, adopted by the National Assembly on July 15, 1960, was written so as not to give any one individual dictatorial powers. Thus, neither the president nor the prime minister could exercise full authority. Also, after twelve years of the Rhee government's dictatorship, the leaders were reluctant to engage in power politics. The American-educated prime minister, Chang Myōn, was a soft-spoken, gentle man who was not by temperament suited for the kind of decisive political action required to handle the unstable South Korean situation of 1960–1961. To make matters worse, the North Korean government took advantage of the internal disorder and stepped up their subversive activities against the South. Many people, including the United Nations commanders, became concerned about this situation. The South Korean government of the Second Republic had limped along without accomplishing much for less than a year when a greatly feared event took place, the military coup of May 16, 1961. Engaged in internal power struggles, the leaders of the Second Republic had paid no attention to the possibility of a coup.

THE THIRD AND FOURTH REPUBLICS: 1961–1979

The Third Republic: 1961–1972

The Third Republic was a dictatorial terror regime, run by a handful of military junta members. A democratic government duly elected by the people of South Korea was crushed by a mere thirty-six hundred gun-wielding soldiers, led by a minor two-star general, Park Chung Hee (Pak Chōng-hi), and several field rank officers, on May 16, 1961. As Walter Easey and Gavan McCormack state in *Korea North and South*,

> Many people in the West understand vaguely that political liberties in South Korea are severely curtailed under the military dictatorship of Park. What is little known is the scope and depth of the comprehensive state apparatus of terror that maintains the regime in power . . . The present regime in South Korea is maintained in power by a judicious combination of the sticks of terror, torture, intimidation and harassment for the masses, with the carrot of wealth and privilege on a gargantuan scale for those bureaucrats and army officers who give Park their cooperation.[3]

Easey and McCormack, writing in 1978, could not have been more correct. Park held on to power for more than eighteen years, until October 26, 1979, when he was shot and killed in an American movie style shoot-out by his own chief of the KCIA, an organization he created to help keep him in power. He had a gangster-like personality and had been imprisoned in 1947 under suspicion of involvement in an army revolt, the Sun-chōn and Yōsu rebellion, for which Park's brother was executed. Park was freed and restored to his rank because during the Korean War trained army officers were in short supply.

When he seized power, Park was stationed in Yōng-dūng-p'o within the Seoul city limits, across the Han River and less than one half hour drive to the capitol building. When Park and his troops struck and occupied the government building, and radio and TV stations, Prime Minister Chang Myōn went into hiding. Three political elements could have stopped Park and his troops: the Army Chief of Staff, Gen. Chang To-yōng, who headed six hundred thousand troops; the president of the ROK, Yun Po-sōn; and the senior UN and American generals. Yet they did nothing, and Park was able to stage a coup d'ètat and rob South Korea of democracy.

Park's first order of business was to arrest the elected officials of both houses of Congress and put them in prison without a trial. Then, Park arrested government leaders, put controls on every segment of Korean society, and instituted martial law and a curfew. He controlled the people with an iron fist. There were no longer any civil liberties in South Korea, and Park made Rhee's dictatorship pale compared to his own. Park was a graduate of a second-rate

Japanese military academy in Manchuria and had received an officer's commission in the Japanese army; he had no concept of what democracy entails.

Park amended the constitution in 1963 and ran for the presidency. He was elected with a narrow margin of 46.6 percent against Yun's 45.1 percent. As Park monopolized all the radio and TV stations, he was reelected to a second term in 1967. The constitution limited the presidency to two terms, but Park amended the constitution again in 1969 to enable himself to be elected for a third term. Once "elected," Park tightened his control over the nation even more. In December 1971, he forced the National Assembly to pass a bill granting him complete power to mobilize the nation and people and to regulate and control everything in the country, including the press and the economy.

In October 1972, Park proclaimed martial law. He dissolved the National Assembly, closed all universities and colleges, imposed censorship on all publications, and banned all political activities.[4] Park's ruthless dictatorship was at its peak. After a few days, he put his new constitution, called *Yusin* (Revitalizing Reforms), on a national "referendum" managed by his own local government officials. Thus the illicit Fourth Republic was born. The new constitution of 1972 allowed Park to succeed himself indefinitely, to appoint one-third of the National Assembly's members, and to exercise emergency powers at will. All of these powers served to satisfy Park's political ambitions and personal greed. He made himself president for life and did not act for the national or people's interest. The Fourth Republic represented the continuation and worsening of Park's dictatorship.

Changes in the Social and Political Complexion of Korea During the Third Republic

Expansion of the education sector continued unabated during the Third Republic. In 1960 about 33 percent of South Korean youth between twelve and fourteen years attended middle school. This increased to 53.3 percent in 1970. In this same period, the proportion of high school age youth increased from 20 to 29.3 percent. By 1970 about 9.3 percent graduated from four-year colleges and universities, producing over thirty thousand graduates annually.[5] These graduates became the backbone of the industrial and technological society of South Korea, promoting rapid economic development. They also became the intellectual groups who took a dim view of the harsh, dictatorial rule of Park and his supporters. They formed the core of opposition in the cities, including Seoul.

At each election, about two-thirds of the urban votes went to opposition candidates running against Park's party members. As the South Korean urban middle class participated in the country's economic boom (the economy was expanding at an annual growth rate of over ten percent), their income grew steadily.

New Village Movement (*Sae-maūl Undong*)

In contrast to the urban areas, the rural areas of South Korea had not fared well. The Park government neglected the farming regions. The average farmer's income was only about one-half that of an urban worker in 1970. This situation caused massive migration from rural to urban areas. The rural areas had been the political base for both the Rhee and Park governments. As the rural population lagged behind the urban population in terms of education, rural residents, unaware of the central government's policies and activities, became the target of the government's enforcement of irregular voting. The incumbent government used a highly centralized channel from provincial regions down to the villages, and the village leaders, *Panjang*, were highly effective at influencing the votes of the rural population. But this political base of the Park government was crumbling with the urban migration. In 1971, Park started to crack down on students and intellectuals even harder in the cities, while he began to adopt new farm policies geared toward stemming the migration from rural to urban areas.

In 1971, the government began to adopt long-delayed measures to increase farm productivity and income. Seeds for higher-yielding rice were imported. More fertilizers and loans were provided with government subsidies. This reduced the rate of migration from farms to cities, although it did not stop it completely. By 1971, when this farm policy was implemented, most South Korean farms were run by women and old men.

In the fall of 1971, toward the end of the Third Republic, the government started the Sae-maūl movement with great fanfare. Local officials under highly centralized organization received orders from Seoul to mobilize the movement, whose objective was to improve the farm and village environment and rural living standards. The projects needed to accomplish this goal were to be carried out by the farmers themselves, with government assistance. Through local agencies, the dictatorial Park government enforced this movement effectively in all of the country's thirty-six thousand villages. New roads and bridges were built; thatched roofs were replaced with tiles, paid for by government subsidies; model villages were built. After a few years, the emphasis shifted toward raising productivity and income. Rural credits, market information, and farm services were provided. Gas and electric lines were installed. The Sae-maūl movement continued into the late 1970s. By the end of the movement, eighty-five percent of villages had electricity, and about sixty percent of farm households had television sets.[6] Fifty percent of farmers' children were entering high schools. Farm families were able to enjoy amenities they could not obtain before this movement. Whatever motive the Park government had for starting the Sae-maūl movement, it had beneficial results for Korean society. But this policy did not stop the urban migration.

The Fourth Republic: 1972–1979

Park promulgated the revised constitution in December 1972 and was "reelected" by an electoral college of two thousand locally "elected" deputies of the National Conference for Unification. These ruthless measures infuriated students and intellectuals, who started a national campaign to revise the Yusin constitution in 1973. As their movement gathered momentum, Park issued a dictatorial emergency decree in January 1974 outlawing all such campaigns. In May 1975, he issued Emergency Measure Number Nine, which made it a crime either to criticize the constitution or to provide press coverage of such an activity, subject to a penalty of more than one year's imprisonment. This harsh measure was akin to the measures of the Japanese occupation army during the colonial period. Park, a former Japanese army officer, had learned well how to oppress people.

As during the period of Japanese oppression, the Korean people began to organize opposition against Park. In response, Park incarcerated students and political leaders of the opposition parties. In August 1973, he sent his KCIA agents to Tokyo to kidnap the opposition leader Kim Dae Jung, causing a serious dent in Korean–Japanese relations. In March 1976, prominent political leaders, including the former president of the ROK, Yun Po-sōn, and Kim Dae Jung had issued the Democratic Declaration demanding the restoration of democracy in South Korea. Park arrested them and sent them to prison for terms of five to eight years.

In August 1979, about two hundred Korean women employees of the Y. H. Industrial Company, which had gone bankrupt, demonstrated. The Park government sent out one thousand riot policemen and killed one woman, an unnecessarily harsh response. The "Y. H. Incident" became a rallying cry of Park's opposition and the Korean people. Park's strongarm measures brought disaster to him and his family, as well. In August 1974, a North Korean agent, who had returned from Japan, tried to kill Park in a theater while he was making a speech. The assailant missed Park but killed his wife, who was seated behind him. After that, Park began to shun public places.

Despite opposition, Park maintained his dictatorship. When a general election was held for the National Assembly in December 1978, Park's Democratic Republican Party won only 30.9 percent of the popular vote, against the opposition New Democratic Party's 34.7 percent and the independents' 27.2 percent.[7] However, Park retained control of the Assembly, because he could appoint one-third of its members in addition to the seats won by his party, as provided in his Yusin constitution.

Park's repressive rule came to an abrupt end when his own KCIA chief, Kim Chae-gyu, shot and killed him and his politically powerful chief bodyguard, Ch'a Chi-ch'ōl, in a restaurant gunfight. Kim Chae-gyu was demanding moderation of Park's harsh rule, which he believed would eventually result in disaster for the Park regime. However, Park and Ch'a opposed Kim's idea. Park, who lived by a gun, died by a gun. After Park was killed on October 26,

1979, the prime minister, Choi Kyu-ha, became the acting president, in accordance with the Yusin constitution. Shortly thereafter, Choi was elected president by the electoral college of the National Conference for Unification.[8] Choi was only a caretaker president, lacking support from civilians and military alike. Lieutenant General Chun Doo Hwan (Chōn Tu-hwan), who was in charge of the prosecution of the KCIA chief Kim, used his position effectively and emerged as the new strongman, succeeding Park.

Economic Development During the Third and Fourth Republics

Some people, including Westerners, have attributed South Korea's phenomenal economic development to the authoritarian economic planning of Park's regime. However, this theory is based merely on assumptions. In fact, there is no solid economic development model in the world which indicates that an authoritarian dictatorship would cause economic takeoff, including the model of South Korea. The five-year plans of the authoritarian states of the Communist countries all failed to produce economic progress, compared to the economies of free world countries. Russia, Poland, Cuba, North Korea, and Romania, to name a few, all became economically bankrupt. Non-Communist dictatorships fared no better. Spain, Argentina, Iran, and Iraq remained underdeveloped nations, although all of them were endowed with significant natural resources.

All of these countries, whether they were Communist nations or not, had one thing in common: they were all under dictatorial governments. An authoritarian, dictatorial government inhibits, rather than stimulates, the economic development of a nation, because free enterprise cannot function properly under strict control. The end of Spain's dictatorship brought prosperity to that country, and relaxation of control in Communist China produced rapid economic growth there. Therefore, it is a fallacy to assume that the authoritarian five-year plans of the Park regime created prosperity in South Korea. In fact, every indication is that his dictatorship hindered natural economic progress. Park's regime interrupted the free exchange of ideas, publications, and learning by closing schools, colleges, and newspapers. Tight control of capital movement caused a skewed concentration of wealth and capital in the hands of a few who supported Park in his political game plans. All of these factors inhibited South Korea's economic development.

Despite the factors working against economic development, the nation went through several economic takeoff stages, which finally ranked South Korea among the world's newly industrialized countries (NICs). The economic growth was made possible by the astronomical growth in South Korea's educated human resources, or in other words, trained and educated manpower. Although poor in natural resources, South Korea has people who were unusually motivated to pursue higher education. No government officials told them to pursue higher education. Few government scholarships were ever awarded. However, that did not discourage the people in their drive for education.

In 1945, there were fewer than three thousand college students in all of Korea. The number rose to one hundred thousand in 1960 and reached close to one million in 1980, by the time the Park government came to an end. Korean students majored in mathematics, engineering, science, business, medicine, architecture, and so on, fields vital to the industrialization of a nation. The proportion of students in higher education institutions in Korea was second only to that of the United States.[9] It was the know-how of the Korean people that built Korean industry, not the government of Park or anyone else.

Once South Korea reached an economic takeoff stage, the manufacturing sector functioned as the main stimulus for the economy, growing from fifteen to twenty-one percent per year from 1962 to 1971. This rapid growth took place without much inflation. As a matter of fact, the South Korean (won) currency's value increased in relation to the U.S. dollar. The example of South Korean economic growth rebuts the theory that rapid economic growth accelerates inflation.

Five-Year Economic Plans instituted during the Rhee regime continued under Park. The Park government had four such Five-Year Plans; however, the plans' actual contribution to South Korea's economic development is unknown. In addition to a highly educated labor force, South Korea also has a diligent populace, willing to work an average of fourteen hours per day, six days per week. With that kind of people, a society will make significant economic progress, no matter who heads the government. Indeed, South Korea's economic progress accelerated even faster in the period 1980–1990, after Park was gone.

From 1970 to 1980 (the second ten years of Park's regime), South Korea moved into heavy industry. Steel, shipbuilding, oil refining, automobile construction, electronics, machinery, chemicals, and weaponry were developed on a large scale. By 1990, South Korea could boast of being in the top ten in many of these production capabilities. Some Korean industries were in first or second place in the world.

Foreign Relations with the United States

The United States was hesitant to support the Third Republic at first but maintained close ties with the ROK government on military, economic, and diplomatic affairs. In 1964, the relationship was further strengthened by the ROK government's decision to send combat troops to Vietnam to aid the United States effort there. Park, having seized power illegally, needed firmer support from the United States. This was a good opportunity to obtain such support. The United States needed allies, especially Asian allies, in a difficult war. South Korea had combat-experienced, well-trained troops. Now the ROK had a chance to repay the United States for the help it had provided in Korea's war of survival. The U.S. government welcomed the ROK's decision.

First, South Korea sent a hospital unit, then an engineering battalion, followed by two combat divisions. Almost fifty thousand South Korean troops were stationed in Vietnam on a rotating basis. As many as three hundred thousand troops gained combat experience. As of February 7, 1970, Korean casualties included 3,094 killed, 3,051 wounded, and four missing in action. In addition to combat troops, South Korea sent civilian contractors, technicians, and workers. The South Korean Tiger and White Horse Divisions fought so well that the Vietcong avoided tangling with Korean troops as much as possible. The ROK also received economic benefits from the Vietnam War. The United States purchased considerable amounts of military supplies from South Korea, stimulating the economy. The U.S. President Lyndon B. Johnson paid a personal visit to South Korea in October 1966 to express his appreciation for the Korean participation.

During the period of 1976–1979, South Korea experienced the Jimmy Carter scare. During his presidential campaign in 1976, Carter pledged that, if elected, he would withdraw all combat troops from South Korea. In 1977, he actually withdrew thirty-six hundred troops. However, once in office, Carter discovered that it was far easier to make campaign promises than to carry them out. He had to whittle down his hopes and ideals, because he could not gain majority support for troop withdrawal.[10] The withdrawal of U.S. troops was suspended. However, Carter continued to demand that Park improve human rights in South Korea, causing ROK–United States relations to reach a low ebb.

Foreign Relations with Japan

During the period of Syngman Rhee's government, South Korean relations with Japan had not progressed smoothly. Rhee had been imprisoned and tortured by the Japanese several times for fighting for Korea's freedom from Japan. It may have been difficult for him to forgive past Japanese wrongdoings. Rhee drew a line in the middle of the Eastern Sea (Japan Sea) and imprisoned any Japanese fishermen crossing over the Rhee Line toward the Korean coast. In addition, he demanded several billion U.S. dollars for reparation of past Japanese aggression. Park, having no such personal animosity against the Japanese and having served as a Japanese army officer during World War II, was much more eager to negotiate with the Japanese. The ROK government under Park normalized relations with Japan. Negotiations began in October 1961 and an agreement was reached in June 1965. Reparation was set at a fraction of the amount demanded by the Rhee government. Japanese fishermen were permitted to come within three miles of the Korean coastline. Japan was to provide loans, investments, and capital for South Korean industrialization. This settlement was denounced by the opposition parties, students, and intellectuals as a sellout. In fact, Park initiated the Japanese economic penetration of South Korea. By 1980, Japanese investments in the ROK had reached U.S. $1.7 billion, sixty percent of all foreign investment.[11]

THE FIFTH REPUBLIC: 1981–1987

The Transitional Period

At the time of Park's assassination, he wielded total dictatorship. He was closely supported by his director of the Presidential Security Force, who was assassinated at the same time. The assassination left South Korea in a political vacuum. The assassin, the director of the KCIA, was quickly arrested by the Martial Law Command and was to be executed later. Ch'oi Kyu-ha, the prime minister under Park, was appointed interim president and later was "elected" president by the rubber stamp electoral college installed by Park in December 1979. But Ch'oi had no political base. During this time, several hundred prisoners, including opposition political leaders such as Kim Dae Jung, were released. Emergency Measure Number Nine, used by Park as an instrument for his dictatorship, was abolished. With the political upheaval, Chun Doo Hwan (Chōn Tu-hwan), head of the Defense Security Command, was given the responsibility of investigating Park's assassination. Lieutenant General Chun, using his position, began to dismantle Park's power base by purging Park government elites, then began to build his own base.

While the ROK military, led by Chun, was consolidating, Kim Young Sam (Kim Yōng-sam), head of the New Democratic Party, demanded a new democratic constitution. The demand was ignored. Kim Young Sam, struggling against the Park dictatorship, was now faced with a challenge within his own party, as Kim Dae Jung was released from house arrest. The government party, the Democratic Republican Party, dormant under Park's personal rule, resumed its activity under Kim Chong-p'il. Although political parties became more active, neither interim president Ch'oi nor the three Kims could exercise any real political power. Chun Doo Hwan continued to consolidate his power by replacing the army chief of staff and head of the KCIA with his own men.

The Kwangju Massacre

Students and intellectuals had been the backbone of Korea's struggle against oppressive forces for nearly a century. During the Japanese occupation period, students demonstrated against the Japanese in independence movements, capped with the March 1, 1919, Movement. Students risked their lives in toppling the dictatorial government of Syngman Rhee. During Park's rule, students never ceased the struggle against his dictatorship, forcing him to adopt unpopular measures which further alienated the people.

College and university students numbered nearly one million in 1980, a far greater number than during Rhee's regime. They had become a great political force in South Korea. These indomitable young people began to demonstrate against Chun's rule. Chun answered the students' demonstration with the May 17, 1980, decree closing colleges and universities and the banning of all political gatherings. In addition, Chun imprisoned all three Kims, leaders of the three South Korean political parties. Even harsher than Park, he was determined to seize power by any means.

Kwangju City, the capital of Chōnla Province, was historically known as a bastion of resistance to oppression. Here a great movement had taken place against the Japanese. It was one of the centers of the old Paekche Kingdom, and the people of Kwangju were always suspicious of the people of Kyōngsang Province, where the old Silla Kingdom was located. Both Park and Chun were from Kyōngsang Province, thus, people in Kwangju did not like them. On the morning after Chun issued the new dictatorial decree, on May 18, 1980, about two hundred students from Chōnnam University demonstrated. By afternoon, the crowd had grown to about one thousand. By 4:00 p.m., Special Forces units, paratroopers trained for assault missions, were dispatched under the Martial Law Command. They killed many unarmed people.[12]

From May 20 to May 25, people gathered for memorial services. On May 25, about fifty thousand demonstrated, demanding the end of martial law and the release of their native son, Kim Dae Jung. This time, Chun dispatched a full army division and encircled the city. The army launched an attack on unarmed civilians, killing an unknown number. The official account of those killed exceeded 240; the unofficial estimate was 1,800. Many more thousands of people were wounded. There was little doubt that these troops were under the orders of Chun himself. After massacring these civilians, Chun tightened his grip even further and organized a junta command.

Chun's Junta Government

Chun organized a junta committee, known as the Special Committee for National Security Measures, to implement dictatorial measures. His close associates were three army generals: Lieutenant General Ch'a Kyohōn, deputy chief of staff of the army; Major General Roh Tae Woo (Lo Tae-u), commander of the Capital Garrison Command; and Major General Chōng Ho-yong, commander of the Special Forces. The junta passed laws and decrees normally the responsibilities of the National Assembly. On August 27, 1980, Chun was "elected" president by the National Conference for Unification, receiving 2,524 votes of 2,525. Once Chun became the ROK president, he began weeding out any element he believed to be "antigovernment." These included thousands of government employees, businessmen, bankers, politicians, and media people. Chun's "Cultural Revolution" was taking its toll.

Foreign Relations of the Chun Regime

Just a few months after the Chun junta brutally massacred hundreds, if not thousands, of people at Kwangju, the newly elected president of the United

States, Ronald Reagan, invited the Chuns to the U.S. White House as the Reagans' first official guests. President Reagan expressed his support for Chun, reinforcing Chun's position in Korea. Korean students and intellectuals began to view the United States as another imperialistic power, favoring anybody who supported imperialist interests. Three years later, in November 1983, Reagan reaffirmed his support of Chun by visiting South Korea. This was a vast departure from the Carter administration's demand for the Park regime to improve human rights issues. The students at the demonstrations during Chun's regime shouted "Yankee Go Home" and "American imperialists." Americans, once the liberators and protectors of South Korea and held in high esteem by the Korean people, were now characterized by such terms by some. This was unheard of. The Korean students not only referred to the United States with contempt, but also attacked the U.S. Information Service (USIS) building in Pusan in March 1982 and again in Seoul in May 1985. All of these student actions were expressions of anger against the Chun regime, not really against the United States. However, they were greatly disappointed by U.S. support of Chun, as the Korean students sincerely believed the United States was a bastion of democracy and human rights. Reagan's support also helped Chun's relationship with Japan. In 1983, Chun secured U.S. $4 billion in loans from Japan and was visited by Japan's prime minister, Nakasone. South Korea improved relations with China and the Soviet Union as well, mainly through sporting and social events.

It is sad to state that the Korean people had to have such government. Korea, with more than five thousand years of shining civilization, did not deserve such contemptible leaders, one after another. However, Chun used the power of the armed forces and stayed on as the president of the ROK for seven years.

The Kwangju massacre haunted Chun all through his presidency. After seven years, he turned the presidency over peacefully, something Rhee and Park were unwilling to do. At the end of his term, he apologized to the people for the Kwangju incident and corruption caused by the illegal financial deals of his in-laws and went to a secluded mountain temple to repent. During Chun's regime, South Korea was rapidly industrialized, and a foreign trade surplus was attained (although Chun had nothing to do with the nation's sustained economic growth). This type of social and economic upsurge had happened many times in the history of Korea. The Korean phoenix was rising again from the ashes of the Korean War.

End of Chun's Rule

Having forcibly seized power, Chun never gained the trust of the people. However, he used the power of the armed forces to remain the president of the Republic of Korea for seven years. There were constant disturbances by students, which, in the end, brought down his regime. Chun hand-picked his successor, Roh Tae Woo, handing over the presidency to him on June 29, 1987.

Thus ended the Fifth Republic. However, the deeds Chun committed to gain power and the corruption of his presidency did not fade away. Eight years later, on December 3, 1995, he was formally charged with critical offenses by the prosecution officials of the South Korean government. Chun was charged with violating military–criminal codes by leading the 1979 military coup. Six insurrection charges were filed, calling for the death penalty. In addition, Chun was also charged with corruption in accepting U.S. $900 million in bribes and killing more than 240 unarmed civilians at Kwangju City in May 1980 (see Chapter 21). He was arrested and jailed.

THE SIXTH REPUBLIC

During the Fifth Republic there was a lingering question about the legitimacy of the government because the Yusin Constitution, on which Chun based his presidency, was the product of the dictatorial Park Chung Hee. Chun was "elected" president of the ROK through government-appointed "electoral college" representatives, not by vote of the people. It was an undemocratic, illegal government, engineered by the army officers. The Park and Chun military dictatorships together held power for twenty-five years. The people of South Korea and political parties demanded solutions to these problems. The army officers realized that they could not hold on to power without massive bloodshed.

Roh Tae Woo, the former army officer designated to succeed Chun, had to amend the constitution to realign its terms with those of the First Republic. The latest constitution required a popular, direct vote for the president, with a five-year term. It also eliminated the appointee system of one-third of the National Assembly members, which guaranteed government control of the congress. It also guaranteed freedom to pursue political activities, as well as freedom of the press, assembly, and speech.

With this new constitution, the Sixth Republic was born on June 29, 1987, and Roh Tae Woo was elected by the people as president. It was the first direct election in sixteen years in South Korea. Roh had to meet all the demands of the opposition. He initiated a roundtable conference with the opposition leaders on a regular basis. These reforms were made possible by the incessant student demonstrations against the military government and Chun's autocratic rule. The military realized that it could not continue its dictatorial way of governing.

On April 26, 1988, an election was held to select the thirteenth National Assembly. The result showed clearly the people's preference to end the military domination. The ruling Democratic Justice Party (DJP) failed to win a working majority. The combination of opposition parties commanded the majority. They were Kim Dae Jung's party for Peace and Democracy (PPD), Kim Young Sam's Reunification Democratic Party (RDP), and Kim Chong P'il's New Democratic Republican Party (NDRP). The National Assembly established a special panel to review irregularities and ill effects of the Fifth Republic as a major task to prevent future recurrences. The panels reviewed the governmental irregularities, the Kwangju incident of 1980, claims of election fraud, controversial laws, and regional rivalry.

In January 1990, the ruling party, DJP, combined its forces with Kim Young Sam's RDP and Kim Chong P'il's NDRP to create a new majority party, the Democratic Liberal Party. In this new party, Kim Young Sam, who had been fighting for civilian rule and democracy, became the leader.[13] Kim Young Sam was willing to join the government party, DJP, as long as he became the party leader. The merger of the parties gave Kim an opportunity to gain control of the government.

Five years after the Sixth Republic was initiated, the second direct election by the people was held. Kim Young Sam, a civilian, was elected president in June 1992. A civilian was finally elected president, thirty-one years after the military took over the ROK government by force. The new government has been functioning well, although there have been some student demonstrations. No students have been killed so far. The ROK is on the right political track, with sustained continuous economic growth. Although South Korea is headed in the right direction toward democracy, there is no guarantee that it will continue to do so, unless the people maintain vigilance against power-hungry people such as Park and Chun. An intelligence network may be necessary to prevent domestic or foreign takeover of government, whether military or otherwise.

In November 1995, it was revealed that the former South Korean President, Roh Tae Woo, who began the Sixth Republic, was the central figure of a massive financial scandal. Roh was accused of creating a secret U.S. $650 million slush fund for himself, hiding the money away in someone else's name. Roh, who was seemingly more democratic than his predecessors Park and Chun, appeared to have been as corrupt financially. The corrupt leaders in the Korean government had sapped the national strength of Korea during the second half of the Li Dynasty, eventually destroying Korea's nationhood. Such recurrent corruption of Korean leaders seems to indicate that they have not yet awakened after the harsh Japanese experience and the division of the country.

THE ECONOMY OF SOUTH KOREA TO THE 1990s

The South Korean economy was almost totally destroyed by the Korean War. As noted, the 1950s were the years for reconstruction of the destroyed economy. Koreans did not waste their time, but used every available resource for education of the young for future expansion of Korea's economy. The building of human resources began to pay off at the beginning of the 1960s, and especially in the 1970s and 1980s. Real gross domestic product (GDP) grew from U.S. $2.3 billion in 1962, to U.S. $223 billion in 1991, and U.S. $445 billion in 1994. Per Capita GDP increased from a meager U.S. $87 in 1962, to U.S. $5,569 in 1991 and U.S. $7,660 in 1994.[14,15] By the end of 1995, South

Korea's GDP at purchasing power parity was U.S. $547 billion, according to the U.S. Central Intelligence Agency *Factbook* report for 1995. This meant that South Korea's per capita GDP exceeded U.S. $12,600, with a population of about forty-five million in 1995 (see Chapter 21). This per capita GDP of South Korea (U.S. $7,660 for 1994) may be compared to other Asian nations' per capita GDP for 1994: the Philippines, U.S. $850; Vietnam, U.S. $170; Indonesia, U.S. $740; China, U.S. $490; Thailand, U.S. $2,110; India, U.S. $300. Most of these nations became independent at about the same time as South Korea. These countries, except Vietnam, did not have war, as South Korea had. Compared to this exceptional South Korean economic expansion, North Korea had a total GDP of U.S. $22.9 billion, and per capita GDP of U.S. $1,038 in 1991 (see the discussion of the North Korean economy in Chapter 18). North Korean GDP has decreased at the rate of five percent per year since 1990, and the decline had continued in the mid-1990s.

An average worker in South Korea earned U.S. $868 per month in 1989,[16] a respectable amount considering the lower living costs in South Korea than in United States or Japan. Surveys of income distribution in South Korea in 1985 and 1988 showed that average household income had risen an average of 14.8 percent per year, from U.S. $8,645 to U.S. $13,081.[17] Again, the purchasing power of the same amount of money in Korea was far greater than in the United States or Japan. Less than ten percent of the population in South Korea lived below the poverty line, compared to over thirty percent in the United States.

The central sector of South Korea's economic development was manufacturing. Steel production increased from 0.5 million ton in 1970 to 19.1 million tons in 1988, with an annual average increase rate of 11.7 percent. South Korea had become one of the major steel producers in the world.[18] The electronics industry produced U.S. $106 million worth of goods in 1970. This was increased to U.S. $23,531 million in 1988, an annual growth rate of thirty-five percent. The world's largest computer-chip-producing firm in 1990 was Korean. Motor vehicle production was 28,920 units in 1970; by 1989, it had increased to 1,869,000 units. South Korea was one of the major auto producers of the world in the 1990s. The shipbuilding industry of South Korea was second only to that of Japan in the late 1980s; by the second half of 1993, South Korea's shipbuilding orders from foreign countries had topped Japan's. Thus, South Korea became the largest shipbuilder in the world; total ships exported totaled U.S. $1.76 billion in 1989. South Korea also became a major producer of petrochemicals. The production increased from 671,000 tons in 1970 to 2,814,000 tons in 1988. Fertilizer production was 1,703,000 tons in 1988.

South Korea's growth in foreign trade and capital formation was even more astounding. Because of rapid industrialization, South Korea had to import capital goods, such as factory machinery, producing an imbalance in foreign trade and increases in foreign debts until 1985. The trade deficit peaked in 1980, with U.S. $-4.38 billion. This was reduced to a mere U.S. $-19 million by

1985. However, once South Korea became industrialized, the trade imbalance turned in its favor, as noted in Table 17.1.

Table 17.1
Balance of Payments on Trade (in U.S. $ Millions)

1975	-1,671
1980	-4,384
1985	-19
1986	+4,206
1987	+7,659
1988	+11,561

Source: Louis R. Mortimer (ed.), *South Korea* (Washington, D.C.: Federal Reserve Division, Library of Congress, 1992), 336.

By 1988, South Korea's annual trade surplus reached U.S. $11.5 billion. However, this did not include hidden earnings of foreign surplus from tourist visits and Korean workers' overseas earnings sent home. In the late 1980s and early 1990s, more than one million Japanese tourists visited South Korea annually, and about two hundred thousand Korean workers were employed in projects overseas, mostly in the Middle East and Southeast Asia. The hidden inflow of annual foreign income from these sources was estimated to be U.S. $5–$10 billion in the early 1990s.

The total of exports from South Korea increased from a mere U.S. $60 million in 1961, to U.S. $ 60.7 billion in 1988, an increase of more than one thousand times in less than thirty years.[19]

Capital formation in South Korea was no less dramatic. Because of its capital investments in massive factories, in the period of 1970 to 1985, South Korea's investments exceeded domestic savings. As a result, Korea had to rely on foreign funds, mostly in the form of loans. This equaled about seven percent of gross national product (GNP) in the first half of the 1960s, rising to 9.3 percent in 1970. However, this situation has now been reversed. South Korea has been recording more savings than investments by eight percent since 1986.[20] South Korea turned into a creditor nation from a prolonged status of a debtor nation in 1989 (see Table 17.2).

Table 17.2
External Debt and Assets (in U.S. $100 Million)

	1987	1988	1989
Total External Debt (A)	356	312	285
Total External Assets (B)	132	239	315
Net External Debt (A minus B); (surplus)	224	73	-30
(External Exchange Holding)	(36	124	200)

Source: Korean Overseas Information Service, *The Handbook of Korea* (Seoul: Korean Overseas Information Service, 1990), 369.

At the end of 1985, South Korea owed U.S. $46.8 billion to foreign creditors, making it the fourth largest debtor in the world. However, both total and net amounts of foreign debt outstanding began to decrease in 1986, as a result of a surplus in foreign trade and domestic savings. Domestic savings grew dramatically from 1986 to 1987, thirty-three percent to thirty-six percent,[21] and continued thereafter. South Korea was able to reduce foreign debt gradually and accumulate external assets through the promotion of exports on credits and overseas investments. South Korea became a creditor country in 1989.[22] The trade balance between South Korea and the United States was U.S. $8.7 billion in favor of South Korea in 1988. However, a strong effort was made to balance trade with the United States. Seoul had brought this figure down to almost nothing by the early 1990s.

South Korea began to invest heavily in the oil-rich countries of the Middle East as well as Indonesia in the late 1980, and in Russia in the 1990's, in order to secure petroleum, which South Korea lacks and needs greatly. South Korea formed partnerships with Indonesia and the new Russia for oil exploration. By 1994, many thousands of South Korean businessmen, engineers, and technicians were in Russia for three major industries: oil, fisheries, and lumber. South Korea granted U.S. $2 billion in foreign aid to Russian in 1993, after two visits by Russian President Boris Yeltsin. Total South Korean investments in Russia reached an estimated several billion U.S. dollars. South Korean companies such as Samsung electronics and Lotte department stores had become well established in Russia by 1994. By the mid-1990s, South Korea was the only Asian nation which was welcomed into Russia. Japan and China were not quite so well received.

The total direct foreign investment in South Korea during the period of 1962 to 1986 had amounted to U.S. $3.631 billion.[23] Direct foreign investment was a small fraction of Korea's economy. Of this, Japan accounted for 52.2 percent and the United States 29.6 percent. In 1987, Japan invested U.S. $494 million, or 44.9 percent of the total U.S. $1.1 billion of foreign investments, mostly in hotels and tourism, to offset some of the spending by the more than one million Japanese tourists who visited Korea annually. One of the major South Korean export items was construction. By 1982, South Korea had racked up U.S. $50 billion in construction contracts to other countries, most of them in the Middle East and Southeast Asia.[24]

In the introduction to *Korea's Man-Made Miracle*, published in 1983, Jon Woronoff states "While the very speed of this [South Korea's] resurgence makes it appear exceptional, perhaps even miraculous, it is only the sort wrought by man. Human beings were Korea's only real natural resource, and even that showed little promise until, in the early 1960s, something happened." This author might add that Korea's human resource development, the fruit of the radical expansion of education during the period 1945–1960, began to ripen in the early 1960s and eventually yielded the miraculous economic expansion of South Korea in the 1980s and 1990s. South Korea has come a long way since

Woronoff's book of 1983, as the true economic miracle of South Korea took place after 1985, far surpassing what Woronoff could have imagined in 1983. This was one more repeat of the resurgence of the Korean people, which has happened so many times in the history of Korea. South Korea had more Ph.D.'s than any other nation in 1990, in terms of population, including the United States. Many of these Ph.D.'s were earned in the United States. In July 1995, when editors of *Business Week* magazine interviewed South Korea's President Kim Young Sam, he stated that South Korea had reached the per capita income mark of U.S. $10,000 in 1995 and will reach U.S. $20,000 in the year 2000. He said that at the turn of the twenty-first century, South Korea's economy will pass the $1 trillion GNP mark. *Business Week* editors noted that South Korea "could well become the first country to establish itself as an Advanced Industrial Power in the world since the emergence of Japan."[25] This was no surprise to people who knew that Korea had attained the highest level of civilization many times in the past, rising from the ashes of near-total destruction of wars. The rapid development of the South Korean economy since the Korean War is no exception.

18

North Korea: 1950–1990s

KIM IL SUNG AND POLITICAL DEVELOPMENTS

The history of North Korea was dominated by one man, Kim Il Sung (Kim Il Sŏng), from 1945 until his death in 1994. Many people considered Kim Il Sung a fake, because he took the name (known to many older Koreans) of a freedom fighter known before this latter Kim Il Sung was born in 1912. This latter Kim Il Sung's given name was Kim Sŏng-ju.

Whether Kim was a fake or not, he had one advantage which other North Korean political leaders lacked. He acquired the ability to communicate in the Russian language with the Soviet commanders of the occupational forces of North Korea, a skill he learned while he was in Far Eastern maritime Russia for five years (see Chapter 14, the section, Korean Partisan in the Korean–Manchurian Region). Kim Il Sung was also helped by his first wife, Kim Chŏng-suk, who also spoke Russian. A vivacious and generous lady, she always cooked enormous amounts of food for the hungry Soviet generals when they visited Kim's house. For this, the Soviets liked her.[1]

The Soviet generals did not trust any native Korean political leaders. Kim, who was a Soviet army officer and had lived in Russia for many years, was considered a part of the Soviet army. Therefore, he was in a unique position to connect the Soviet Union to North Korea. Kim was set up by the Soviets to lead the Koreans, and to help Soviet occupation forces administer the Soviet policies in North Korea.

Kim Il Sung, who was a minor guerrilla unit leader in Manchuria, did not have a significant following in North Korea among Koreans, notwithstanding his special connections with the Soviet generals. In order to gather support of Koreans, he had to use several front men. A Nationalist leader, Cho Man-sik, was one. As soon as his usefulness was gone, he disappeared, and was never heard from again. There were two other powerful Communist groups, the Yenan (Yan'an) group, who returned from Communist China, headed by Kim Tu-bong, and the South Korean Communist group, led by Pak Hōn-yōng, who was from South Korea. Both groups had a longer history in the Communist movement than Kim Il Sung's group.

Kim Il Sung's group had one advantage over the others. It was a newer group and much more active. His group arrived in Korea in October 1945, two months after the liberation of North Korea. Kim Il Sung was introduced by the Soviet commanders to the Korean people as the national hero who had fought for Korea's independence. Kim's group had the support of the Soviet Union from the beginning (see Chapter 15, the section, North Korea: August 1945–September 1948).

Kim Il Sung and his backers launched an image-building propaganda campaign early in 1946, which never ceased up to his death in 1994. Many of those claims formulated to build up his image were not founded in truth. However, they were effective in convincing masses of North Korean people that their *Widae-han Chidoja* (great leader) had performed unimaginable, wonderful feats. The way Kim Il Sung built himself up to be "the great leader" was almost unconscionable, even megalomaniacal. He had his own statue erected everywhere, some as high as ten-story buildings. He made his birthplace a national shrine while he was still alive. Even the kings of old dynasties in Korea would not dare do such things. However, Kim did so without hesitation; there was no trace of modesty in him. Kim's propaganda machine was in operation, full power, endlessly. Young children of North Korea were brainwashed continuously. Thus, he created a nationwide Kim Il Sung cult, which worshipped him as a demigod.

The North Korean dictatorship under Kim had been the most rigid, irrational regime seen anywhere in the world, including Communist and third world nations. Since the late 1940s, from twelve to fourteen percent of the population of North Korea has been enrolled in the Communist party, compared with one to three percent party enrollment in most Communist countries.[2] Kim's control of the North Korean population was complete. In 1949, as Kim Il Sung was contemplating the invasion of South Korea, in order to gain support of South Korean Communists, the Korean Workers' Party (KWP) was formed by the merger of the Communist parties of North Korea and South Korea. This South Korean element was headed by Pak Hōn-yōng.

The Korean War venture was a total disaster for Kim Il Sung and North Korea (Chapter 15). Kim Il Sung was largely responsible for over three million deaths in the war; many millions more were wounded. Almost all of the factories in North Korea, which the Japanese had left behind, were destroyed, including hydroelectric plants destroyed by American B-29 bombers. The North Korean cities were in ruins. The North Korean population in 1950, when the war started, was 9.62 million. However, over 500,000 people were killed, and another 650,000 North Koreans escaped to South Korea during the war, reducing the population to 8.49 million by 1953.[3] North Korea lost more than ten percent of its population as a result of the war started by Kim Il Sung.

Despite the fact that the Korean War adversely affected North Korea, Kim Il Sung used it to his political advantage. Once he found out that the South Korean Communists were of no more use to him, Kim set out to use the domestic Communists, mostly from South Korea, as scapegoats for the disasters of the Korean War. Pak Hōn-yōng and his twelve associates were falsely accused as American spies and were executed in 1953. In the mid-1950s, Kim eliminated both the Soviet and Yenan factions of the Communists to become the undisputed dictator of North Korea by 1958. The Korean guerrillas, including Kim Il Sung and Ch'oe Yōng-gōn of the Korean People's Army, who fought against the Japanese army in Manchuria, had proved to be too tough for any other political groups in North Korea. Kim Il Sung and his associates of the former Korean guerrilla forces in the Korean–Manchurian border region near the Paekdu Mountains seized complete control of North Korean politics, economy, and society. These conditions continued into the 1990s. The backbone of the power of Kim Il Sung was the faithful Korean People's Army (KPA), controlled by former partisans.

THE *CHUCH'E* (SELF RELIANCE) IDEA OF NORTH KOREA

Chuch'e has been Kim Il Sung's political philosophy, which has influenced North Korea's political, military, economic, and social events for four decades. North Korea is a totalitarian state that has almost no comparison in the modern history of the world. This *Chuch'e* idea determined every possible segment of North Korean lives.

In the word *Chuch'e, chu* means "main; master; self." This root is used to form such words as *chu-jang* (self-assertion), *chu-ui* (ideology), *chu-gwan* (main thought). *Ch'e* means "body; organization." This forms such words as *sin-ch'e* (physical body), and *tan-ch'e* (organization). *Chuch'e* could be translated, word for word, as the main body or self-asserted organization. This was the sort of "Kim-Il-Sung"ism which emphasized the self-reliance of a nation which aimed for all things done in North Korea to be done to benefit the nation of North Korea and no other nation.

It was a form of nationalism. However, Kim Il Sung denied that it was nationalism; he called it socialistic patriotism. Kim failed to describe the difference between nationalistic patriotism and socialistic patriotism. North Korea applied this concept in practice, becoming a nation that is abnormal by world standards. Kim Il Sung and his associates had an attitude of contempt of world public opinion, policies, or agreements between nations. As long as they considered that any international agreement was not in the interests of North Korea, they did not hesitate to change or discard it. The policy-makers' opinions varied from period to period, and even among themselves. Any international agreement signed with North Korea was good only as long as it agreed with their self-conceived national interests. This was the reason North Korea has vacillated on such international agreements as the Treaty of Non-Proliferation of Nuclear Weapons.

The *Chuch'e* idea was enforced in the economic development and military expansion of North Korea. The planned economy of North Korea eventually stagnated, to the point that after 1991, the North Korean GNP actually began to decline from a total of only U.S. $22.9 billion by five percent per year.[4] This pales in comparison to South Korea's total GNP of U.S. $237.9 billion in that same year. North Korea's self-contained economy was less than one-tenth the size of South Korea's, an economy that was still expanding rapidly in international markets in the early 1990s.

North Korea's *Chuch'e*, or self-reliance principle gave the nation a rapid military expansion from 650,000 troops in 1979 to 1.2 million in 1994, while South Korea steadily maintained a little over 650,000 troops. For North Korea, which has one-tenth of the South Korean economic power, and only fifty percent of the population, with twenty-one million people in 1991, the maintenance of such a large force has been a heavy burden, which cannot be sustained for very long. *Chuch'e* in North Korean military terms was clearly causing a severe strain on every aspect of North Korean society. In 1989, the North Korean military expenditure was U.S. $6 billion, or about thirty percent of the total GNP of that nation.[5] South Korea, on the other hand, spent U.S. $9 billion, or fifty percent more than North Korea spent in 1989, as the South Korean national military became highly sophisticated, with the latest high technological weapons. South Korea has a well-trained, battle-experienced reserve of 1.24 million to back up the modern army. The total military expenditure of U.S. $9 billion amounts to only four percent of South Korea's total GNP and does not cause any strain on the society. It is obvious that *Chuch'e* yields no solutions to North Korea's many problems.

Kim Il Sung began to talk about *Chuch'e* in 1955, when he was involved in the power struggle with the pro-Soviet faction in North Korea. On December 28, 1955, Kim delivered his first speech about *Chuch'e*, while attacking his political foe Pak Ch'ang-Ok, the leader of the Soviet–Korean group. He demanded that North Korea's imitation of the Soviet Union be stopped.[6] Once the Soviet–Korean political influence was removed, he did not mention it again until 1963.[7] Therefore, Kim's *Chuch'e* had been politically motivated from the beginning.

During the period from 1955 to 1963, when Kim never talked about *Chuch'e*, Kim paid frequent visits to the Soviet Union and the People's Republic of China to elicit financial aid. However, the best he could obtain was short-term loans, which he had to pay back in short order. China was far more generous than Russia, because while the Soviet Union demanded repayment of all the loans, China forgave some. In the meantime, China had gone through political and economic convulsions of its own. The Great Leap Forward of

1958–1960 was a total failure, reducing China's production by as much as forty percent in some sectors. Then there was the Cultural Revolution, followed by the rampage of China's Red Guards, who labeled Kim Il Sung a revisionist. Kim was condemned in China.

The Sino–Soviet dispute had intensified in the late 1950s and 1960s, and Kim took a neutral stance. However, he was forced to accept the position that North Korea must stand alone and survive. In truth, *Chuch'e* was forced upon him whether he liked it or not. Kim never had a formal higher education and was not a Marxist–Leninist theoretician. Yet he tried to tie his *Chuch'e* idea to Marxism–Leninism. It did not work, because the Communist ideology of Marxism–Leninism was irrelevant to "Kim Il Sung"ism, the self-reliance of a nation. Nevertheless, Kim spent a great deal of money to export his idea to the third world countries, creating schools which preached *Chuch'e*, entirely supported by funds from the scarce financial resources of North Korea. There is no indication that this attempt produced any results for North Korea.

In reality, Kim's actions speak louder than his idea or his words. Despite all his talk of government for the benefit of the people, his totalitarian actions enslaved the North Korean people in a way unseen in any other nation. In fact, his actions bespeak an individual captivated by the idea of establishing a dynasty, with his oldest son, Kim Jung Il, his successor. Transmitting political power by blood relation is, in fact, a sin in the Communist world; no other Communist nation ever attempted to establish lineage in this manner of old-time kingship. Kim Il Sung was nothing more than a self-interested monarchist in this regard.

NORTH KOREAN ECONOMIC DEVELOPMENT

The South Korean economic system was founded on capitalistic principles, and the North Korean economy is based on the Communist system, with total control by the state. These nations provide a model of contrasting economic systems. The contrast is unparalleled, except by the German example of East and West. The Korean example is more meaningful because of the relative sizes of North and South, and the same type of beginnings. These two economies have produced such huge differences in industry, total GNP, and per capita incomes that the North Korean economy was at a level of only three percent of the South Korean economy by 1995. This difference developed in only thirty years, in the period from 1965 to 1995.

The South Korean economy grew as a function of a natural market economy of supply and demand. Governmental control played very little role in South Korea's economic growth. As a matter of fact, the South Korean government's efforts to interfere with the economy through five-year plans had adverse effects (see the discussion of the South Korean economy in Chapter 17).

The North Korean economy was based on a series of North Korean Governmental Development Plans: the Two-Year Plans of 1947–1948 and

1949–1950; the Three-Year Post-War Reconstruction Plan of 1954–1956; the Five-Year Plan of 1957–1960; the first Seven-Year Plan of 1961–1967, which was extended three years, to 1970, to strengthen the defense industry; the Six-Year Plan of 1971–1976; the second Seven-Year Plan of 1978–1984; and the Third Seven-Year Plan of 1987–1993.

The North Korean economy developed rapidly in the first twelve years, until 1960, by which time it had grown at a rate of thirty percent and twenty-one percent.[8] This was possible because the economic expansion was caused by reconstruction of war damages. The North Korean government was able to marshal labor and materials in a concentrated effort to rebuild an almost totally destroyed economy. Simple economic principle dictated that when there was a very low level of economic base, any additional input would produce a quick increase in rate of production. However, as this continued, the law of diminishing returns set in. Also, all the work done to reconstruct the destroyed cities and their results were taken into account as part of the growth. However, once these works were completed, the rate of growth for the North Korean economy began to slow after 1960.

North Korea had a population of ten million in 1960 against South Korea's twenty-five million. South Korea's economy grew slowly until its educated manpower could effectively generate eventual general economic growth, at the beginning of the 1960s. North Korea, which could forcibly allocate raw labor, produced a higher rate of per capita national output than South Korea, although the total GNP was still smaller than South Korea's until 1960. However, North Korea began to have economic difficulties and economic growth slowed, while South Korea reached the stage of economic takeoff in the mid-1960s and grew at an annual rate varying between ten and fifteen percent. For thirty years, South Korea maintained sustained economic growth, seldom falling below the ten percent level in any year.

North Korea, in the meantime, experienced difficulty in planning, allocation of resources, bureaucratic mismanagement, political favoritism, and transportation bottlenecks. For example, after the Five-Year Plan ended in 1960, the government lacked a succeeding plan and spent more than a year formulating the first Seven-Year Plan. North Korea formulated the *Ch'ŏllima* (flying horse that can fly one thousand li in one hour) mass production economic plan, modeled after China's Great Leap Forward in 1958, forcing people to produce more in all sectors of the economy. Similar to the profound failure of China's economic plan, *Ch'ŏllima* produced chaos in all sectors of the North Korean economy. More forced input of raw labor, driving people to work unreasonable numbers of hours, eventually exhausted people after a few years, just as in the Chinese economic example. The economic principle of diminishing returns came into play. The first Seven-Year Plan of North Korea was a failure. The unsatisfactory results forced them to extend the plan to ten years. The subsequent Six-Year Plan and the second Seven-Year Plan were both disappointing. North Korea had to roll the goals over into the next plans.

While the South Korean economy went through a second takeoff stage in the 1980s and expanded rapidly into world markets, the North Korean economy bogged down to a no-growth situation in the second half of the 1980s. In fact, it began to decline in 1991, at the rate of 5.2 percent per year, and this decline has continued through the 1990s. The North Koreans have been secretive about this fact, and definite economic figures are scarce. However, economists know that North Korea had less than one-tenth the GNP of South Korea, U.S. $22.9 billion (North Korea) against U.S. $237.9 billion (South Korea) in 1991. The per capita income of North Korea was U.S. $1,038 in 1990, compared to South Korea's U.S. $5,569 in the same year. North Korea keeps its economic figures secret. However, the total GNP of North Korea dropped to below the estimate of U.S. $20 billion in 1994. In contrast, South Korea's GNP grew to about U.S. $329 billion, with per capita GNP of U.S. $7,660 in 1994.[9] A more striking fact was that the North Korean per capita income sank to less than U.S. $800, while the South Korean per capita income was approaching the level of U.S. $10,000 in the mid-1990s (see the discussion of the South Korean economy in Chapter 17). South Korea's economy has been expanding at an average of nine percent in the 1990s, while the North Korean economy has been shrinking at an estimated rate of five percent per year.

The world's economists classified South Korea as a newly industrialized country (NIC) in the early 1990s, and it moved into the rank of the advanced industrialized powers of the world in the mid-1990s, the only such development except the Japanese model. Such a classification was given to only a few countries, that is, South Korea and Brazil, among more than 150 developing countries in the world in the fifty-year period since the end of the Second World War. South Korea went through a devastating war; Brazil did not. Yet South Korea rose to the level of a truly industrialized nation, more so than some of the Western European nations.

North Korea is far from the NIC categorization as yet. North Koreans are also Koreans who are industrious. With the proper political and economic climate, they have the capacity to do as the South Koreans have. In this regard, the South Korean business firms have begun to show a keen interest in expanding their business in the North. After all, they are already involved in business enterprises on a large scale in Communist China, and they do significant amounts of business with the Soviet Union. Perhaps the commercial cooperation of North and South might provide the basis of reunification of a German type, if a politically initiated reunification is impossible.

One point is quite certain: the cocoon concept of Kim Il Sung's *Chuch'e* was a serious mistake. It simply did not work. The new Russia and Eastern European countries turned to free enterprise, and even Communist China would rather trade with South Korea than North Korea. North Korea has become increasingly isolated from the world politically and economically. This isolation has become even more severe since North Korea defaulted on several billion dollars' worth of loans in late 1976 and acquired notoriety among nations. Interest was mounting on the unpaid loans, and U.S. $6.78 billion was owed in 1989, increasing to U.S. $7.86 billion in 1990. It has been this way not only in economic matters, but also with international treaties and agreements. North Korea has discarded international agreements without any reason given. As pointed out in earlier chapters, northern Koreans, unlike southern Koreans, have had the tendency to be untrustworthy. The history of betrayal by northern Koreans goes back many centuries. There have been numerous rebellions and treasonous betrayals.

The South Korean *Chaebol* (business conglomerates) such as Hyundai and Daewoo have had business contacts with North Korea since 1989. Daewoo, for example, signed a U.S. $30 million contract to invest in North Korea in 1992, with the agreement that North Korea would provide labor and land. Any agreement must be carefully safeguarded, lest North Koreans violate it without hesitation. It is in North Korea's self-interest to be trustworthy.

As North Korea has become increasingly isolated, its leaders have begun to develop closer ties with renegade regimes in Iran, Iraq, and Libya, forming a sort of outlaw group. There remains a question of nuclear armament by this group. Nuclear armament is a wrong approach and will not solve the problems of North Korea. It may bring some oil or cash in the short term. However, North Korea has been risking international contempt on a long-term basis, which will make the country an international outcast. For many years to come, North Korea will face economic difficulties. The only solution may come from two sources, Japan and South Korea, especially South Korea, the archrival. The general economic condition of North Korea, including agriculture, has been getting worse year by year, to such an extent that in 1995 many people in North Korea were dying of starvation. As if to underwrite such a report, North Korea purchased three hundred thousand tons of rice from Thailand, and in May 1995, it turned to its archrivals South Korea and Japan for help with an emergency supply of rice, in the range of one million tons. This was unheard of for North Korea, a nation which always depicted itself as a worker's paradise. The reality had finally caught up with the make-believe. The cause of most of the problems was the overburdened North Korean economy, which had been taxed beyond its capacity to maintain a standing military force of 1.2 million people.

On June 21, 1995, after five days of secret talks with South Korean representatives in Beijing, setting aside pride and the self-reliance idea, impoverished North Korea agreed to accept U.S. $270 million, including one hundred fifty thousand tons of rice, in emergency aid from South Korea.[10] This aid money bought shipments of food from Japan as well. Historically, Koreans had proved that they were indeed a compassionate people, who aided even their enemies in distress. That is the mark of a civilized people (Chapter 14, the section, the End of World War II and Korea's Liberation). South Korean aid was more proof that South Korea and North Korea must unify.

MYSTERY MAN KIM JUNG IL (KIM CHŌNG-IL) AND HIS POWER BASE

In order to guarantee the succession of power by his son, Kim Jung Il, and thereby extend the Kim dynasty of North Korea, Kim Il Sung carefully groomed his son for succession for over twenty years. Citing his failing eyesight (perhaps a pretext), Kim Il Sung let his son control videotaped inputs needed for final decisions involving every detail of state affairs. Before his death on July 8, 1994, Kim Il Sung appointed his son supreme commander of the Korean People's Army, with the rank of marshal. Thus, the younger Kim became the head of the North Korean armed forces. He also became the chairman of the DPRK National Defense Commission. These were two of the most powerful defense positions in North Korea. Yet puzzles remain. Nearly three years after his father's death, Kim Jung Il had failed to gain his father's topmost positions, that of the general secretary of the Workers' Party of Korea (WPK) and president of the Democratic People's Republic of Korea (DPRK).

Kim Il Sung, in order to build Kim Jung Il's power base, surrounded him with longtime faithful partisan members, giving them high-ranking positions and privileges. In North Korea Kim Il Sung stood alone as the military leader, known as *Tae-wōnsu* (great marshal), above all other military personnel. However, after his death, the other military leaders became more visible. Most of Kim Jung Il's public appearances were related to the military, and the younger Kim's entourage was composed of military personnel.[11] Before October 8, 1995, Kim Jung Il was the only marshal in North Korea. But on that day, Choe Guang and Li Ul-sol were both promoted to the rank of marshal. In 1996, Kim Jung Il was sharing the rank of marshal with two others. This could have meant the transfer of power within the North Korean military from sole control to shared control. Neither the Central Committee of the Worker's Party of Korea nor the Supreme People's Assembly (SPA) of the DPRK met for two years after the death of Kim Il Sung. The SPA normally approved North Korea's annual budget and settled the previous year's accounts. Who controlled the national budget became a mystery.

There were other puzzling questions about Kim Jung Il. He never made public speeches. His longest utterance was on April 25, 1992, when he read one sentence from a written note, shouting "Glory to the officers and soldiers of the heroic Korean People's Army."[12] His father had made annual speeches at the SPA, some lasting as long as three to four hours. And public speeches were required of the head of the Communist state. Kim Jung Il's inability to speak in public may have seriously affected his ability to carry out his duties as head of the North Korean armed forces or as the head of the government. This may have been one of several reasons that both the SPA and the WPK were suspended, because Kim Jung Il did not deliver required speeches or lead these organizations. Both the SPA and the WPK are bodies of the people's representations. Without them the people are completely shut off from the government. The North Korean military was given more power than ever before. Three KPA generals were promoted to vice-marshal (equivalent to a five-star rank) in October 1995, making a total of eight vice-marshals. There were a total of eleven marshals, including Kim Jung Il, in the North Korean military. Military expenditures in North Korea were twenty five percent of the total GNP, and more than fifty percent of the government's gross revenue in 1995. In order to consolidate his power base, the military, Kim Jung Il had sweetened military leadership with large-scale promotions in 1995–1996. These military leaders and their families, including the second generation of old partisan members, most of whom were midlevel military, formed a special privileged class. As long as they were loyal to Kim Jung Il, his position was secure. It is believed that Kim Il Sung planned it this way. To strengthen its position, North Korean leadership demanded that the people work harder and put in longer hours. There was further indoctrination in 1995–1996.

The key figures who supported Kim Jung Il in 1996 were Choe Guang, Minister of Defense; Kim Yong-chun, Chief of General Staff; Kim Guang-jin, Vice Minister; Li Ul-sol, Chief of the Guard Bureau; Choe Myong-nok, Chief of the Political Bureau of the Military. All of these people were marshals or deputy marshals with five-star-general ranking. They were in their seventies and eighties, hard-line, former partisans who had fought against the Japanese army in the Korean–Manchurian border areas in the 1930s–1940s. Although Kim Jung Il represented a military regime of the North Korean government, he was never a proficient military leader. When he was young, he was sent to East Germany to attend the East German Air Force Academy. But he flunked the courses and could not finish the school. He was installed by his father as the head of the military, so that Kim Jung Il could continue the dynasty of the Kim family founded by Kim Il Sung. This Kim dynasty cast doubt about the future unification of Korea, because such an event would destroy the power base of Kim Jung Il.

There was another aspect to Kim Jung Il. He seemed to be interested in motion picture production and directing. In North Korea, all the enterprises were state-owned. This gave Kim Jung Il free access to movie production as the producer and director. He could control the hiring of personnel, including actors. He was involved in movie projects as director. He would involve himself in the work until late in the evening. When the day's work was over, he would dive into orgies with the actors and actresses until morning. This was his life-style. He lacked his father's charisma, leadership, and background as a revolutionary, qualities needed by a credible, forceful leader. And his main interest was not in state affairs. In order to prove his qualifications, Kim Jung Il had directed international terrorist activities, including bombing incidents in Rangoon, Burma, and the Korean airliner in the Middle East, in which several hundred people were killed. He led documented terrorist activities (see Chapter 19, the section, North Korean Armed Infiltration and Terrorist Activities). This made Kim Jung Il an even more dangerous man.

In addition to Kim Jung Il's inability to lead and conduct the WPK and the SPA, he had other major problems which prevented him from succeeding his father as the leader of the DPRK. Despite prolonged efforts over two decades to make Kim Jung Il his heir, Kim Il Sung had become disappointed with his son's dismal failure in managing the third Seven-Year Plan (1987–1993), which had been entrusted to him. When Kim Jung Il withdrew North Korea from the world's Non-Proliferation Treaty (NPT) on Nuclear Weapons on March 12, 1993, without his father's approval, Kim Il Sung became very angry. Kim Jung Il's action further isolated North Korea from the world, putting it in the category of renegade regimes with Iran, Iraq, and Libya. Kim Il Sung took himself out of semi-retirement to take political matters into his own hands. At the same time, he suspended Kim Jung Il's official title in the WPK. This happened in mid-1993 and was not retracted until Kim Il Sung's death. This was a reason that Kim Jung Il could not assume the general secretary's position in the WPK, according to one research report.[13]

In December 1993, Kim Yōng-ju, Kim Il Sung's brother, who was purged by Kim Jung Il for eighteen years, was restored as a Central Committee member of the WPK by Kim Il Sung, and appointed vice president of the DPRK. The uncle had been a longtime political enemy of Kim Jung Il. Kim Jung Il's stepmother, Kim Sōng-ae, Kim Il Sung's second wife, was also a bitter political rival of Kim Jung Il.[14] Kim Jung Il was out of favor with his father a few months before his father's death and faced hostile clan members in 1995–1997. In order to hold on to his power base, the military, Kim Jung Il promoted a large number of general officers in 1995. However, this created a consensual power bloc of military officers. North Korea appeared to move into an oligarchy, run by about twelve people including Kim Jung Il. North Korea was limping along without a national congress, a political party, or a national budget. This was a dire situation for any nation at the turn of the twenty-first century. North Korea was overburdened with the 1.2 million men of the armed forces. On top of all this, it was suffering man-made severe annual floods caused by overcutting of trees in the mountains, which sent sediment to the riverbeds. The shallow rivers and streams could no longer handle the water and flooded farmlands and towns annually. This was the result of one more of Kim Jung Il's blunders of economic planning. As Kim Il Sung noted before his death, North Korea was faced with an unprecedented national crisis. Kim Jung Il lacked the leadership to solve these problems. His talk and actions were consistently those of a hard-line extremist who would hinder any improvement in North Korea's political and economic situation.

Notes to Part VI

CHAPTER 15

1. Louis R. Mortimer (ed.), *South Korea* (Washington, D.C.: Federal Research Division, Library of Congress, 1992), 27.

2. Ibid.

3. Claude A. Buss, *The United States and Republic of Korea* (Palo Alto, CA: Hoover International Studies, 1982), 30.

4. Nena Vreeland, Shinn, Just, and Moeller, *Area Handbook for North Korea* (Washington, D.C.: American University, 1975), 28.

5. Louis R. Mortimer (ed.), *South Korea*, 95.

6. Ibid., 115.

7. Nena Vreeland et al., *North Korea* (Washington, D.C.: American University, 1976), 30.

8. Ibid., 31.

CHAPTER 16

1. Claude A. Buss, *The United States and Republic of Korea*, 31.

2. Louis R. Mortimer (ed.), *South Korea*, 30.

3. Rosemary Foot, *The Wrong War* (Ithaca, NY: Cornell University Press, 1985), 34.

4. Claude A. Buss, *The United States and Republic of Korea*, 31.

5. Louis R. Mortimer (ed.), *South Korea*, 31.

6. Ibid.

7. Claude A. Buss, *The United States and Republic of Korea*, 31.

8. Nena Vreeland et al., *North Korea*, 32.

9. *Britannica*; vol. 6, *Korean War* (London: 1992), 963.

10. Ibid., 962.

11. Jon Woronoff, *Korea's Economy: Man-Made Miracle* (Arch Cape, OR: Pace International Research Inc., 1983), 15.

CHAPTER 17

1. Louis R. Mortimer (ed.), *South Korea*, 34.
2. Ibid.
3. Gavan McCormack and Mark Seldon (eds.), *Korea North and South: The Deepening Crisis* (New York: Monthly Review Press, 1978), 77–78.
4. Louis R. Mortimer (ed.), *South Korea*, 40.
5. Ibid., 46.
6. Ibid., 47.
7. Ibid.
8. *Handbook of Korea* (Seoul: Korean Overseas Information Service, 1990), 118.
9. Louis R. Mortimer (ed.), *South Korea*, 40.
10. Claude A. Buss, *The United States and Republic of Korea*, 79.
11. Ibid., 106.
12. Louis R. Mortimer (ed.), *South Korea*, 55.
13. *Handbook of Korea*, 120.
14. Louis R. Mortimer (ed.), *South Korea*, 112.
15. *U.S. News and World Report*, June 5, 1995, 45.
16. Louis R. Mortimer (ed.), *South Korea*, 176.
17. Ibid., 177.
18. *Handbook of Korea*, 378–379.
19. Ibid., 369.
20. Ibid., 368.
21. Louis R. Mortimer (ed.), *South Korea*, 191.
22. *Handbook of Korea*, 369.
23. Louis R. Mortimer (ed.), *South Korea*, 185.
24. Jon Woronoff, *Korea's Economy: Man-Made Miracle*, 150–151.
25. "Korea Headed for High Tech's Top Tier." *Business Week*, July 1995, 54–64.

CHAPTER 18

1. Dae-Sook Suk, *Kim Il Sung: The North Korean Leader* (New York: Columbia University Press, 1988), 52.
2. Louis R. Mortimer (ed.), *North Korea* (Washington, D.C.: Federal Research Division, Library of Congress, 1994), 37.
3. Aidan Foster-Carter, *Korea North and South* (New York: Monthly Review Press, 1978), 120.
4. Louis R. Mortimer (ed.), *North Korea*, 112.
5. Ibid., 244.
6. Dae-Sook Suk, *Kim Il Sung: The North Korean Leader*, 143.
7. Ibid.
8. Louis R. Mortimer (ed.), *North Korea*, 113.
9. Ibid.
10. Associated Press Wire Service, June 22, 1995, Report from Beijing.

11. B. C. Koh, *Recent Political Developments in North Korea*, presented at the Conference North Korea After Kim Il Sung: Continuity or Change?, The Hoover Institution, Stanford University, February 27, 1996, 7.

12. Ibid.

13. Sato Katsumi, Nishioka Tsutomu, *Is the Secretary General (of the Liberal Democratic Party of Japan) Kato Koichi a Puppet of North Korea?* (Tokyo: Bunkei Shunshu, December, 1995), 116–127.

14. Ibid.

Part VII

The Arms Race and Unification Efforts of the Two Koreas

19

National Security of South and North Korea

THE MILITARY STRENGTH OF SOUTH KOREA AND NORTH KOREA

South Korea's population was always about twice that of North Korea. South Korea's population in 1953 was about twenty-two million, against North Korea's less than nine million. In 1960 these numbers had increased to twenty-five million for South Korea and ten million for North Korea. In 1995, the South Korean population was about 45.5 million, against the North's 23.5 million. Coupled with this large difference in population, the South Korean GDP was U.S. $547 billion, against North Korea's GDP of about U.S. $18 billion (estimate) in 1995. The North's GDP was less than one-thirtieth that of the South (see Chapter 17, and Chapter 21).

These figures show clear-cut advantages for South Korea in resources and potential national power. In order to counterbalance these huge disadvantages and as a result of the insecurities of being a smaller nation, North Korea had been increasing in military manpower and weaponry. These efforts had taxed North Koreans' lives and economy to such an extent that, in 1990, about twenty-five percent of the GNP was allocated to maintenance of a huge armed force of about 1.1 million. This continued to increase to 1.2 million in 1994. Such an overtaxing of the North Korean economy had adverse effects, to the extent that it started to shrink at an annual rate of five percent, while it was already small compared to South Korea's GDP (see the discussion of the North Korean economy, Chapter 18). As the Soviet Union had overtaxed itself during the Cold War period, and finally collapsed internally, North Korea had had serious problems. However, North Korea, unlike the Soviet Union, had totally enslaved its people by government and Communist Party actions. Any political dissent would be severely punished. Thus, the people had no voice in this matter. They had been absolutely quiet.

The whole nation of North Korea became one huge armed camp. It was the most heavily armed nation in the world, relative to its size. In 1950, the imbalance of military strength in favor of North Korea was two to one over that of South Korea. In 1950, the two hundred thousand well-equipped troops of North Korea were far superior to the less than one hundred thousand poorly equipped and poorly trained South Korean army personnel. This weakness of the South Korean military forces caused the Korean War, together with the U.S. State Department decision to abandon the Korean Peninsula. This military imbalance of two to one in favor of North Korea was almost identical in 1995, with 1.2 million troops of North Korea against just a little over 600,000 South Korean military forces. And the North Koreans were far better equipped than the South Koreans in 1995. This clear imbalance (see Table 19.1) may tempt the North Koreans once again. This was one reason why the North Koreans became very belligerent in the mid-1990s.

To this large imbalance of military personnel and weaponry North Korea added possible nuclear weapon development. It is possible that they had developed several nuclear bombs in their arsenal by 1994. North Korea successfully blackmailed South Korea, Japan, and the United States into an agreement to provide them with less dangerous light-water nuclear reactors (which would cost South Korea U.S. $4.5 billion), plus annual deliveries of 500,000 metric tons of heavy fuel oil. This was pure appeasement of North Korea, without solid guarantees of any reciprocation. Before the Second World War, England and France appeased the rearmed Germany. However, appeasement failed to stop the war. Giving North Korea the two expensive nuclear reactors and much-needed fuel would never guarantee a stop to the North Korean nuclear armament program. North Korea had been a highly secretive country, with a long history of contempt for international agreements. The two nuclear reactors could only strengthen the North Korean economy, and hence its national resources, and ultimately its military might.

The growth of the North Korean armed forces was remarkable. The North Korean military was almost decimated by the UN forces in the early stages of the Korean War in 1950. The Korean War was sustained by the input of the Chinese "volunteer" forces, which eventually increased to 850,000 men at the peak of the war. This Chinese force was withdrawn in 1958. The North Korean forces expanded steadily and were still increasing in the mid-1990s.

The total expenditure on the military in the South and North showed quite a different story. However, caution must be applied here, because some of the North Korean military expenditures were hidden in nonmilitary sectors of the economy. Nevertheless, Table 19.2 indicates the trend of military expenditures.

Table 19.1
Total Military Strength of South and North Korea

Year	*South Korea*	*North Korea*
1950	100,000	200,000
1960	600,000	250,000
1970	610,000	390,000
1979	640,000	700,000
1981	600,000	780,000
1983	600,000	780,000
1985	600,000	790,000
1987	600,000	840,000
1989	650,000	1,100,000
1992 to 1994	650,000	1,200,000*

* Estimate: Of these 1.2 million North Korean troops, about one hundred fifty thousand men were assigned to the civilian construction works, while still fulfilling their military duties.

Source: Louis R. Mortimer (ed.), *North Korea* (Washington, D.C.: Federal Research Division, Library of Congress, 1994), 242 (original source: *World Military and Arms Control*, 1991); Louis R. Mortimer (ed.), *South Korea.* (Washington, D.C.: Federal Research Division, Library of Congress, 1992), 278 (original source: *World Military and Arms Control*, 1991).

Table 19.2
South and North Korea's Military Expenditures, 1979–1989 (in U.S. $ billions)

Year	South Korea	North Korea
1979	5.0	6.8
1981	6.0	6.1
1983	6.5	6.0
1985	7.0	6.0
1987	7.8	6.1
1989	9.1	6.0

Source: Louis R. Mortimer (ed.), *North Korea* (Washington, D.C.: Federal Research Division, Library of Congress, 1994), 244 (original source: *World Military and Arms Control*, 1991).

South Korean Defense Industry

In the early 1990s, South Korea was spending fifty percent more on the military than North Korea. This was due to the deployment of the expensive high-tech military equipment used by the South Korean military forces.

South Korea has been manufacturing much of its weaponry. This includes M-16 rifles, M-88 tanks, McDonnell Douglas 600-MD attack helicopters, TOW antitank weapons, Northrop F-5E/F fighter planes, and transport equipment. Additionally, many naval vessels, including destroyers and landing craft, were produced in South Korea, in cooperation with U.S. firms and with the permission of the U.S. government.

Russia and China on Korean Security

Because the Soviet Union, which had been the main supplier of North Korean armaments, met its demise in the early-1990s, Kim Il Sung's *Chuch'e* idea of self-reliance based on military power became even more important. The new Russian regime is in no condition, nor does it have the willingness, to supply North Korea with weapons, unless, perhaps, North Korea pays for them with cash, something North Korea does not have the capacity to do. At any rate, the new Russia is too firmly committed to South Korea, by South Korean economic aid to Russia and business deals and contracts, to offend South Korea by providing any help to North Korea.

Communist China is in a similar situation. South Korea is more important than North Korea to them. In 1994, the Chinese prime minister, Li Peng, visited Seoul, and South Korea returned the courtesy in 1995 with a visit by its prime minister, Lee Hong Koo, to Beijing. China has been rapidly moving into a market economy, and South Korea has become deeply involved in it. Trade between South Korea and China reached U.S. $5 billion in 1993.

North Korean Military Readiness

In this situation, North Korea had been stockpiling enough ammunition, food, petroleum oil, and other military necessities in hardened underground facilities. By 1994, North Korea had stockpiled some 990,000 tons of ammunition, an amount sufficient for four months of combat.[1] This is hardly enough to launch a major war. In contrast to North Korea's situation, South Korea can draw almost unlimited military weaponry from the United States and Japan, if and when a war should start again on the Korean Peninsula. Although the North Korean armament was quantitatively greater qualitatively it was inferior to that of South Korea (see Tables 19.2–19.5).

Following the principle of *Chuch'e*, North Korea has developed an extensive defense industrial capacity, although most equipment is of old Soviet or Chinese design, much of it outdated. Some equipment has been redesigned by the North Koreans: armored personnel carriers, self-propelled artillery, light tanks, high-speed landing craft, Romeo class submarines, SCUD-derived surface-to-surface missiles, antitank missiles of the SA-7's, SA-14's, SA-16's, and possibly SA-2's. Aircraft production is believed to have begun in 1995. North Korea has 134 arms factories, many of them underground.[2]

The Ground Forces of South Korea and North Korea

With 3,600 tanks, more than ten thousand units of field artillery pieces and rocket launchers, and close to one million ground troops, North Korea poses a significant threat to South Korea. However, most of the tanks are medium to light tanks. The breakdown of the number of tanks in 1992 was as indicated in Table 19.5:

Table 19.3
Major Armament for the Ground Forces of South Korea and North Korea, 1995–1996

Category	*South Korea*	*North Korea*
Army (military effective)	520,000	About 1,000,000
Major units	Three mechanized infantry divisions	Twenty-six motorized and regular infantry divisions
	Nineteen infantry divisions	Fourteen armored brigades
	Two independent infantry divisions	Twenty-three motorized/mechanized infantry brigades
	Seven special forces brigades	Five independent infantry brigades
	Three air defense artillery brigades	Twenty-two light infantry brigades
		Six heavy artillery brigades
		Fourteen artillery brigades
SSM	Three SSM battalions	One independent Scud regiment
		Fifty-four FROG-3/-5/-7
		Thirty Scud-C

Source: Hideshi Takesada, "North Korean Military Threat Under Kim Jung Il," paper presented at the conference on "North Korea after Kim Il Sung: Continuity or Change?" Hoover Institution, Stanford University, Palo Alto, CA, February 27–28, 1996.

Table 19.4
Equipment 1992

	South Korea	*North Korea*
Tanks	1560	3600
Armored personnel carriers	1550	1960
Field artillery pieces	4,200	7,800
Multirocket launchers	140	2,500
Mortars	5,300	11,000
Surface-to-surface missiles	12	70

Source: Louis R. Mortimer (ed.), *South Korea* (Washington, D.C.: Federal Research Division, Library of Congress, 1992), 278 (original source: *World Military and Arms Control*, 1991).

Table 19.5
North Korean Tanks

Tank Type	Number of Tanks
T-54/55/59	2,200 +
T-62	600
T-34	NA
Others	800

Source: Louis R. Mortimer (ed.), *North Korea*, 287.

The Gulf War showed that Soviet-built tanks were no match for American-built tanks and attack helicopters, which South Koreans have been manufacturing in the 1990s. South Koreans have also been manufacturing TOW antitank guided missiles. They possess a higher-quality, more technologically advanced weaponry than North Korea, which has equipment that is outdated and becoming obsolete. However, most of the North Korean weapons are still operational. The huge number of North Korean troops and equipment poses a problem for South Korea.

Korean Terrain

Perhaps the best ally of South Korea is the topographical features of the Korean Peninsula. About eighty percent of the peninsula is rugged mountain regions. These areas are almost impassable for tanks, self-propelled artillery pieces, or armored personnel carriers. Unlike in Vietnam, the Korean mountains are covered with relatively short pine trees, and these trees do not provide good coverage. Thus, any vehicular movement could be easily spotted. Also, the millions of trees form an effective barrier to advancing mechanized forces, although they will not stop infantry. Flat plains are found only along the west coast and in the central valley. However, these plains and relatively low hills are covered with divided and terraced rice paddies that are filled with water, knee deep, with a foot of mud underneath. Usually these rice paddies are less than one half acre in size and divided by vertical earthen dikes, averaging four feet wide and five feet high, forming property boundary lines. Millions of these dikes criss-cross the farmlands. During the dry season of winter, the dikes become frozen, rock-solid walls, impassable for any military vehicle, thus forming natural barriers. Whether it is summer or winter, the only passable places for an invading army are the few roads running north to south. These roads can easily be blocked with destroyed vehicles or roadblocks, forming a killing field for the backed-up mechanized columns, just as happened in Kuwait during the Gulf War. During the beginning of the Korean War, the invading North Korean tank columns were quickly destroyed by the planes of the UN Forces.

Defense of Seoul and U.S. Troops

The most vulnerable spot is Seoul, with over ten million people only twenty-eight miles from the demilitarized zone (DMZ) line. If war comes again to Korea, Seoul will suffer some damage. However, total destruction of Seoul would be impossible because of the city's massive size. It would take years of pounding and unlimited ammunition, which North Korea does not have; North Korea has only a four-month supply. To back up South Korean ground troops, thirty-two thousand U.S. Army personnel were in Korea in 1990, along with another 12,500 U.S. Air Force and Navy personnel. These U.S. Army troops are the "trigger" force that would guarantee U.S. involvement in the event of a

North Korean attack and serve as a standing warning to North Korea. In 1994, the U.S. forces introduced the Patriot antimissile missile to counter North Korean missiles.

Air Forces of South Korea and North Korea

The air forces of South Korea and North Korea are in a similar situation in quantity and quality. North Korea has more fighters and bombers; however, the equipment is much older than that of the South Korean forces. There were forty thousand air force personnel in South Korea, while North Korea had seventy thousand in 1993 (see Table 19.6).

Table 19.6
Combat Equipment for the Air Forces of South Korea and North Korea in 1995–1996

	South Korea		*North Korea*	
Combat fighters	F-16	60	MIG-17	110
	F-5 A/E	195	MIG-19	130
	F-4 D/E	130	MIG-21	130
			MIG-23	46
	Antiguerrilla aircraft	23	MIG-29	40
Reconnaissance	RF-42	18	SU-7	18
aircraft	RF-5A	10	SU-25	35
U.S. Air Force				
in Korea	F-16	72		
Total		**508**		**509**
Transport		37		282
Armed helicopters		400		80
Bombers		0	H-5	80
Support aircraft		263		0
SAM			SA-2	240
			SA-3	36
			SA-4	24

These figures were derived from 1995–1996 reports on fighters, together with 1992 reports on other aircraft. These figures change annually, as both the ROK and DPRK manufacture their own equipment.

Source: Hideshi Takesada, "North Korean Military Threat Under Kim Jong-Il."

The F-16 C/D's have been proved to have much higher performance than the MIG-29's. In the 1990s, the South Korean defense industry has produced F-5's, while North Korea has not produced any fighter aircraft. Most of the North Korean fighter planes are MIG-17's and 21's that are becoming obsolete. North Korea has built underground facilities to store and protect their combat airplanes.

Beginning in November 1995, South Korea started production of F-16 C/D's, the world's most advanced combat fighter aircraft at that time. This was done with U.S. $5 billion under the Korea Fighter Program, which gave South Korea 120 more fighter planes. This was the first production of F-16 C/D's outside the United States,[3] indicating that South Korea has attained the highest level of technological development.

U.S. Air Force in Korea

In 1995, the United States Air Force stationed twelve thousand personnel in South Korea to support the South Korean Air Force, with two fighter squadrons of seventy-two advanced F-16's operating from Osan and Kunsan Air Bases. The advanced U.S. Air Force combat planes provide significant added deterrence to any possible North Korean attack. In case of hostility on the Korean Peninsula, the United States and South Korea also have an agreement to utilize the U.S. Air Bases and their combat planes from Japan and the Philippines.

Naval Forces of South Korea and North Korea

The navies of South Korea and North Korea in the 1990s have distinctly different characteristics (see Table 19.7). The South Korean navy of thirty-five thousand men is built around forty-nine destroyers and frigates, while the main component of the North Korean Navy of forty thousand men has been twenty-five submarines. South Korea also has two well-trained marine divisions, with twenty-five thousand troops. Both Koreas have capabilities and have been building their own naval vessels. North Korea sent spies to infiltrate the South Korean Navy during the peak period of the late 1970s and early 1980s, to sabotage, interrupt, and terrorize South Korea, using submarines and patrol boats. To counter these North Korean activities, South Korea built up a formidable naval fleet composed of destroyers and frigates and was able to check the North Korean activities in the late 1980s and 1990s.

Table 19.7
South Korean and North Korean Naval Forces, 1995–1996

		South Korea	*North Korea*
Vessels	Frigates	33	3
	Destroyers	16	
	Submarines	6	25
	Missile patrol boat	10	42
Marine troops			
	Divisions	2	0

Source: Hideshi Takesada, "North Korean Military Threat under Kim Jong-Il," Paper presented at the Conference on "North Korea after Kim Il Sung: Continuity or Change?" Hoover Institution, Stanford University, Palo Alto, California, February 27–28, 1996.

The South Korean shipbuilding industry has become one of the largest in the world (see Chapter 16). It built 250,000-ton tankers, fully computerized and automated, that were sold on the world markets. The overseas shipbuilding orders for South Korea surpassed Japan's orders in 1993. By the early 1990s, South Korea was capable of building any naval ship, including aircraft carriers if necessary.

The U.S. Navy had five hundred sailors and marines as contingency, bringing the total U.S. armed forces personnel stationed in South Korea to 44,500 in 1993. The entire U.S. Navy stationed in the Pacific region could participate on short notice, if needed in the event of war. This situation of stationing U.S. forces continued indefinitely as of the publication date.

A SUMMARY OF THE MILITARY STRENGTH OF SOUTH KOREA AND NORTH KOREA

North Korea, with about half the population and less than one-thirtieth of the wealth of South Korea in 1995, had mobilized its resources to the maximum on a war footing. North Korea's total standing military personnel numbered 1.2 million in 1995, seriously straining the North Korean economy. In the early 1990s, the North Korean expenditures on military have been roughly twenty-six percent of its total GNP of about U.S. $22 billion. This overly expanded, non-productive expenditure on the military stressed the North Korean economy to such an extent that the North Korean GNP had actually been shrinking at the rate of five percent per year since 1990. Compared to this, the South Korean economy was about U.S. $547 billion in 1995 and has been continuously expanding at the rate of about nine to ten percent per year in the 1990s. South Korea was spending U.S. $9 billion on defense, amounting to only 3.6 percent of the total GDP, while North Korean expenditures were U.S. $6 billion, about thirty-five percent less than South Korean expenditures. In addition, South Korea paid a large part of the expenses for the U.S. forces stationed in South Korea.

The 1.2 million men of the North Korean military forces in 1995 were roughly twice the size of the South Korean forces of 650,000. In addition, North Korea had twice the quantity of military equipment, including 3,600 tanks, 7,800 field artillery pieces, and 11,000 mortars, against South Korea's 1,560 tanks, 4,200 artillery pieces, and 5,300 mortars. There was a definite imbalance of military power between South and North Korea.

While North Korea increased its military forces steadily from 250,000 in 1960 to 1.2 million in 1994, South Korea maintained its from about 600,000 in 1960 to about the same size, 650,000, in the 1990s. While North Korea increased its military forces five times over a thirty-year period, South Korea had not increased its military forces much. South Korea had neglected its defenses. In 1995, the ratio of two to one in military strength in favor of North Korea was similar to the situation that existed in 1950, immediately before the Korean War, when North Korea invaded. With this difference in military strength in 1950, North Korea almost succeeded, until the United States intervened. It seemed that South Korea was allowing this old situation to recur in the 1990s.

South Korea, with its well-established industry and new factories, coupled with weaker military forces to guard them, has become an attractive target for the North Koreans, who are in serious economic difficulties. There is a chance that North Korea will be tempted to gamble with their larger military forces.

The United States–Republic of Korea Mutual Defense Treaty and the presence of 44,500 U.S. military personnel in South Korea has been the guarantee of U.S. involvement in the event of the onset of war on the Korean Peninsula. In addition, acrimonious relationships which have developed between North Korea and its former allies, Russia and China, may somewhat discourage the North Korean leaders from launching a war against South Korea.

Nevertheless, North Korea has been dominated by unstable, irrational leaders, and further, there is no absolute guarantee that the United States will come to the aid of South Korea in the end. In fact, increasing numbers of U.S. politicians have advocated a reduction in the U.S. commitment to Korea, as exemplified by the actions of the former U.S. President Jimmy Carter.

Ultimately, it would be necessary for South Korea, for its security, to match the military strength of North Korea. This is the only guarantee. It can easily be done with South Korea's economic strength. South Korea has much to lose, while North Korea has little.

The weakness in relative military strength creates another problem. It creates weakness at the negotiation table. There have been several negotiations between South Korea and North Korea. Negotiations on unification and nuclear armament are the most important. The overwhelmingly stronger North Korean conventional military forces make North Koreans rigid and tougher at the negotiation table.

The nuclear disarmament "bargain" struck in June 1994 between the former U.S. President Jimmy Carter and North Korean Kim Il Sung was one-sided in favor of North Korea and forced South Korea to pay for two light-water nuclear reactors to be installed in North Korea. This was estimated to cost South Korea as much as U.S. $4.5 billion, without any benefit for South Korea, in exchange for a "promise" from North Korea to allow international teams to inspect North Korean nuclear facilities. They can change their mind at any time, and have done so in the past.

Since the death of Kim Il Sung in July 1994, the new leaders of North Korea have reneged on the original agreement. They initially refused to accept the South Korean-manufactured reactors and insisted on German-manufactured reactors paid for by South Korea. This North Korean attitude opened a new, dangerous passage in East Asia. Both South Korea and Japan have long possessed the technology and wealth to produce their own nuclear weapons. North Korea may force a nuclear arms race in East Asia.

North Korea, with its two-to-one advantage in conventional forces over South Korea, has been putting pressure on South Korea for an arms race. It appeared that Kim Jung Il, the oldest son of Kim Il Sung, was in control of the North Korean armed forces in 1996. Kim Jung Il was known to be a man of unstable personality and had a record of terrorism. This makes the situation on the Korean Peninsula even more precarious. He may strike South Korea when his position becomes weak, in order to strengthen it. The Cold War in Europe is over between the United States and the Soviet Union, but it is not over on the Korean Peninsula. North Korea, a Stalinist state (more so than the original model ever was), is out to arm itself to an extreme.

The U.S. President Bill Clinton warned North Korea on several occasions in 1994 and 1995 that the use of nuclear weapons against South Korea or Japan would surely provoke retaliation that would wipe North Korea off the map. He reiterated that in such an event, there would be no more North Korea as it existed at that time. His words were not meant as an empty threat. The United States was obligated to do so by the treaties with South Korea and Japan. An extreme militarism led to the demise of Nazi Germany and Imperialist Japan. The Stalinist Soviet Union met a similar demise. North Korea could have a similar end if it overplays its hand with militarism.

NORTH KOREAN ARMED INFILTRATION AND TERRORIST ACTIVITIES

North Korean subversive and terrorist activities against South Korea have continued since Korea was divided in 1945. Before the Korean War, North Korean Communist leaders coordinated closely with the South Korean Communist Party and infiltrated South Korean government offices, especially the military and police. During the early period of the United States military government in Korea, in 1945–1946, the South Korean Communist Party, led by Pak Hōn-yōng, operated in the open as a legitimate political party. However, after it was discovered that they were printing counterfeit money in large quantities, the U.S. military government in South Korea outlawed the party and the Communists went underground.

The Korean Communists infiltrated the Republic of Korea Army and instigated the army revolt of Cheju Island and Yōsu-Sunch'ōn Rebellions, which caused the death of tens of thousands of military personnel and civilians in 1948. The ROK army purged many of its members, weakening its effectiveness. For this, the leader of the South Korean Communist Party, Pak Hōn-Yōng, was awarded the position of vice premier in the North Korean government when he went to North Korea in 1949. Later, he lost a power struggle against Kim Il Sung and was executed in 1953.

Even after the armistice in 1953, North Korean infiltration never ceased. In the 1960s, North Korean agents disguised as students continuously agitated South Korean society through demonstrations and unrest. The South Korean governments of Rhee and Park, from the 1950s to the 1970s, became more dictatorial, using this unrest as a pretext. Communist activities were made a crime, and at the same time the civil and human rights of South Koreans were suppressed. In the late 1960s, North Korean tactics toward South Korea increasingly shifted to violence, in order to destabilize South Korea. North Korea dispatched armed commando units into South Korean coastal regions and engaged South Korea police and armed forces. On some occasions, the use of artillery was involved. North Korea was conducting a guerrilla war against South Korea. In the peak year of 1968, North Korea attempted six hundred infiltrations and firefights. Most of these attempts failed as a result of effective South Korean coastal defenses.

As North Koreans discovered that pirate like coastal raids were ineffectual, the leaders changed tactics and began to employ terrorist activities. In 1968, North Korea dispatched thirty-one members of the North Korean 124th Army Unit, who came within five hundred meters of the South Korean presidential residence, the "Blue House," undetected. Finally, a firefight broke out, killing twenty-eight heavily armed North Korean infiltrators and thirty-seven South Korean security guards. In 1969, North Koreans attempted one hundred fifty armed infiltrations. As all of them failed, North Koreans put more emphasis on terrorism, covert networks, and intelligence gathering.

North Koreans began to focus their terrorism on attempts to assassinate high-ranking South Korean government officials, including the presidents of the ROK. In 1970, one North Korean infiltrator was killed while planting a bomb at the Seoul National Cemetery, attempting to kill President Park Chung Hee. In 1974, a Korean from Japan, directed by North Korea, shot at President Park, instead killing Park's wife, who was seated behind him. In the late 1970s and 1980s, armed infiltration by North Korean agents continued. All of them were stopped by the South Korean security forces, who were becoming increasingly effective as they gained experience. However, North Korea had not abandoned its terrorist policy.

In October 1983, when South Korean President Chun Doo Hwan was touring Southeast Asian nations, North Korea seized its opportunity to assassinate him and dispatched a three-man team from North Korean intelligence services. These North Korean agents set a time-bomb at a state reception ceremony welcoming Chun at Rangoon, Burma. The bomb exploded a little too early, as Chun was detained elsewhere. Chun escaped; however, eighteen South Korean officials, including four cabinet ministers, were killed, and fourteen others were injured. One of the North Korean agents was killed, and two others were captured. One of them confessed that they were sent by the North Korean government.[4]

North Korean terrorism did not abate. On November 29, 1987, a bomb exploded aboard a Korean Air jetliner, returning from the Middle East, killing all 135 people on board. Two agents of North Korea, who got off the plane just before it took off, were captured. One was an older man, and the other was a young woman. They both carried a cyanide pill, which they were instructed to swallow if they were captured. The old man swallowed the pill and died, but the young woman could not swallow it. She was taken to Seoul and confessed that the North Korean government had ordered her to place the bomb. She also told the South Korean authorities that Kim Jung Il, the oldest son of Kim Il Sung, directed them to do so in order to discredit South Korea before the 1988 Seoul Summer Olympics. Four years earlier, the Rangoon bombing had also been masterminded by Kim Jung Il, according to the confession of one of the North Korean agents there.[5] North Korean armed incursions continued to occur into the 1990s. On September 19, 1996, a group of infiltrators attempted unsuccessfully to land on the South Korean shore off Kangnūng, using a submarine. Eleven North Korean spies and crewmen committed suicide; thirteen were killed by South Korean forces, and one was captured. Kim Jung Il had not abandoned his decades long terrorist activities, even while North Korea was experiencing severe famine conditions in 1995–1997. This same man, Kim Jung Il, was in control of the 1.2 million North Korean armed forces in the mid-1990s.

These events proved that South Korea had absolutely no room to be complacent, with its armed forces outnumbered two to one. All these records discredit North Korea as a reasonable and respectable regime. North Korea has become an isolated nation. A former ally, the Soviet Union, is gone, and with it any military technology North Korea might have obtained. Even Communist China can no longer be considered a North Korean ally. In 1995, while North Koreans were dying of starvation, China refused to provide a supply of rice unless North Korea paid for it in cash. After all the terrorist activity by North Koreans, South Korea announced that it was willing to help North Korea alleviate the hunger by supplying rice in May 1995. The overseas South Koreans also initiated emergency assistance of food to North Korea. The South Korean Chapter of World Vision International in California purchased ten thousand tons of Chinese corn with cash and delivered it by railcars to Namyang on the border of China and North Korea in mid-1995.

This was done for humanitarian reasons prompted by the world news (reported by the Associated Press) that poverty had become widespread in North Korea and people were starving. On June 21, 1995, at the Beijing Conference between South and North Korea, North Korea, setting aside traditional pride, agreed to accept U.S. $270 million from South Korea, including 150,000 tons of rice. With that money and credit, North Korea was able to purchase an additional 300,000 tons of rice from Japan in July 1995, to stave off starvation in a critical period. Compassion has been a tradition of Korea throughout history.

20

Unification Efforts by International Organizations and South and North Korea

The most fervent wishes of all Koreans, South Koreans and North Koreans alike, is that the two parts of Korea be united and become one nation. Korea was one nation ever since the Silla Kingdom united all of Korea in 676 A.D. Through the Silla, Koryō, and Chosōn Kingdoms, for over twelve hundred years, Korea maintained independence and unity except during the twentieth century, one of the worst centuries Korea had ever gone through in more than five thousand years of its history. Events have been adverse to Korea ever since Japan annexed Korea in 1910. Koreans, who enjoyed magnificent civilizations many times over, had to suffer oppression and humiliation by the cruel foreign occupational power of Japan for thirty-five years. When the liberators came, Koreans rejoiced. However, they soon learned that their nation was to be divided into two occupation sectors, of the United States and the Soviet Union. Korea was divided at the 38th Parallel, in order to disarm the Japanese forces, by the United States and Soviet forces. Fifty years later, in 1995, after a major conflict, the Korean War, the Korean Peninsula was still divided. The worst was that these two parts had become mortal enemies. Nearly two million armed troops were glaring at each other across the demilitarized zone (DMZ), each ready to pounce on the other at the first opportunity. Aggressiveness had been much more apparent with smaller North Korea, with about half the population and one-thirtieth of the wealth (1995 GDP figures) of South Korea.

Both international bodies, the United Nations and special international conferences, and South and North Koreans themselves, have tried to promote Korean unification. However, all of these efforts have been fruitless. International efforts to unify Korea have been boycotted either by South Korea or by North Korea. The negotiations between South and North Koreans have all been rejected also. The causes of continued failed efforts are several:

First, South and North Korea have fundamentally different political and economic doctrines and systems that cannot permit compromise. Second, there is deep-seated distrust between the two Koreas. No matter what the proposal is from one side, the other party always interprets it with suspicion. Third, those in power in each of the two Koreas would never give up their own power and control, but always maneuver to gain power and control from the other side. Fourth, the objectives and methods of approach to unification by South and North Korea are so different that they are all unacceptable to the other party.

Despite the fundamental differences, the two Koreas have moved toward reconciliation through numerous proposals and moves. The Korean War, by which North Korea and Kim Il Sung attempted to occupy all of Korea by military force, was, in fact, an attempt to unify by force. But the Korean War alienated South Koreans and increased their distrust of North Koreans, so much so that Korean unification moved further away than ever. The ensuing North Korean hard-line policy, which employed armed infiltration and terrorist tactics, did not help Korea's unification efforts.

However, both sides have pushed aside the difficulties and continued their efforts. In the latter part of the 1980s and early 1990s, when the North Korean economy was sliding downward while the South Korean economy was projected into one of the world's greatest economic powers, North Korea seemed to open its door to South Korean business enterprises. North Korea had become increasingly isolated from the world community, and it had become impoverished. Therefore, it was a matter of necessity to turn to South Korea for salvation.

There was some possibility that a German-type unification could be implemented. Kim Il Sung, the center of the difficulties between South and North Korea, was gone in 1994, yet his son, Kim Jung Il, survived, supported by aging hard-line leaders of the old-time partisans. In 1995, Kim Jung Il's leadership quality was yet to be tested. The old-time partisan supporters of Kim Il Sung were in their late seventies and eighties. Maintenance of the 1.2 million military forces, which drew every resource of the small impoverished nation, may force the eventual downfall of the country. Perhaps the unification of Korea may occur sooner than everyone expects it, and again it may not. The demise of the Communist Soviet Union opened the possibility of Korea's unification, just as it did the unification of East and West Germany.

INTERNATIONAL EFFORTS FOR KOREA'S UNIFICATION

After the Korean War, an international conference was held in Geneva, beginning on April 27, 1954, to seek a peaceful settlement of Korean affairs. This Geneva Conference was attended by South Korea and its sixteen allies, on one hand, and on the other North Korea and its allies, the Soviet Union and Communist China. On June 15, 1954, the conference broke up because the parties could not agree on the three major issues, which South Korea and its allies proposed and North Korea rejected. These issues were UN authority in Korean affairs; UN-sponsored general elections in North Korea based on population (one half of South Korea); and stationing of UN forces in Korea until establishment of a unified, independent, and democratic Korea. Upon the failure of the conference, the United Nations General Assembly reaffirmed the goals stated in the conference to create a unified, independent, and democratic Korea on December 11, 1954. North Korea did not pay much attention to this resolution. Almost every year the UN discussed Korean issues without much result.

In 1990 and 1991, the United Nations began to take a new course toward Korea. Instead of insisting on a unified Korea, the United Nations began to consider separate memberships for both South Korea and North Korea. This move was initiated by South Korea, which sought UN membership. The South Korean foreign relations with the Soviet Union and Communist China had become increasingly warmer, and both nations were agreeable to South Korea's UN membership in 1991. The South Korean intention was to get UN membership as a sole representative of all of Korea. South Korea did not work for North Korean membership. North Korea was vehemently opposed to South Korean membership, claiming that such a move would make the division of Korea permanent.

With the backing of the United States, in September 1991, the United Nations General Assembly voted to admit both South Korea and North Korea as separate members. Thus both South Korea and North Korea became independent states recognized by the world body. In reality, this move consolidated the separate nationhood of both South and North Korea, making unification even more difficult.

SOME SOUTH AND NORTH KOREAN DIALOGUES

Both South Korea and North Korea have proposed numerous unification plans over the years, and each time such proposals were rejected by the other side. The major proposals were as follows:

On March 25, 1948, the North Korean Democratic National Front proposed a joint conference of political parties and organizations, and a conference was held in P'yōngyang. On April 20, 1948, 564 representatives of fifty-six southern and northern organizations participated.[1] From South Korea, some leaders such as Kim Koo and Kim Kyu-sik participated. Syngman Rhee refused. The meeting called for the withdrawal of all foreign troops and the creation of an all-Korea political council. Nothing came of the meeting.

On June 7, 1950, the North Korean Democratic Front for the Unification of the Fatherland called for a general election throughout Korea. It was an empty call.

After the war, on November 23, 1953, President Syngman Rhee of South Korea proposed a general election be held in North Korea to choose representatives to fill the seats reserved for them in the ROK National Assembly (about one-third of the total seats).

On October 2, 1954, the ROK National Assembly passed a resolution calling for unification through UN-supervised general elections in North Korea to choose representatives to the National Assembly in Seoul. A similar resolution was passed on September 10, 1957.

On September 20, 1957, Kim Il Sung proposed the withdrawal of all foreign troops, the reduction of armed forces in both South and North Korea to 100,000 each, and free travel, postal, and cultural exchanges. He made similar proposals several times, as late as 1994, immediately before his death.

On August 14, 1960, Kim Il Sung proposed a confederation of South and North as a step toward unification. He repeated similar proposals several times after that.

On August 27, 1960, Prime Minister Chang Myōn of the ROK proposed a UN-supervised general election to unify Korea.

On November 2, 1960, the South Korean National Assembly called for a similar UN-sponsored general election.

On November 15, 1961, Chairman Park Chung Hee issued a joint communiqué in Washington, D.C. with U.S. President John F. Kennedy, calling for peaceful unification on the principles reaffirmed by the UN General Assembly.

On August 12, 1971, the ROK Red Cross proposed to link the dispersed families in South and North Korea. On August 14, 1971, the North Korean Red Cross accepted the ROK proposal. It was the first time any agreement was reached between South and North. The Red Cross meetings were held on and off for ten years without achieving any results.

On July 4, 1972, both South and North Korea issued a historic South–North Joint Communiqué indicating that they would stop slandering and defaming each other, create a South–North Coordinating Committee, and open a direct telephone line between Seoul and P'yōngyang. On March 10, 1973, the first Executive Council meeting of the South–North Coordinating Committee opened at P'anmunjōm.

On January 18, 1974, Park proposed a South–North non-aggression agreement. It was rejected by North Korea on January 26, 1974, by an editorial of the *Rodong Shinmun*, the organ of the North Korean Labor Party. Park proposed a non-aggression pact several times over the years.

On March 19, 1978, North Korea suspended the Red Cross talks.

The South–North dialogue was suspended for a year, but some exchange of letters was made to prepare for a future meeting.

On January 12, 1981, South Korea's President Chun Doo Hwan proposed an exchange of visits between South and North "without any condition, and free of obligation." This proposal was rejected by North Korea a week later. Chun again proposed a summit meeting on June 5, 1981. Again, North Korea rejected his proposal.

Several South and North Korean organizations, including the Red Cross, proposed ideas for several years for an agreement, but each was rejected by the other side. For thirty years, there was no significant progress in the South–North talks toward unification, until the mid-1980s.

The major threads of South Korea's repeated proposals were to hold a nationwide general election supervised by the UN, based on population distribution. This idea was simply unacceptable to North Korea because it was outnumbered almost two to one by South Korea in population. Also, the South Korean people were strongly anti-Communist; this meant that North Korea would lose political control if a national election were held. That was why Kim Il Sung proposed the idea of a confederacy of South and North, with equal status for both. This was not acceptable to South Korea.

In 1984, when South Korea was hit by a typhoon, causing devastating floods, North Korea, on its own initiative, delivered relief goods. Such goodwill had positive effects. The following year, in 1985, an exchange of visits by performing artists took place. On July 7, 1988, South Korea's President Roh Tae Woo proposed building a single "national commonwealth," and solicited help from Washington, D.C., Tokyo, Moscow, and Beijing. However, the North Korean response was negative. Kim Il Sung reiterated the idea of a Democratic Confederate Republic of Korea. By 1988, however, South and North Korea began to enter a new phase in inter-Korean relationships through trade. South Korea lowered tariffs and liberalized trade with North Korea. The countries still had to go through a third party, such as Japan or Hong Kong.

In 1988, North Korea asked Seoul to meet three points: repeal the National Security Act, which designated North Korea as an enemy; declare non-aggression; and establish a "Peaceful Reunification Committee." South Korea attempted to meet those demands but could not quite complete the task. At the United Nations on October 18, 1988, Roh advocated convening a six-nation consultative conference to accomplish a permanent peace settlement in Korea, with North Korean partnership.

On January 1, 1989, Kim Il Sung extended an invitation to several South Korean religious leaders. However, nothing came of it toward the unification effort. During 1989, South Korean businessmen from *Hyundai Chaebōl* (conglomerates) and *Chōng Chu-yong* obtained a visiting permit from North Korea through an intermediary in Japan. They were received by Ho Tam, North Korea's chairman of the Committee for the Peaceful Reunification of the Fatherland, as well as the North's business leaders, who were eager to discuss tourism. This was a breakthrough. In the same year, a South Korean religious leader, a national assemblyman, and a dissident student visited North Korea without the South Korean government's approval. They were sentenced to a harsh fifteen years of imprisonment. South Korea did not want its citizens making unauthorized contact with North Korea and made sure everyone became aware of it. This response did not please North Koreans. In addition, South Korea's joint maneuver "Team Spirit" with the U.S. troops became a sore point for the North Koreans.

INITIAL ECONOMIC COOPERATION

Despite the political difficulties, inter-Korean economic cooperation progressed into a new stage in 1989 and 1990. This was primarily due to North Korean necessity, as North Korea had lost its main trading partners, Soviet Russia and the East European nations. In 1988 and 1989, South Korea purchased North Korean clams and artwork. In 1990, South Korean Christians donated eight hundred tons of rice. In 1990, a direct business deal was signed between a small South Korean firm and a North Korean company for five hundred South Korean refrigerators and two hundred forty color televisions in exchange for North Korean cement, artifacts, and paintings.

On March 29, 1991, the South Korean Cheongji Trading Company signed a trade agreement with North Korea's Kumgang-san International Trade and Development Company to exchange one hundred thousand tons of South Korean rice for eleven thousand tons of cement and thirty thousand tons of coal from North Korea. South Korea's Chaebol shipped thirty thousand barrels of high-sulfur diesel oil, worth U.S. $1.4 million, to North Korea, payable in cash. Samsung, Hyundai, and Sangyong, South Korean firms, imported sheet steel, zinc ingots, gold bullion, farm crops, and yarn and exported color televisions, sugar, and refrigerators to North Korea. According to South Korean figures, the two-way trade increased from U.S. $23.34 million in 1989, to U.S. $190 million in 1991. In 1992, North Korea ordered U.S. $800 million to U.S. $1 billion worth of consumer goods from South Korea to celebrate Kim Il Sung's eightieth birthday.[2] In 1992, the South Korean firm Daewoo signed a contract to build an industrial park in Chin-Nam-P'o, North Korea, with an initial investment of U.S. $10–$20 million. Trade and investment between South and North Korea have been rapidly increasing in the 1990s.

UNITED NATIONS MEMBERSHIP FOR BOTH KOREAS AND INITIAL POLITICAL BREAKTHROUGHS

A politically important breakthrough in inter-Korean relations began with a series of prime ministerial talks in 1990 and 1991. In October 1991, a month after the two Koreas were admitted to the United Nations, at the fourth prime ministers' meeting in P'yŏngyang, South and North agreed to work toward a non-aggression pact. A document, the Agreement on Reconciliation, Non-aggression, Exchange and Cooperation, was signed in Seoul on December 13, 1991, and became effective in February 1992.

At the sixth prime ministers' meeting in December 1991, both Koreas also signed a document barring either side from possessing or using nuclear weapons. These were essentially "promises," and nothing was concrete. South and North Korea were yet to sign a peace treaty, and the non-aggression agreement was not formalized, although what they agreed upon was a step toward such a goal. North Korea seemed to have reneged on its promises and appeared to be in the process of making nuclear weapons in 1994. South Korea agreed to pay U.S. $4.5 billion for two light-water nuclear reactors to replace existing North Korean reactors which produced weapons-grade plutonium. Because there had been a consistent North Korean record of breaking promises at will, such a huge investment could never guarantee anything.

In May 1995, more than one hundred seventy nations of the world agreed to extend the Treaty on the Non-Proliferation of Nuclear Weapons in perpetuity. An isolated, impoverished small country could buck the world system only so long without bringing disaster on itself. In the early 1990s, North Korea seemed to be in dire need of South Korea's help. North Korea did not mind receiving goods and industrial materials from South Korea as long as it was not revealed in public that the goods were produced in South Korea.

North Korea purchased various types of consumer merchandise from South Korea, worth close to U.S. $1 billion, to celebrate Kim Il Sung's eightieth birthday, distributing such goods as toothbrushes, toothpaste, clothes, television sets, electronic equipment, and washing machines to people as gifts. North Koreans insisted that the South Koreans must not attach labels of South Korean brand names to such goods. Public recognition of South Korea's industrial well-being seemed to hurt North Korea's self-respect. For a time, North Korea rejected the idea of receiving two light-water nuclear reactors manufactured in South Korea. However, they indicated in June 1995 that as long as an international body determined the place of manufacture and the two light-water nuclear reactors did not have labels indicating South Korean origin, the North Koreans would not question the origin of the reactors.[3] For the pride of the "workers' paradise," North Korea seemed to go to any length to hide the truth, although it was nothing more than make-believe. Nevertheless, North Korea's turnaround toward South Korea was a welcome indication of improving relationships between the two parts of the Korean Peninsula.

21

Future Prospects for Unification and Potentiality for Korea

The unification of Korea is the most important, urgent, and difficult problem facing all of the Korean people in the twenty-first century. It was none other than the Korean leaders themselves who endlessly bickered with each other and who could not come to an agreement that could unify the country. Instead, they put their greed for power above the interest of people and unification of the country, and let unification slip away from the people of the Korean nation.

The twentieth century has been a harsh century for the Korean people. The Chosōn Dynasty, after more than five centuries of existence, became so feeble and corrupt that it could not even defend itself, but was at the mercy of the surrounding powers of China, Russia, and Japan. When China and Russia were defeated by Japan, Korea fell victim to Japanese imperialism, which was one of the most cruel forces in the history of mankind. Koreans somehow survived thirty-five years of intolerable Japanese colonial rule, keeping their cultural heritage intact, only to find their country divided for over one half century. This nightmarish twentieth century, full of horrific events rarely seen in Korean history, is giving way to a new century which could bring the unification of Korea, if and only if the leaders of South Korea and North Korea give up their selfishness, greed for power, and mutual suspicion and set out earnestly to unify the country and the people.

The focal points of disagreement are that South Korea, with twice the population of North Korea, has insisted that, on the basis of the democratic principle of one vote per person, the distribution of political power must be based on the population proportions. North Korea, on the other hand, having a little over one half of the territory of the Korean peninsula, has been insisting on equal sharing of the political power. They will not recognize the difference in population size.

There have been other differences in economic structure of both South and North Korea. South Korea is a fully capitalistic country, which recognizes private ownership of land, industry, and production. This system has been highly successful in South Korea. South Korea became one of the greatest economic powerhouses of the world in the 1990s.

In North Korea, the state owns everything. The farmlands are operated by highly centralized communes. The production of the industries is state-directed, according to the central plan. There have been serious bottlenecks, and coordination among sectors of the economy has not taken place smoothly. Therefore, the North Korean economy has been shrinking at an annual rate of five percent per year since 1990. Visitors to North Korea in the mid-1990s noticed that the whole population looked gaunt and thin. Indeed, in 1995, news leaked out of North Korea that many people had died of starvation.

State ownership of all lands is nothing new in East Asia. This system of state ownership of land and production goes back more than ten centuries to the T'ang Dynasty of China. The T'ang Dynasty, which was founded in 618 A.D. and lasted until 906 A.D., had farmland distribution systems which started with the land law of 624 A.D. Each adult male was allocated one ch'ing of land (15.13 acres), which was returned to the government at his death. A widowed wife or concubine received thirty mou (thirty percent of male). All land belonged to the state. A farmer paid grain as rent (*tsu*), and in addition, contributed silk or cloth (*t'iao*) and performed labor services as part of the rent payment to the government. The Korean kingdoms of Silla and Koryō modeled their land systems after that of the T'ang Dynasty, implementing similar systems. This was also the case with Japan during the Heian period (794–1192). All of these systems eventually failed, because the distribution of land could not keep pace with the population increase and people had little incentive to improve the land they did not own. The difficulty in North Korea of raising enough food to feed people may have stemmed from the same causes. Insistence of the North Korean government on a communal system may have had adverse effects on the economy. In the final analysis, the commune system is not worth enough to block a process as vital as the unification of the nation.

NECESSITY OF COMPROMISE

In order for South and North Korea to come to an agreement, each side must acknowledge the other's points and reach an agreeable common ground. North Korea, with the one-party system of a Communist dictatorship, has been insisting on a confederate type of unification, with autonomous regions in both South and North Koreas. According to this plan, which Kim Il Sung insisted on for over four decades, each confederate state would be allowed to have its own political and economic system under one Korean flag and a unified central government of Korea. Kim also insisted that the present leaders of the ROK government be barred from participation in the new central government. This was an unreasonable demand. In fact, to achieve unification, the security and future vital role in the new government for the present leaders of both countries must be guaranteed. During the Silla and Koryō unification of Korea, the leaders of rival states were given the highest ranks and posts in the new government. The present leaders of South and North Korea must learn from history. They must be generous, compassionate, and forgiving of rivals to bring about unification.

There is nothing wrong with the idea of forming a temporary confederate government until a more democratic universal government can be installed with a general election. North Korea, with a one-party system and with fifteen percent of its population belonging to the Communist Party, would have a difficult time organizing a South Korean-type general election in short order. The North should be given five to ten years to prepare for a democratic general election with two or more political parties.

It would be feasible to combine the unification ideas of both South and North Koreas. First, combine South and North Korea into a single confederate state of Korea, with built-in stages toward a democratic nation. There is nothing wrong with having a Communist party among several political parties. Russia, France, Italy, Japan, and even the United States have had Communist parties. Let the people decide through democratic voting processes their political preferences. However, after five to ten years of preparation, Korea should adopt a form of government which would be freely elected by universal vote of the people. That is the only democratic way.

INTEGRATION OF BUSINESS STRUCTURES

A unified Korea has great potential, with a combined population of sixty-five million people and one of the highest levels of education in the world. Korea would be on par with France, England, and Italy in its national power in every aspect. The Korean people are diligent, industrious people, who have been gladly working more than ten hours per day, six days per week. That is how South Korea built itself up as an industrial power in such a short time, after the complete destruction of the Korean War. South and North Korea would be able to pull together economically, utilizing their human resources together, building a unified economic power.

North Korea has a wealth of concentrated mineral deposits, rarely seen in any other part of the world. This would form an added resource to South Korea's acquired high level of technology and industry. South Korea's business know-how, capital, and industrial equipment should be welcomed into North Korea, and the two Koreas must integrate economically as one unit. That is the only way to solve North Korea's poverty problem. In the first half of the 1990s, there were some signs that North Korea might welcome South Korean business firms. However, the business deals were on a small scale and were not significant.

Communist China had been moving toward a private enterprise system in the late 1980s and 1990s, welcoming business investments from the United States and Europe. China even started a stock market system. South Korean business firms have actively invested in Communist China's industrial markets. If Communist China and the former Soviet Union could welcome South Korea, there is no reason North Korea could not also do so. In fact, North Korea's economic salvation can only come from South Korea. This was proved by the fact that on June 21, 1995, South Korea agreed to provide a sum of U.S. $270 million in emergency aid, including 150,000 tons of rice, to impoverished North Korea. President Kim Young Sam of the ROK called it an economic turning point between South and North Korea. South Korea also agreed to provide two light-water nuclear reactors worth U.S. $4.5 billion, manufactured in South Korea, in exchange for dismantling of the atomic weapon producing reactors of North Korea. Such events will be the beginning of business and industrial integration of South and North Korea's economies, if they do not betray each other.

Once the economic integration takes shape, the political integration will come easier. It is possible, perhaps in the twenty-first century, that the two Koreas may achieve true unification as did Germany. The situation of South and North Korea is very similar to what had been the situation for West and East Germany. The North Korean leadership has been struggling to prevent this from happening. However, conditions in North Korea have deteriorated to such an extent that they have no choice but to turn to South Korea for aid. The unification seems to have become a matter of necessity for Korea, as it was for Germany.

POLITICAL INTEGRATION IN SEVERAL STAGES

For over four decades, since the 1950s, both South and North Korea have made numerous unification proposals. However, none of them was acceptable to the other side. The main reason was that each side considered its own political situation and ignored the conditions existing on the other side. The South Korean demands for an immediate UN-supervised general election were unacceptable to North Korea, because it was ruled by one party and an election involving several parties in a democratic way was impossible. It may require at least several years to prepare for such a democratic elective system.

North Korea has been proposing a united Korea composed of two confederate states, with equal status. However, this ignores the South Korean population, which is twice that of North Korea. Under the democratic principle of one vote per person, this proposal is not acceptable to South Koreans. This would be the ultimate goal for a united Korea. All the new Soviet republics and East European nations have adopted this Western form of democracy and have been functioning very well.

Given the existing North Korean political situation, it may be feasible to adopt a confederate system as an interim measure, with a time limit attached, perhaps from five to ten years, during which time political parties could be established in both South and North Korea. It would be essential to educate the people on democratic processes, especially in North Korea. This interim period may be utilized to integrate the economic structures of both Koreas. Once the preparations are completed, a general election in proportion to population can be carried out to form a centralized government. Any form of unified government would be better than a divided nation, where each part must maintain a million-man standing army to defend itself from the other. This is an intolerable situation. North Korea has become bankrupt because of it. Everyone will benefit, including the leaders, if Korea unites. The world will benefit also, as one of the most dangerous political hot spots will be cooled.

ALLIANCE OR NEUTRALITY FOR KOREA

Eventually, Korea must choose whether to maintain alliances with the United States, and later to include Japan to form an East Asian power bloc of the three nations, or to be neutral. The memory of Japan's aggression on the Korean peninsula in the first half of the twentieth century is still fresh in the minds of many Koreans. It is doubtful that Koreans would wholeheartedly take Japan into an alliance. There has been too much bitterness in their relationship, going back many centuries. However, once Korea becomes unified, it is possible to form an East Asian alliance of these three countries, to counterbalance the growing power of China in Asia. As NATO has for Western European nations, such an alliance could safeguard the security of Korea. In the European example, France, England, and Germany, which had a long history of conflict, learned to live cooperatively together. Korea and Japan could walk together on the road of true prosperity, under the tutelage of the United States. Or Korea could maintain a separate alliance with the United States, as it has since World War II.

This alliance became uncertain several times. Depending on who occupied the White House and State Department, the abandonment of Korea was seriously considered several times. Dean Acheson's and Jimmy Carter's decisions were such examples of the United States moving to abandon the security of Korea. The disastrous Korean War was the result of such a decision. In a democratic nation such as the United States, public opinion sways widely, and politicians must follow the mood of the country. Isolationism sweeps the United States occasionally, as it has since before World War II through to the Vietnam War. There has been some evidence that some politicians in America prefer isolationism in the late 1990s.

There is an alternative course, which Korea could take if and when the American people become preoccupied with isolationism. It is the course of strict neutrality, like that of Switzerland, which is sandwiched among the much larger nations of Germany, France, and Italy. To survive under such geopolitical circumstances, Switzerland has adopted a policy of strict neutrality with a strong potential to be a great military power. To ensure the security of the nation, the Swiss maintain universal military training. Any nation which tampered with Swiss neutrality would have to deal with three-quarters of a million armed troops. For this reason, even Nazi Germany left Switzerland alone. Korea, toward the end of the Li Dynasty in 1904, announced neutrality, hoping to free itself from the encroachment of Japan. However, neutrality did not work, because Korea did not have a military force to safeguard the announced neutrality. Korea was completely occupied by Japan in 1905.

If South and North Korea unite, perhaps in the twenty-first century, the leaders may have to decide whether to adopt neutrality. Korea is surrounded by the four greatest powers of the world, the United States, China, Russia, and Japan, far more powerful than those neighboring Switzerland. Korea must maintain a strong military self-defense force, as Switzerland has.

South Korea and North Korea should never abandon the effort to unify, no matter how discouraging it may become at some points. Integrate the social and economic sectors first, because these are easier to integrate than the political. Then integrate the political, diplomatic, and military sectors, stage by stage, regardless of the degree of progress. This is the only avenue left for Korea's survival and full independence. Once united, Koreans will have the capacity to create a true Fifth Golden Age of Korea.

INTERNATIONAL AND DOMESTIC REASONS FOR UNIFICATION

In October 1995, Japan's Prime Minister Tomiichi Murayama made a declaration to the Japanese parliament that the Japan–Korea Annexation Treaty was signed by the Korean government in 1910; thus the annexation was "legal."[1] He failed to mention that it was signed by the Japanese puppet Li Wan-yong, who was illegally installed as Korea's prime minister by the Japanese resident-general, Terauchi Masatake. The treaty was forced upon Li by Terauchi. It was as if the present German government declared that the World War II occupation of France was legal because agreements were signed with the French puppet Vichy government.

This proved that there was no contrition among the Japanese leaders about past Japanese imperialism and militarism toward Korea. They have not yet abandoned many centuries of aggressive tendencies toward Korea. This is all the more reason why South and North Korea must unite and cease the pointless internal struggles which reduce the overall strength of the Korean nation. The unification of South and North Korea should take first priority over all other matters. If the two Germanys could unite, so can the two Koreas.

In addition to subtle threats by the Japanese political leaders, domestically both Koreas are undergoing a very difficult period in the latter part of the

1990s. North Korean society is dominated by a rampant black market economy. The country has become impoverished to such an extent that people were literally starving to death in the spring of 1995. Emergency economic aid from South Korea in the amount of U.S. $270 million helped North Korea buy nearly 450,00 tons of rice (150,000 from South Korea, 300,000 from Japan). Thus, North Korea was able to stave off mass starvation temporarily. However, as if to indicate that such suffering was not enough, during the summer of 1995, torrential flooding inundated North Korea. It was reported that five million people, or twenty-five percent of the population, lost their homes. Forty percent of the farmland was destroyed in August 1995. The threat of starvation carried over to 1996 and 1997 as a result of continued severe flooding. North Korea's economic problems are compounded by political chaos. In early 1997, two and one-half years after Kim Il Sung's death, North Korea is still without an official head of state.

South Korea has had its own difficulties since 1995. The country was going through political turmoil. An opposition party congressional member uncovered secrets about former President Roh Tae Woo, who took massive bribes from business firms. Roh Tae Woo was accused of creating a secret slush fund of U.S. $370 million for himself, which he hid away under fictitious names. Roh was arrested on November 17, 1995, and sent to jail. He was formally indicted by prosecutors.

Roh's legal difficulties have triggered people's demand for the prosecution of Chun Doo Hwan, who was responsible for the massacre of at least two hundred forty people and the wounding of thousands of unarmed civilians during the 1980 Kwangju pro-democracy uprising. Chun was charged with violating the military–criminal code by leading the 1979 military coup, as well as killing hundreds or perhaps thousands of people. The six insurrection charges filed against him call for the death penalty. Chun was arrested on December 3, 1995. While Roh faced ten years to life imprisonment, Chun's possible penalty was death.

In addition to the charges described, in January 1996, the ROK's prosecuting officials made formal charges against the imprisoned Chun and Roh, for ordering the 1980 massacre of more than 240 unarmed, peaceful demonstrators at Kwangju.[2] On August 26, 1996, a three-judge tribunal sentenced Chun to death for mutiny, treason and bribery. Roh was sentenced to twenty two years, six months in prison. In addition, Chun was fined U.S. $270 million, and Roh was fined U.S. $350 million. Chun's death sentence was commuted to life-imprisonment by the South Korean Appellate Court on December 16, 1996.

Although South Korea was undergoing political convulsions in the late 1990s, they may produce positive results. A precedent has to be established that no one is above the law, and that violators, sooner or later, have to face justice. South Korea will be far stronger and democracy would be more secure after this turmoil. South Korea will be in a stronger position to deal with the ultimate goal, the unification of South and North Korea, in the twenty-first century.

Perhaps the difficulties faced by both South and North Korea can force these two parts to unite and create a stronger society and nation. Kim Young Sam, the first true democratically elected president of the Republic of Korea in a half century, has proclaimed on several occasions that he is determined to wipe out corruption from South Korea and create a true democratic state while working for the unification of Korea. It would be a significant event if some of his stated goals could be accomplished.

Even without such a desired unification of the two Koreas, South Korea alone seems to have the promise of a bright future. According to the U.S. Central Intelligence Agency (CIA) *Factbook* 1995 citation of an article by Richard Halloran,[3] South Korea achieved a gross domestic product (GDP) at purchasing power parity of U.S. $547 billion for 1995. This was much higher than economists' projections. The South Korean economy was one of the world's ten largest economies in 1995. By 2020 it is expected to be the sixth largest economy in the world with GDP of U.S. $3.412 trillion, according to the same CIA publication and World Bank growth estimates.[4]

If South Korea alone can generate such economic power, it would be a simple matter to project the potential of a united Korea of South and North. North Korea has almost unlimited concentrations of mineral resources locked in the mountains. If the wealth of South and North Korea could be combined, prosperity on the Korean peninsula would be assured. This can be achieved only through peaceful negotiations. Korea has too much to lose. The Korean phoenix is now soaring again. This progress must not be interrupted.

Notes to Part VII

CHAPTER 19

1. Louis R. Mortimer (ed.), *North Korea* (Washington, D.C.: Federal Research Division, Library of Congress, 1994), 251 (original source: *World Military and Arms Control*, 1991).

2. Ibid.

3. *Korea Update* (Washington, D.C.: Korean Information Office, Embassy of the ROK, November 13, 1995) vol. 6, no. 23, 3.

4. Louis R. Mortimer (ed.), *North Korea*, 262.

5. Ibid.

CHAPTER 20

1. *Unification Endeavors by the Republic of Korea* (Seoul: Korean Overseas Information Service, 1982), 38.

2. Louis R. Mortimer (ed.), *North Korea*, 160.

3. *New York Times* and *Washington Post*, June 11 and 12, 1995.

CHAPTER 21

1. Associated Press, Osaka, Japan, November 19, 1995.

2. Associated Press, Seoul, South Korea, December 3, 1995.

3. Richard Halloran, "The Rising East," *Foreign Policy*, Spring 1996, 11.

4. Ibid.

Chronology

Period and Dates	Korea	World
Paleolithic	Cultures	
500,000 B.C. to 400,000 B.C.	P'yōngyang and Hūk-ku-li	Peking man
100,000 B.C.	Ham-kyōng North Province, Kul-bo-li	
30,000 B.C.	Ch'ung-ch'ōng North Province, Sōk-jong-li	Farming in Northern Iraq 8000 B.C.
Neolithic–Bronze Age		
5000 to 3000 B.C.	Comb motif pottery	
		Bronze Age in China 3000 B.C.
3018 B.C. to 2333 B.C.	Mythological founding of Tangun Chosōn Kingdom of Korea; bronze culture appears 3000 B.C.	Hsia Dynasty of China 2205 to 1766 B.C.
3000 to 2000 B.C.	Farming culture begins	Shang Dynasty of China 1766 to 1122 B.C.

Period and Dates	Korea	World
Old Chosōn: Iron Age		
1500 B.C.	Rice culture begins	
1122 B.C.	Kija Chosōn Dynasty	Greek city–states 1100 B.C.
1000 B.C.	Iron Age begins	
500 to 200 B.C.	Wide use of iron tools	Warring period in China begins 452 B.C.; unification of China by Emperor Ch'in Shih Huang-ti 221 B.C.
195 B.C.	Wiman takes Chosōn Kingdom east of Liaotung (Manchuria)	
108 B.C.	Chinese Han Empire creates four provinces, including Nang-nang, in northern Korea; however, the three Korean Han Kingdoms remain independent in southern Korea	
Three Kingdoms		
	Three new kingdoms are established in the territories of Chin-Han, Ma-Han and Pyōn-Han	
56 B.C.	Koguryō Kingdom by Chumong	Death of Julius Caesar 44 B.C.
37 B.C.	Silla Kingdom by Pak Hyōk-kō-se	Augustus as Roman Emperor Beginning of Pax Romana 27 B.C.
18 B.C.	Paekche Kingdom by King On Chō	
42 A.D.	Kaya (Imna) Kingdom founded	

Period and Dates	Korea	World
313 to 391 A.D.	Koguryŏ destroys Chinese Han province of Nang-nang around P'yŏnyang, occupies all of Manchurian region	Korean settlers introduce new Japanese Yayoi culture: new pottery, iron tools, rice cultivation 200 B.C. to 400 A.D.
		Creation of Yamato state in Japan by Korean settlers 360 A.D; Japanese imperial clan descends from Koreans
372 A.D. 384 A.D.	Buddhism introduced to Koguryŏ, and Paekche Kingdoms	
		Division of Roman Empire into East and West 395 A.D.
532 A.D.	Silla annexes Kaya (Imna)	
		Buddhism introduced to Japan from Korea 538 A.D.
598 A.D.	Koguryŏ annihilates Sui Chinese invading army of one million troops, led by Emperor Yang-ti	Construction of world's oldest wooden building, Horyu-ji Temple, in Nara, Japan, by Korean architects from Paekche 607 A.D.
645 A.D.	Koguryŏ defeats T'ang Chinese forces at Ansi Castle	Hegira of Mohammed year 1 of Moslem calendar 622 A.D.
660 A.D.	T'ang–Silla allied forces destroy Paekche	Old Mayan civilization flourishes in the region of present-day Guatemala 317 to 987 A.D.

Period and Dates	Korea	World
668 A.D.	T'ang-Silla forces destroy Koguryŏ; beginning of unified Silla	
Unified Silla and Palhae		
676 A.D.	United people of the Three Kingdoms defeat T'ang forces and cleanse them from the Korean Peninsula	
698 A.D.	Koguryŏ people retake Manchurian region and create Palhae Kingdom	
700 A.D. or earlier	World's first printed material with wooden block encased in Pulkuksa Temple stone pagoda	Unsuccessful Arab siege of Byzantium; high-water mark of Moslem expansion toward Eastern Europe 717 A.D.
726 A.D.	Palhae opens foreign relations with Japan	
751 A.D.	Silla builds Pulkuksa Temple in Kyungju	Japan's Heian period; a golden age begins 794 A.D.
		Over one-third of Japan's 1,200 nobles registered in official register as Korean descendants in the ninth century, during the Heian period 815 A.D.
		Kingdom of England founded 828 A.D.

Period and Dates	Korea	World
846 A.D.	Silla's Chang Kung-bok revolt (Chang Kung-bok had built maritime empire linking China, Korea, and Japan)	
892 A.D.	Later Paekche founded	
904 A.D.	Later Koguryō founded	
		Downfall of T'ang Dynasty of China and beginning of the Five Dynasties 907 A.D.
Koryō		
		Founding of Khitan (Liao) Empire
918 A.D.	Wang Kōn reunites Korean Peninsula and founds Ko(gu)ryō Kingdom	
	Koryō moves capital to Kaekyōng	
926 A.D.	Palhae destroyed by Khitans	
935 A.D.	Last Silla king finally surrenders to Koryō	
		Otto the Great of Germany crowned emperor of the Holy Roman Empire 962 A.D.
		Sung China established 979 A.D.
1125	Korean descendants of Palhae; Chin (Nuchen) destroys Khitan (Liao)	

Period and Dates	Korea	World
1127	Chin occupies Northern China, builds a vast empire	Sung escapes to South China (South Sung) 1127
		Genghis Khan unites Mongolia 1206
1234	Mongols destroy Chin, invade Koryō	
1234	World's first movable metal types invented in Koryō	Mongol army of Batu invades Europe and defeats allied forces of Europe in Germany 1236
1274 and 1281	Koryō participates in Mongol invasion of Japan	
1353	Japanese pirate activities, begun in 1223, become severe	Renaissance begins in Italy 1330s
1356	People of Koryō cleanse Mongols from Korea	Ming China eliminates Mongols from China 1368
Chosōn		
1392	Li Sōng-ge establishes Li Dynasty of Chosōn	
1403	Korean government establishes Office of Casting movable metal types and publishes thousands of books using them	Gutenberg's Bible: first use of movable metal types in the West 1454 (220 years after the Korean invention)
1446	Invention of scientific Korean alphabet (Hangūl)	Christopher Columbus discovers the new world of America on October 12, 1492

Period and Dates	Korea	World
1590	Invention of world's first iron-clad warships	Martin Luther breaks with Catholicism; begins translation of Bible 1521
1592	Japan invades Korea with 150,000 troops	
	Admiral Li destroys Japanese fleet	
1597	Second invasion by Japan	
1598	Disorganized retreat of Japanese troops from Korea under defeat	British establish East India Company, 1600
		Demise of Toyotomi's forces in Japan, weakened by defeat in Korea, at Sekigahara battle 1600
		Tokugawa Iyeyasu begins new Shogunate 1603
		Jamestown, Virginia: first of thirteen colonies in North America 1607
1627	Descendants of Korean Kingdoms of Koguryō and Palhae; Chins (Nuchen or Yōjin) coin a new name—Manchu—for themselves and invade Korean Peninsula	

Period and Dates	Korea	World
1636	Second invasion of Korea by Manchu; Manchu forces brother–brother relationship on Korea	Manchus conquer Ming China, then Burma, Tibet, and Vietnam; establishment of Ch'ing Empire of China 1644
1785	Korea prohibits Western learning	United States Declaration of Independence from England 1776
1801	Persecution of Catholics in Korea	
	Freeing of government slaves	
1840	Western ships appear on Korean waters	American Civil War 1861–1865
1866	Incident of American merchant marine ship, *General Sherman*	Tokugawa Shogunate ends; Meiji Period begins in Japan 1868
1871	American fleet attacks Kanghwa Island	
1876	Korea–Japan Friendship Treaty	
1882	Korea-U.S. Friendship Treaty	
1894	Sino–Japanese War	Spanish–American War ends with the secession of Puerto Rico, Guam, and the Phillipine Islands to the United States 1898
1904	Russo–Japanese War	Anglo–Japanese Alliance 1902
1905	Japan forces Treaty of Protectorate on Korea	

Period and Dates	Korea	World
Colonial Regime		
1910	Japan forces annexation of Korea	
		World War I 1914–1918
		Soviet government established in Russia 1917
		U.S. President Wilson declares principle of self-determination of nations 1918
1919	Korean independence movement of March First	
	Koreans establish provisional government of Korea in Shanghai, China	
1910 to 1934	Japanese confiscate about fifty-nine percent of the farmlands in Korea	
1923	During Tokyo earthquake, Japanese officials encourage Japanese people to massacre six thousand Koreans to divert their minds from the disaster	
		World economic depression begins 1929
		Japanese seize Manchuria 1932
1937	Korean partisans attack Po Ch'ōnpo Japanese base in Korea	Japanese start Second Sino–Japanese War 1937

Period and Dates	Korea	World
1937–1941	Japanese ban all freedoms, Korean names, and use of Korean language by Koreans in Korea	Japanese attack Pearl Harbor, Hawaii (U.S.) 1941 U.S. enters Second World War
1941–1945	Korean volunteer forces of one hundred thousand join Chinese forces to fight Japanese	Second World War ends 1945; Japan surrenders to U.S. United Nations established 1945
Occupational Period		
1945–1948	U.S. and USSR forces occupy Korea, divide peninsula at the 38th parallel	New Japanese constitution 1946
New Republics		
South (ROK) and North (DPRK)	Establishment of two occupational governments: South and North	
1948	Establishment of Governments of the Republic of Korea and Democratic People's Republic of Korea	People's Republic of China established 1949 North Atlantic Treaty Organization (NATO) established 1949
1950–1953	Korean War: UN forces aid South Korea	Chinese Communist Army intervenes in Korean War December 1949

Period and Dates	Korea	World
1953	Kim Il Sung executes rival Pak Hōn-yōng (North)	Egypt seizes Suez Canal 1956
1958	Kim Il Sung executes rival Cho Pong-am (North)	
1960	Student uprising topples ROK President Rhee's government (South)	
	Chang Myōn forms government (South)	
1961	ROK military seizes government (South)	Cuban missile crisis 1962
		US bombing of North Vietnam begins 1965
1968	Kim Il Sung establishes absolute dictatorship (North)	Chinese Cultural Revolution 1966
	Kim Il Sung declares *Chuch'e* (self-reliance) idea at national conference of Labor Party (North)	
1969	ROK President Park Chung Hee enforces a new constitution and creates a dictatorial regime (South)	
1971	Red Cross Conference of South and North: beginning of dialogue between two Koreas	Communist China admitted to UN 1971; Taiwan expelled from UN

Period and Dates	Korea	World
		North Vietnamese capture Saigon; U.S. withdrawal from South Vietnam 1975
1979	Assassination of ROK President Park	
1980	ROK President Chun Doo Hwan crushes Kwangju uprising and kills hundreds of civilians	
	Chun appoints himself president (South)	
1987	ROK President Roh Tae Woo announces new constitution for democratic, civilian-controlled government (South)	North Korea and South Korea both admitted to UN 1991
1992	Kim Young Sam becomes (civilian) president (South)	Demise of Soviet Union and Communist regimes in Eastern Europe 1990–1991
1995	ROK's GDP surpasses US $547 billion and per capita income of US $12,600	Persian Gulf War 1991
	North Korea suffers economic poverty and starvation	Bosnian Peace Accord 1995
1995–1996	Former ROK Presidents Chun and Roh sent to jail on charges of treason, bribery, and massacre of people	

Bibliography

American Enterprise Institute. "Withdrawal of U.S. Troops from Korea?" *Defense Review*, no. 2 Washington, D.C., 1977.

Amsden, Alice H. *Asia's Next Giant: South Korea and Late Industrialization*. New York: Oxford University Press, 1989.

Asia Watch Committee. *A Stern, Steady Crackdown: Legal Process and Human Rights in South Korea*. Washington, D.C.: Asia Watch, 1987.

Baik Bong. *Kim Il Sung, Biography II*. Tokyo: Mirasha, 1970.

Beasley, W. G. *Japanese Imperialism, 1894–1945*. Oxford: Clarendon Press, 1987.

Blair, Clay. *The Forgotten War: America in Korea, 1950–1953*. New York: Times Books, 1988.

Bond, Douglas G. "Anti-Americanism and U.S.–ROK Relations: An Assessment of Korean Students' Views." *Asian Perspective*, (Seoul) 12, Spring–Summer 1988.

Britannica, vol. 6. *Korean War*. London: 1992.

Burnett, Scott S. *Korean–American Relations*. Honolulu: University of Hawaii Press, 1989.

Buss, Claude A. *The United States and Republic of Korea: Background for Policy*. Stanford, CA: Hoover Institution Press, 1982.

Ch'on He-Pong. *La-Ryo Inshesul-ui Yonku* (Research on Printing Technology of Silla–Koryō). Seoul: In-mun-hwa-sa, 1982.

Chung Chin-wee. *Korea and Japan in World Politics*. Seoul: Seoul Computer Press, 1985.

Chung Kyung Cho. *Korea Tomorrow*. New York: Macmillan Co., 1956.

———. *New Korea*. New York: Macmillan Co., 1962.

———. *The Third Republic*. New York: Macmillan Co., 1971.

———. *The Korea Guidebook*. New York: Houghton Mifflin, 1987.

Chung Sei-wha. *Challenges for Women*. Seoul: Seoul Ewha Woman's University Press, 1986.

Clark, Donald N. *Christianity in Modern Korea.* Lanham, MD: University Press of America, 1986.

———. *The Kwangju Uprising: Shadows over the Regime in South Korea.* Boulder, CO: Westview Press, 1988.

Conroy, Hilary. *The Japanese Seizure of Korea: 1868–1910.* Philadelphia: University of Pennsylvania Press, 1960.

Covell, Jon Carter. *Korea's Colorful Heritage.* Seoul: Si-sa-yong-o-sa, 1985.

Covell, Jon Carter and Alan Covell. *Korean Impact on Japanese Culture.* Elizabeth, NJ: Hollym International Corp., 1984.

———. *The World of Korean Ceramics.* Seoul: Si-sa-yong-o-sa, 1986

Cumings, Bruce. *The Japanese Colonial Empire.* Princeton, NJ: Princeton University Press, 1984.

Fairbank, John K., Edwin O. Reischauer, and Albert M. Craig. *East Asia: Tradition and Transformation.* Boston: Houghton Mifflin, 1973.

Foot, Rosemary. *The Wrong War.* Syracuse, NY: Cornell University Press, 1985.

Foster-Carter, Aidan. *Korea North and South.* New York: Monthly Review Press, 1978.

Gray, Ralph (ed.). "The Ainu of Japan." *National Geographic*, December 1969, vol. 48. no. 13

Ha Young-sun. *Nuclear Proliferation: World Order and Korea.* Seoul: Seoul National University Press, 1983.

Hahn Bae-ho and Tadashi Yamamoto. *Korea and Japan: A New Dialogue Across the Channel.* Seoul: Asiatic Research Center, Korea University, 1978.

Halloran, Richard. "The Rising East." *Foreign Policy*, Spring 1996.

Han Sung-Joo. *The Failure of Democracy in South Korea.* Berkeley: University of California Press, 1974.

Han Woo Keun. *The History of Korea.* Translated by Lee Kyung Shik and Grafton Mintz. Honolulu: University of Hawaii Press, 1971.

Headquarters, Department of the Army. *U.S. Government: United States Army Handbook for Korea*, 1958.

Henthorn, William E. *A History of Korea.* New York: The Free Press, 1971.

Hoefer, Hans Johanees. *Korea.* Hong Kong: Apa Productions, 1981.

Hulbert, Homer B. Edited by C. N. Weems. *History of Korea* (two vols.). New York: Hillary House Publisher, 1962 (revised reprint).

Hyde, Georgie D. M. *South Korea: Education, Culture and Economy.* Basingstake, Hampshire, England: Macmillan Press, 1988.

Ienaga, Saburo. *Nihon Bunkasi* (Cultural History of Japan). Tokyo: Iwanami Bunko, 1982.

Ilyon. *Samguk Yusa.* Translated by Ha Tae Hung and Grafton Mintz. Seoul: Yonsei University Press, 1973.

Kajimura, Hideki. *Chosen-shi* (History of Korea). Tokyo: Kodansha Kendaishinsho, 1989.

Kim Chong-won. *Divided Korea: The Politics of Development: 1945–1972.* Cambridge, MA: East Asia Research Center, Harvard University Press, 1975.

Kim Dong-wook, et al. *Korean Culture and Arts.* Seoul: The Korean Culture and Arts Foundation, 1981.

Kim Gi-dong. *The Classical Novels of Korea.* Seoul: The Korean Culture and Arts Foundation, 1981.

Kim Hak-joon. *The Unification Policy of South and North Korea*. Seoul: Seoul National University Press, 1978.

Kim Hong-hak. *The Prehistory of Korea*. Translated by Richard and Kazue Pearson. Honolulu: University of Hawaii Press, 1970.

Kim Jeh-young. *Toward a Unified Korea*. Research Center for Peace and Unification of Korea, 1987.

Kim Kyong-dong. *Man and Society in Korea's Economic Growth*. Seoul: Seoul National University Press, 1979.

Kim Won-yong. *Art and Archaeology of Korea*. Seoul: Daekwang Sorim, 1986

Kim Yung-chung. *Women of Korea: A History from Ancient Times to 1945*. Seoul: Ehwa Woman's University Press, 1976.

Kin Tatsu-Shu. *Chosen* (Korea). Tokyo: Iwanami Shin-sho, 1990.

King Sejong the Great. Seoul: King Sejong Memorial Society, 1981.

Koh B. C. *Recent Political Developments in North Korea*. Presented at the Conference on "North Korea After Kim Il Sung: Continuity or Change?" Palo Alto, CA: The Hoover Institution, Stanford University, February 27, 1996.

"Korea Headed for High Tech's Top Tier." *Business Week*, July, 1995.

Korea Update. Washington, D.C.: Korean Information Office, Embassy of the ROK, November 13, 1995.

Ku Dae-yeol. *Korea Under Colonialism: The March First Movement and Anglo–Japanese Relations*. Seoul: Royal Asiatic Society, 1985.

Kuno, Takeshi and Kakiji Suzuki. *The Art of Japan: Hory-ui (Horyu-ji)*. Tokyo: Shogakkwan, 1966.

Kwak Tae-hwan, Wayne Patterson, and Edward A. Olsen. *The Two Koreas in World Politics*. Masan: Kyungnam University Press, 1983.

Kwon Jene K. (ed.). *Korean Economic Development*. New York: Greenwood Press, 1990.

Lee Chong-Sik. *Japan and Korea: The Political Dimension*. Stanford, CA: Hoover Institution Press, 1985.

Lee Hoon K. *Land Utilization and Rural Economy in Korea*. New York: Greenwood Press, 1969 (originally published by Chicago University Press, Chicago: 1936).

Lee Hye-kyu. *Essays on Korean Traditional Music*. Translated by Robert C. Provine. Seoul: Royal Asiatic Society, 1980.

Lee Ki-baik. *A New History of Korea*. Seoul: Ilchokak, 1984.

Lee Tong Ju. *Korean Paintings in Japan (Ibon sok ui Han Hwa)*. Seoul: Somundang, 1973.

Leinwand, Gerald. *The Pageant of World History*. Boston: Allyn & Bacon, 1971.

Li Chin Hi. *Kokaito-O Oryuhi-no Kenkyu* (Research on Memorial Stone of King Kwang-kae-t'o). Tokyo: Yoshikawa Kobunsha, 1972.

Li Dun J. *The Ageless Chinese*. New York: Charles Scribner's Sons, 1971.

Li Hui-Sung et al. *Han-Kuk Inmyong Tae-sa-jon* (Encyclopedia of Historic Names of Korea). Seoul: Shin-Ku Mun-Hwa-sa, 1982.

Li P'yōng-do. *Kuksa Taekwan* (Overview of National History). Seoul: Po MunGak, 1985.

Maruyama, Masao. *Studies in the Intellectual History of Tokugawa Japan*. Translated by Mikiso Hane. Tokyo: University of Tokyo Press, 1974.

McCormack, Gavan and Mark Seldon (eds.). *Korea North and South: The Deepening Crisis*. New York: Monthly Review Press, 1978.

McCune, Evelyn B. *The Arts of Korea*. Rutland VT: Charles E. Tuttle, 1962.

———. *The Inner Art*. Seoul: Po Chin Jai, 1983.

McCune, Shannon. *Korea's Heritage: A Regional and Social Geography*. Rutland, VT: Charles E. Tuttle, 1956.

Mortimer, Louis R. (ed.). *North Korea*. Washington, D.C.: Federal Research Division, Library of Congress, 1994.

———. *South Korea*. Washington, D.C.: Federal Research Division, Library of Congress, 1992.

Myers, Ramon H. and Mark R. Peattie. (eds.). *The Japanese Colonial Empire, 1895–1945*. Princeton NJ: Princeton University Press, 1984.

Nahm, Andrew C. (ed.). *Korea Under Japanese Colonial Rule*. Kalamazoo: Center for Korean Studies, Western Michigan University, 1973.

Noguchi, Kakuchu. *Yakimono-to Tsurugi* (Pottery and Sword). Tokyo: Kodansha, 1981.

———. *Kara-to Wa* (Ancient Korea and Japan). Tokyo: Kodansha, 1978.

Okongi, Masao. *North Korea at the Crossroads*. Tokyo: Japan Institute of International Affairs, 1988.

Olsen, Edward A. "The Societal Role of the ROK Armed Forces." In Edward A. Olsen and Stephen Jurika (eds.). *The Armed Forces in Contemporary Asian Societies*. (Westview Special Studies in Military Affairs). Boulder, CO: Westview Press, 1986.

Ooka, Minoru. *Temples of Nara and Their Art*. Translated by Dennis Lishka. New York and Tokyo: Weatherhill-Heibonsha, 1974.

Park Jae-kyu. *The Foreign Relations of North Korea*. Masan: Kyungnam University Press, 1987.

Park Jae-kyu, and Joseph H. Ha. *The Soviet Union and the East Asia in the 1980s*. Masan: Kyungnam University Press, 1983.

Preston, Antony. "Trends in Asian Navies." *Asian Defence Journal*, Kuala Lumpur 18, no. 8. August 1988.

Reishcauer, Edwin O. *Japan: The Story of a Nation*. New York: Alfred Knopf, 1970.

The Report of the International Conference on the Problems of Korean Unification (August 24–29, 1970). Seoul: Asiatic Research Center, Korea University, 1971.

Republic of Korea. "Article 42 of the Court Organization I. [Pōpwōn chojikpop], Law 3992, December 4, 1987, as last amended by Law No. 4017." Seoul: August 5, 1988.

———. *The Handbook of Korea*. Seoul: Korean Overseas Information Service, 1990.

———. Ministry of Culture and Information. Korean Overseas Information Office. *Facts About Korea*. Seoul: Hollym, 1985.

———. Ministry of Culture and Information. Korean Overseas Information Service. *An International Terrorist Clique: North Korea*. Seoul: 1983.

———. Ministry of National Defense. *Defense White Paper, 1989*. Seoul: 1990.

Robinson, Michael E. *The Japanese Colonial Empire, 1895–1945*. Princeton, NJ: Princeton University Press, 1984.

Sakamoto, Taro. *Nihonshi Shojiden* (Encyclopedia of Japanese History). Tokyo: Yamakawa Publishing, 1970.

Sato, Katsumi and Tsutomu Nishioka. *Is the Secretary General (of the Liberal Democratic Party of Japan) Kator Koichi a Puppet of North Korea?* Tokyo: Bunkei Shunshu, December, 1995.

Scalapino, Robert A. and Lee Hongkoo (eds.). *Korea–U.S. Relations: The Politics of Trade and Security*. Berkeley: Institute of East Asian Studies, University of California, 1988.

Shiba, Ryutaro, Masateru Yamata, and Tatsushu Kin. *Nihonno Chosen Bunka* (Korean Culture in Japan). Tokyo: Chuko Bunko, 1990.

Sohn Pow Key, Kim Choi Chun, and Hong I Sun. *The History of Korea*. Seoul: The Korean National Commission for UNESCO, 1970.

Song Byung-Nak. *The Rise of the Korean Economy*. Hong Kong: Oxford University Press, 1990.

Stokes, Henry Scott. "Cracking Down in Korea." *New York Times Magazine*, October 19, 1980.

Suh Dae-Sook. *Kim Il Sung: The North Korean Leader*. New York: Columbia University Press, 1988.

Takesada, Hideshi. "North Korean Military Threat Under Kim Jung Il." Paper presented at the Conference on "North Korea after Kim Il Sung: Continuity or Change?" Palo Alto, CA: The Hoover Institution, Stanford University, February 27–28, 1996.

Tanaami, Hiroshi. *Shin-Nihonshi-no Kenkyu* (New Research on Japanese History). Tokyo: Obunsha, 1967.

Tamura, Jitsuzo. *Sekai no Rekishi* (World History). Tokyo: Chuko-Bunko, 1981.

Ueda, Masaaki. *Waikoku-no Sekai* (World of Wai, Ancient Japan). Tokyo: Kodansha, 1989.

Unification Endeavors by the Republic of Korea. Seoul: Korean Overseas Information Service, 1982.

Vreeland, Nena, Rinn-Sup Shinn, Peter Just, and Philip W. Moeller. *Area Handbook for North Korea*. Washington, D.C.: The American University, 1975.

Weinstein, Franklin B. (ed.). *U.S.–Japan Relations and the Security of East Asia*. Boulder, CO: Westview Press, 1978.

Willliams, Nick B. "1980 Uprising: Memories of Kwangju Haunt Korea." *Los Angeles Times,* November 3, 1987.

Woronoff, Jon. *Korea's Economy: Man-Made Miracle*. Arch Cape, OR: Pace International Research, 1983.

Yang Sung Chul. "North and South Korean Arms Race and a New Alternative." *Korean Journal of International Studies* Seoul 20, no. 3, Fall 1989.

Yi Sang-u. *Security and Unification in Korea*. Seoul: Sogang University Press, 1983.

Ziring, Lawrence and C. I. Eugene Kim. *The Asian Political Dictionary*. Santa Barbara, CA and Oxford: ABC-Clio Inc., 1985.

Index

About the Author

KENNETH B. LEE has held positions as Chairman and Professor of the Korean Department, Chief Research Division, and Dean of the Germanic Language School of the U.S. Defense Language Institute. Born in southern Korea and raised in northern Korea, he studied at Korea University, New York University and Stanford University, and received his Ph.D. from the University of Southern California. He has also been Professor of East Asian Studies at Chapman University and Program Chief of Korean and Japanese Studies at Monterey Institute of International Studies. He has published widely on Korea.

ISBN 0-275-95823-X
90000>
EAN
9 780275 958237

HARDCOVER BAR CODE